"Harlem Gallery"
and Other Poems of
Melvin B. Tolson

"Harlem Gallery"
and Other Poems of
Melvin B. Tolson

Edited by
Raymond Nelson

Introduction by
Rita Dove

University Press of Virginia
Charlottesville and London

Acknowledgments for previous publication appear on page ix.

The University Press of Virginia
© 1999 by the Rector and Visitors of the University of Virginia
All rights reserved
Printed in the United States of America

First published 1999

♾ The paper used in this publication meets the minimum requirements of the
American National Standard for Information Sciences — Permanence of Paper for
Printed Library Materials, ANSI Z39.48-1984.

Library of Congress Cataloging-in-Publication Data

Tolson, Melvin Beaunorus.
    Harlem gallery, and other poems of Melvin B. Tolson / edited by
    Raymond Nelson ; introduction by Rita Dove.
        p. cm.
    Includes bibliographical references.
    ISBN 0–8139–1864–2 (cloth : alk. paper). — ISBN 0-8139-1865-0
    (paper : alk. paper)
        1. Afro-Americans — Poetry. 2. Harlem (New York, N.Y.) — Poetry.
    I. Nelson, Raymond, 1938–   II. Title.
    PS3539.O334A6   1999
    811'.52 — dc21   98-52063
                                        CIP

Contents

Acknowledgments

Grateful acknowledgment is given Melvin B. Tolson Jr. and the publishers for permission to reproduce or reprint the published poems of Melvin B. Tolson.

Harlem Gallery: Book I, The Curator. New York: Twayne Publishers, 1965.
Libretto for the Republic of Liberia. New York: Twayne Publishers, 1953.
Rendezvous with America. New York: Dodd, Mead & Co., 1944.

"Abraham Lincoln of Rock Spring Farm." In *Soon, One Morning: New Writings by American Negroes,* ed. Herbert Hill, pp. 57–77. New York: Alfred A. Knopf, 1963.
"African China." *Voices* 140 (winter 1950): 35–38.
"E. & O. E." *Poetry* 78 (Sept. 1951): 330–42, 369–72.
"A Long Head to a Round Head." *Beloit Poetry Journal* 2 (summer 1952): 19–21.
"The Man from Halicarnassus." *Poetry* 81 (Oct. 1952): 75–77.

The list of Tolson's published works is drawn from Robert M. Farnsworth's exhaustive bibliography in his *Plain Talk and Poetic Prophecy* (University of Missouri Press, 1984). Permission is gratefully acknowledged.

Introduction

Rita Dove

> Art
> is not barrel copper easily separated
> from the matrix;
> it is not fresh tissues
> —for microscopic study—
> one may *fix*:
> unique as the white tiger's
> pink paws and blue eyes,
> Art
> leaves her lover as a Komitas
> deciphering intricate Armenian neums,
> with a wild surmise
>
> "Delta," *Harlem Gallery*

"I will visit a land unvisited by Mr. Eliot."[1] With this self-confident boast, Melvin B. Tolson throws down his glove before the pantheon of Modern Poetry. Like many of his more public utterances, this sentence scribbled in a notebook bristles with half-tones and quarter-tones. Is Tolson merely staking out his particular poetic territory and in effect confirming the southern poet-critic Allen Tate's smug pronouncement that "the distinguishing Negro quality is not in the language but in the subject-matter, which is usually the plight of the Negro segregated in a White culture"[2]—in other words, stick to your side of the tracks and we'll stick to ours? Or is he challenging T. S. Eliot, claiming a larger vision than that of the Disgruntled Modernists; could he find a way of reclaiming the wasteland of postwar disillusionment without turning to religion or to other heavily structured systems of thought as Eliot, Pound, Yeats and some of their lesser Anglo-Saxon contemporaries did? And what of the exquisitely formal address: is "Mr. Eliot" an expression of respect, distance, or irony?

With Tolson one can safely say: all of the above. A glance at nearly any passage from the poems reprinted here will confirm that one is in the presence of a brilliantly eclectic mind determined not to hide its light under a bushel. In an interview the year before his death in 1966, Tolson stated: "I, as a black poet, have absorbed the Great Ideas of the Great White World, and interpreted them in the melting-pot idiom of my people. My roots are in Africa, Europe, and America."[3] Tolson contained multitudes and did not shy away from the contradictions therein to look for single-minded issues or simple solutions; he had no problem harboring the paradoxes of the melting-pot—indeed, he was able to refine from that cruel matrix a golden, ostentatious lyricism, drenched in the pain and beauty of the blues: "The blues is an impulse to keep the painful details and episodes of a brutal experience alive in one's aching consciousness, to finger its jagged grain, and to transcend it, not by the consolation of philosophy but by squeezing from it a near-tragic, near-comic lyricism. As a form, the blues is an autobiographical chronicle of personal catastrophe expressed lyrically. . . . Their attraction lies in this, that they at once express both the agony of life and the possibility of conquering it through sheer toughness of spirit."[4] In short, he takes up the challenge of Countee Cullen's lament: "to make a poet black, and bid him sing!"

When urged toward the end of his life to write his memoirs, Tolson refused. "A man's a jack-in-the-box," he protested. "But analyze his writing carefully and you'll have him. There's where you'll find the distilled essence of the man."[5] And so—with a biographical nod to send us in the right direction—let us turn to the writing.

> O ye of the Samson Post,
> let the remembrance
> of things past
> season with tolerance
> the pigs in baskets.
>
> "Pi," *Harlem Gallery*

Melvin Beaunorus Tolson was born on February 6, 1898 in Moberly, Missouri. His father, a minister in the Methodist Episcopal church, moved the family from one small Missouri or Iowa town to another. The eldest of four, Melvin enjoyed a warm and tolerant childhood: he painted and read incessantly; his mother composed impromptu verses, and his father discussed Plato and Aristotle with him. All the children played instruments, and the family convened for musical evenings.

From an early age, then, Tolson was confronted with the culture of the Western world and given the confidence to enjoy it on his own terms. Teachers, many of them white, encouraged his zeal for reading and introduced him to black heroes like Paul Laurence Dunbar and Touissant L'Ouverture. His undergraduate education, beginning at Fisk University in 1918 and culminating in graduation with honors from Lincoln University in 1923, was conducted exclusively at black institutions, affording him a solid community within which to explore his interests in drama, classics, debating, and football. Upon graduation he became an instructor of English at Wiley College (also a black school) in Marshall, Texas; during a brief interlude at Columbia University in New York, Tolson undertook a master's program in English and comparative literature and completed everything but the bibliography to a thesis on prominent figures of the Harlem Renaissance. In 1947 he moved to yet another black college, Langston University near Oklahoma City, where he taught for the rest of his life.[6]

It is significant that Tolson chose to center his life in the black community. His commitment to teaching was legendary; coaching sessions with the debate students would go deep into the night, and he watched with glee as Wiley's debate team defeated the champions from the University of Southern California. He did not believe in misplaced modesty and blind acceptance; instead he pushed himself and others to the limits of human capacity. On more than one speaking occasion his uncompromising oratory incurred the wrath of whites in the audience. He once told a student: "You know where white folks put information they want to hide from you? Books and magazines and newspapers—that's where!"[7] Tolson's lifelong endeavor was to make that information available—to reveal the glories of ancient black civilizations and the follies of Western thought. He delighted in using his mind to the nth degree, and he saw no reason why others shouldn't enjoy the exhilaration of his intelligence, too.

> I see America in Joe DiMaggio,
>   As his bat cuts a vacuum in the paralyzed air;
> In brown Joe Louis, surged in white acclaim,
>   As he fights his country's cause in Madison Square.
>
>   "Rendezvous with America"

A glance at the section titles to Tolson's first collection of poetry, *Rendezvous with America* (published by Dodd in 1944), gives one an idea not only of the poet's scope but of his basic attitude toward the larger cultural landscape. "Rendezvous with America," "Woodcuts for America," "Dark Symphony," "A Song for Myself," "Of Men and Cities," "The Idols of the Tribe," "Tapestries of Time"—here is a poet prepared to take on the world. The title poem displays some of the visionary largesse of Carl Sandburg and Hart Crane, as well as the prepositional trope:

> Into the arteries of the Republic poured
> The babels of bloods,
> The omegas of peoples,
> The moods of continents,
> The melting-pots of seas,
> The flotsams of isms,
> The flavors of tongues,
> The yesterdays of martyrs,
> The tomorrows of utopias.

Tolson makes quite clear his commitment to his country as well as the bone of contention he intends to pick. The rendezvous of the poem's title is a promise and a warning.

Initial critical response tended to center around the long poem "Dark Symphony," which won first prize at the American Negro Exposition in Chicago in 1939. "Dark Symphony" is a lyrical tour de force, a sweeping review of black American history in musical vocabulary. The poem is divided into six sections, and each section is assigned a musical signature. The upbeat optimism of *Allegro Moderato* describes the black contribution to the Revolutionary War effort. This early idealism is made drear by the escalating horrors of slavery, exquisitely rendered in *Lento Grave* ("slow and stately") in the second section, horrors that are then made spiritually bearable only by the nourishment of gospel, what W. E. B. Du Bois calls the Sorrow Songs. The iambic trimeter of *Andante Sostenuto* underscores the abeyance of those years when the emancipation promise of "forty acres and a mule" had soured into the institution of sharecropping:

> They tell us to forget
> The Bill of Rights is burned.
> Three hundred years we slaved,
> We slave and suffer yet:
> Though flesh and bone rebel,
> They tell us to forget!

The dawning of the Harlem Renaissance heralds the birth of Alain Locke's famous "New Negro"; the fourth section, aptly marked *Tempo Primo*, both points toward the future and harkens dramatically back to the ungrounded optimism of the Revolutionary War period. Sure enough, the next section (*Larghetto*) rebukes white America for its failures: each stanza begins with the refrain "None in the Land can say / To us black men Today," followed by examples of the violence and deceit plaguing the Depression years. The final section regales in march time (*Tempo di Marcia*) the determination of the New Black American to advance "Out of the dead ends of Poverty" and "Across barricades of Jim Crowism" to a better world.

Rendezvous with America is a precocious, even brash, first book. Admittedly, it is the work of an aspiring poet flexing his muscles; many of the poems are derivative, and Tolson's voice, except in portions of the title poem and in "Dark Symphony," has yet to achieve its eclectic exuberance. The dark humor works best when wry observations are posited against the "straight man" of a mainstream culture. Thus, his Shakespearean sonnets are not devoted to love; rather, they employ the narrative strategies of African fable to examine historical violations of human rights.[8] "Dark Symphony" plucks from the standard musical repertoire a bluesy orchestral sound. In the section "Woodcuts for Americana" the rustic, static portraiture typical of patriotic crafts is the norm against which Tolson carves his grain, bathing archetypes and symbols with his fresh and sardonic eye— such as Dame Justice from the antiballad of "An Ex-Judge at the Bar," who begins "to laugh / Like a maniac on a broken phonograph." If the terse poem "Song for Myself" pokes gentle fun at Whitman, if its constrictive iambic dimeter line stands in diabolical opposition to Whitman's expansiveness, it is also a tribute to the egalitarian spirit they share:

> Jesus,
> Mozart,
> Shakespeare,
> Descartes,
> Lenin,
> Chladni,
> Have lodged
> With me.

Tolson's mixture of homage and critique is ferreted out with panache. The most original poems in *Rendezvous with America* are showcases for Tolson's catholic curiosity and keen morality, tempered by an ironic grace.

O Calendar of the Century,
red-letter the Republic's birth!
O Hallelujah,
oh, let no *Miserere*
venom the spinal cord of Afric earth!
Selah!

"Ti," *Libretto for the Republic of Liberia*

The younger poet of *Rendezvous with America* staked his claim among the districts of traditional prosodic forms; *Libretto for the Republic of Liberia* announces a poet who has advanced beyond apprenticeship and is now striking out for the territories. In 1947 Tolson was appointed Poet Laureate of Liberia; he wrote *Libretto* in honor of the centennial of the founding of that African country. With its litany of African/Asian/European heroes, its griot rhapsody and telescoped aeons, this work rises above the circumstances of its genesis. No trace of the occasional lingers in this unique poetic celebration: a public ode that gives us not only the scoop on the nitty-gritty nasties of Western history but also, in a propulsive finale, predicts the rise of African nations.

Divided into eight sections corresponding to the notes of the scale, the *Libretto* has a built-in progression, a rising and compelling tension. The first "DO" contains eight stanzas, each beginning with the rhetorical question "Liberia?" This query is countered by images of what Liberia most emphatically is not—neither "micro-footnote in a bunioned book" nor "caricature with a mimic flag"—followed in turn by positive images of Liberia as the "iron nerve of lame and halt and blind" and "the quicksilver sparrow that slips / The eagle's claw." After a lamentation ("RE") for the lost glory of the golden empires of Africa, "MI" gives credit to various American abolitionists and church leaders for their role in the plans to settle Liberia with former slaves. "FA" provides a moment's respite from instances of historical aggression; this "interlude of peace," however, is troubled by images of suspended violence: a giant snake ("fabulous mosaic log") poised to strike, a predatory bird (the American eagle?) looming over its stilled victim. History grinds on in "SOL" as the freed slaves set sail for Africa. Their reverse travail through the long terror of the Middle Passage is accompanied by the communal chant of the griot (the elder assigned the task of memorizing tribal history) reciting African proverbs:

The diplomat's lie is fat
at home and lean abroad.

> It is the grass that suffers when
> two elephants fight.

"LA" devotes seven stanzas to the geological formation of the Liberian coastline and the advance of Christianity as the former slaves struggle to survive the ravages of nature. "TI" abounds with allusions and foreign phrases, French spilling into Latin even as Banquo's ghost mingles with the outrageous tyrants of World War II. "You want erudition? I'll give you erudition," Tolson seems to be saying, mocking the champions of the Western world by summarizing this dizzying sweep through history—largely a progression of wars and ravishment—as "unparadised nobodies with maps of Nowhere / ride the merry-go-round! / Selah!"

"DO" completes the octave. And though there are structural parallels between the first section and the eighth (the question-and-answer pattern of section one has, in section eight, become an elaborate call-and-response around key terms such as the United Nations, Bula Matadi, and Parliament of African Peoples), this conclusion explodes the boundaries of free verse. It resembles the stylized sermon of a charismatic black minister, borne along by the intensity of his vision.

Tolson takes the form of a libretto—literally a "little book" but usually understood as a text to the musical theater—to its limits. The melodrama of man's ambitions is swirled across a canvas that begins with prehistoric glaciers and tumbles into the Futureafrique—pageantry and intrigue abreast on a tide of high-fidelity language. With Libretto, Tolson learns to sing in the operatic mode.

As a book, Libretto for the Republic of Liberia finally appeared in 1953 under the imprint of Twayne Publishers. In his foreword Allen Tate accurately describes the conundrum of Tolson's achievement: "Here is something marvellous indeed. A small African republic founded by liberated slaves celebrates its centenary by getting an American negro poet to write what, in the end, is an English Pindaric ode in a style derived from—but by no means merely imitative of—one of the most difficult modern poets."

No less marvelous, one is tempted to add, than a foreword written by a southern Fugitive poet who had once refused to attend a party in honor of Langston Hughes and James Weldon Johnson because they were black![9] To confuse matters even more, Tate commends Tolson for not going the way of poets such as Gwendolyn Brooks and Langston Hughes, "who supposed that their peculiar genius lay in 'folk' idiom or in the romantic creation of a 'new' language within the English language." That Tolson would allow himself to be praised at the expense of his fellow poets, and by so dubious a personality, was disturbing indeed. But the real storm still lay ahead.

Although
the moment's mistone
and the milieu's groan
sharp an unbearable ache
in the f of the age's bone,
this pain is only the ghost of the pain
the artist endures,
endures
—like Everyman—
alone.

"Delta," *Harlem Gallery*

When Tolson published part 1 of his projected epic poem, *Harlem Gallery*, in 1965, critical response was immediate and controversial.[10] Whereas many mainstream literati were enthusiastic, proclaiming Tolson's piece as the lyrical successor to *The Waste Land, The Bridge,* and *Paterson,* proponents of the rapidly solidifying Black Aesthetic were less impressed— to say the least. Part of the controversy was sparked by Karl Shapiro's well-meaning foreword. "Tolson writes and thinks in Negro," Shapiro pronounced, prompting poet and essayist Sarah Webster Fabio to remark: "Melvin Tolson's language is most certainly not 'Negro' to any significant degree. The weight of that vast, bizarre, pseudo-literary diction is to be placed back into the American mainstream where it rightfully and wrong-mindedly belongs."[11]

Shapiro describes *Gallery* as "a narrative work so fantastically stylized that the mind balks at comparisons." Divided into twenty-four sections corresponding to the letters in the Greek alphabet, *Harlem Gallery* contains allusions to Vedic gods, Tintoretto and Minyan pottery, as well as snippets in Latin and French. No wonder many of his black contemporaries thought he was "showing off."

To be sure, the timing was bad for such a complex piece. The Civil Rights movement was at its peak, and black consciousness had permeated every aspect of Afro-American life, including its literature. Black writers rejected white literary standards, proclaiming a black aesthetic that was distinctly oral, where poems and fiction used the language patterns and vocabulary of the street to arouse feelings of solidarity and pride among Afro-Americans.

Although Shapiro prefaced his precocious linguistic analysis with a righteous outburst against the "liberal" politics of American tokenism, the suspicion had already been raised that Melvin B. Tolson was the white critics' flunky. "A great poet has been living in our midst for decades and is almost totally unknown," Shapiro exclaimed; Paul Breman, however, declared that Tolson "postured for a white audience, and with a wicked sense of humour gave it just what it wanted: an entertaining darkey using almost comically big words as the best wasp tradition demands of its educated house-niggers."[12] But could the white man's "darkie" be the same man who taught at black colleges all his life? And is this that most "unNegro-like" voice that Fabio protested:

> but often I hear a dry husk-of-locust blues
> descend the tone ladder of a laughing goose,
>   syncopating between
>   the faggot and the noose:
>   "Black Boy, O Black Boy,
>   is the port worth the cruise?"

In the controversy over racial loyalties and author's intent, few bothered to read *Harlem Gallery*. Its virtuoso use of folktale and street jive was forgotten as soon as the reader stumbled across a reference to "a mute swan not at Coole." The poem—and its story—got lost in the crossfire.

Harlem Gallery, Book I: The Curator is the first part of a proposed five-part poem delineating the odyssey of the black man in America. *Book II, Egypt Land*, was to be a delineation of slavery; *Book III, The Red Sea*, an analogy of the Civil War; *Book IV, The Wilderness*, was to deal with Reconstruction; *Book V* was titled *The Promised Land*. In *Book I: The Curator* (the only one Tolson had completed by the time he died in 1966), the role of the black artist is examined on several levels. The narrator, a mulatto of "afroirishjewish origins" and ex-professor of art, is Curator of the Harlem Gallery. His gallery allows him ample opportunity to observe the shenanigans of the black bourgeoisie; his dealings with starving artists such as John Laugart, as well as his friendship with other black cultural figures, afford him glimpses into all strata of black life. The Curator's friend, Dr. Nkomo, is his alter-ego, his stronger, more prideful counterpart; taken together, their observations build a dialectic of the position of blacks—and most specifically, the black artist—in a white-dominated society.

The Curator muses on the predicament of being black and an artist in America. "O Tempora, / *what* is man?" he asks in "Beta"; "O Mores, / what *manner* of man is this?" Spliced into this highly stylized ode are little stories—dramatic monologues, vignettes—that serve to illustrate the philosophical stance of the more discursive parts. These stories exhibit classical

narrative techniques, as well as several storytelling "riffs" which are rooted
in the Afro-American oral tradition. "Metaphors and symbols in Spirituals
and Blues / have been the Negro's manna in the Great White World," sighs
one character; perhaps the most vivid declaration of this appears in "Iota":

> In the Harlem Gallery, pepper birds
> clarion in the dusk of dawn
> the flats and sharps of pigment-words—
> quake the walls of Mr Rockefeller's Jericho
> with the new New Order of things,
> as the ambivalence of dark dark laughter rings
> in Harlem's immemorial winter.

In an attempt to answer the Curator's questions, *Harlem Gallery* charts
the lives of three black artists. We meet the first, a half-blind, destitute
painter named John Laugart, in "Zeta." The Curator visits Laugart in his
"catacomb Harlem flat"; Laugart has just finished his masterpiece, *Black
Bourgeoisie*, a painting certain to arouse the ire of the patrons of his gallery.
Yet Laugart refuses to compromise his art in order to pay the rent. The con-
sequences? "He was robbed and murdered in his flat, / and the only witness
was a Hamletian rat."

John Laugart's tragic fate is sandwiched between the shimmering over-
ture of the first five sections and the underworld glimmer of Harlem in the
thirties. The Curator leaves Laugart to his chill vigil and stops in at Aunt
Grindle's Elite Chitterling Shop to shoot the philosophic bull with his ace
boon coon, Doctor Obi Nkomo. They are next seen at a Vernissage at the
Harlem Gallery, where sublimated versions of black history and its heroes
hanging on the wall provide ironic contrast to the ignominious private lives
of the prospective buyers, exemplified by Mr. Guy Delaporte III, "the sym-
bol of Churchianity" to the "Sugar Hill elite." At this point, Tolson's second
black artist bursts into the hushed gallery—Hideho Heights, the "poet lau-
reate of Harlem." Those sections of *Harlem Gallery* devoted to boisterous
and irreverent Hideho Heights display a virtuoso rendering of narrative lay-
ers—a tribute, perhaps, to Heights' own extravagant linguistic paeans. In
"Xi," the Zulu Club provides a backdrop to Hideho's recitation—a rather
militant version of the John Henry ballad—that is interrupted by the verbal
antics of the "Zulu Club Wits," whose tableside conversation ranges from
an anecdote about service in a Jim Crow Restaurant to the moral implicit in
a newspaper illustration of a frog trying to free itself from the fangs of a
snake. In fact, many of the characters in *Harlem Gallery* exhibit a fondness

for animal stories. Reminiscent of the tales of Brer Rabbit (which draw their spirit from African trickster stories), these highly charged fables are allegories demonstrating survival strategies of mistreated minorities in America—consider, for example, Hideho's "strange but true" story of the sea turtle and the shark in section "Phi": Driven by hunger to swallow the sea turtle whole, the shark is utterly helpless as the "sly reptilian marine" "gnaws / . . . and gnaws . . . and gnaws . . . / *his* way to freedom."

The dialogues in the Zulu Club scenes show how close Tolson's baroque surface mirrors typical black street speech. When Heights pinches a "fox," she whirls around and "signifies": "*What* you smell isn't cooking," she says. Hideho's John Henry poem ("The night John Henry is born an ax / of lightning splits the sky, / and a hammer of thunder pounds the earth, / and the eagles and panthers cry!") is right in the tradition of great black ballads, even as it incorporates the bawdiness of a "toast." In her excellent study on black speech patterns, Geneva Smitherman describes the toast: "Toasts represent a form of black verbal art requiring memory and linguistic fluency from the narrators. Akin to grand epics in the Graeco-Roman style, the movement of the Toast is episodic, lengthy and detailed. . . . Since the overall narrative structure is loose and episodic, there is both room and necessity for individual rhetorical embellishments and fresh imaginative imagery. . . . the material is simply an extension of black folk narrative in the oral tradition."[13]

The whole of *Harlem Gallery*, in fact, is very much like the toasts featuring Shine and Stag-o-lee, those mythic "bad-man" heroes in black oral tradition. In Tolson's case, however, his hero is the archetypal black artist.

The third Harlem artist is Mister Starks, conductor of the Harlem Symphony orchestra, who appears in sections "Rho" through "Upsilon." To relate the circumstances of Starks's mysterious death, Tolson uses all the devices of the criminal drama, right down to the Smoking Gun and the Deep Dark Secret Revealed in the Secret Papers. Starks is found with a bullet in his heart; the gun is found in the toilet bowl of a character named Crazy Cain. Now we know "who-dun-it": but in order to understand the motive, we need to read the manuscript Starks left behind: *Harlem Vignettes*, a collection of poetic portraits that begin with a painfully honest self-portrayal. Starks is aware that he has compromised his talents by writing boogie-woogie when he should have been pursuing the excellence of his one triumph, the *Black Orchid Suite*. The *Harlem Vignettes* (section "Upsilon") are incisive thumbnail sketches of many of the characters already encountered in the Gallery, including John Laugart, Hideho Heights, and the inscrutable Curator. In Crazy Cain's sketch we learn that Mister Starks had fired him

from the Harlem Symphony; he was also the illegitimate son of Mr. Guy
Delaporte III and Black Orchid, Starks's wife.

Can we get a Witness? Because what Tolson has been doing all along
is testifying, which is nothing more than to "tell the truth through story."
The *Vignettes* are important not only as an advancement of the plot but
for their function as narrative history—a sort of literary counterpart to the
African griot.

A host of other characteristics typical of black speech appear in *Harlem
Gallery*—mimicry, exaggerated language, spontaneity, the persona of the
braggadocio. There is one narrative technique, however, that informs the
overall structure of Tolson's piece. Smitherman calls this mode of presenta-
tion "narrative sequencing" and observes that many Afro-American stories
are actually abstract observations about the larger questions of life rendered
into concrete narratives:[4] "The relating of events (real or hypothetical) be-
comes a black rhetorical strategy to explain a point, to persuade holders of
opposing views to one's own point of view. . . . This meandering away from
the 'point' takes the listener on episodic journeys and over tributary rhetori-
cal routes, but like the flow of nature's rivers and streams, it all eventually
leads back to the source. Though highly applauded by blacks, this narrative
linguistic style is exasperating to whites who wish you'd be direct and hurry
up and get to the point."

Tolson doesn't stop there, but employs another important aspect of
black/African storytelling, what Smitherman calls "tonal semantics": using
rhythm and inflection to carry the implication of a statement. "Oh yes, it
bees that way sometimes," an old blues lyric goes; Tolson syncopates his pas-
sages by erratic line lengths strung on a central axis, thus propelling our eye
down the page while stopping us up on short lines:

The school of the artist

is

the circle of wild horses,

heads centered,

as they present to the wolves

a battery of heels.

Harlem Gallery is composed according to Tolson's "S-Trinity of Parnas-
sus"—the melding of sound, sight, and sense. *Sound* refers to the oral na-
ture of the poem; Tolson intended his lines to be read aloud. The visual im-
pact of the centered lines contributes to the forward thrust that a lively oral
recitation would possess. *Sense* refers to both meaning and the sensory as-
pect of language.

Tolson's extravagant verbiage pays homage to the essence of style; he mixes colloquial and literary references as well as dictions; irony and pathos, slapstick and pontification sit side by side. And if we look closely at *Harlem Gallery*'s dazzling array of allusions—one component of what Sarah Webster Fabio chose to call Tolson's "vast, bizarre, pseudo-literary diction"—we find no favoritism for any social or cultural group. His allusions range freely from Balaam's ass to the eagle who thought he was a chicken to Byzantine texts to eggaroni. If anything, Tolson is deliberately complicating our preconceived notions of cultural—and, by further comparison, existential—order.

Even the title of Tolson's poem can be taken a thousand different ways. Its primary meaning—the art gallery in Harlem which the Curator runs—is embellished by a host of secondary connotations: (1) the peanut gallery (cheaper balcony seats in a movie theater, where blacks were relegated in segregated establishments); (2) the art gallery as symbol, suggesting a reading of the poem as a series of portraits; and finally (3) the sense of gallery as a promenade where Tolson's characters can "exhibit" themselves.

Tolson certainly makes a case for the hero as stylist. For Hideho Heights, Mister Starks, the Curator, and Doctor Nkomo, style *is* being. As critic Ronald Wallace has noted: "For Melvin Tolson, the victories attainable through style are not only real, considerable and worthy of record, but they are indicative as well of his people's invincible sense of the possible. . . . style, if one takes it seriously as an expression of vision, *is* substance, insofar as it reflects and determines one's experience, assessment and response being what experience, after all, is about."[15]

Harlem Gallery is not merely a showcase for Tolson's linguistic and lyrical virtuosity; neither is it a hodgepodge of anecdotes and small lives set like cameos in the heavy silver of philosophical discourse. It is to be viewed *not* as the superficial "Sugar Hill elite" inspected the art works hanging at the exhibition in the Curator's gallery. Rather, the lives of John Laugart, Hideho Heights, and Mister Starks should be seen as illustrations of the three possibilities/alternatives for the black artist. One can embrace the Bitch-Goddess of Success: "My talent was an Uptown whore," says Mister Starks; "my wit a Downtown pimp." One can, like Laugart, remain uncompromising and be spurned. Or one can lead the double life of Hideho, producing crowd-pleasers while creating in secret the works one hopes will last. The Curator discovers Hideho's double life one night when he brings the drunk poet home in a taxi; on the table the Curator discovers a poem "in the modern idiom" called *E. & O. E.*—which just happens to be the title of a

psychological poem for which Tolson received *Poetry* magazine's Bess
Hokim Award in 1952.

Where does Tolson place himself among the three artists, this "trinity that
stinks the ermine robes"? Certainly not with Mister Starks, although he is
sympathetic to Starks's weakness. And, similarities notwithstanding, he does
not identify himself with the Poet Laureate of Harlem. Although he admires
Hideho's flair and to a great extent believes in Heights's aesthetic manifesto
("A work of art is a two-way street, / not a dead end, / where an artist and a
hipster meet. / The form and content in a picture or a song / should blend
like the vowels in a diphthong"), Tolson certainly didn't hide his "difficult"
poems from the public.

Tolson's meditation on the plight of the black American artist emerges
most clearly in "Psi." The Curator places himself in America's kitchen—
"Black Boy," he begins, "let me get up from the white man's Table of Fifty
Sounds / in the kitchen; let me gather the crumbs and cracklings / of this au-
tobio-fragment / before the curtain with the skull and bones descends." The
kitchen is the place for servants, but it is also the place where scraps of song
and gossip blend to become a marvelous "kitchen talk."

Paradoxically, it is John Laugart, the artist given least space in *Harlem
Gallery*, who most exemplifies Tolson's own sense of artistic responsibility.
And though Tolson did not die destitute and anonymous—in fact, he re-
ceived the annual poetry award of the American Academy of Arts and Let-
ters a few months before his death, from cancer, in 1966—he was misun-
derstood by those he loved most, by those to whom he dedicated his
energies in the creation of his last work—the black *literati*. No one under-
stood this predicament better than Tolson himself. As he has the Curator
say near the end of *Harlem Gallery*:

> Poor Boy Blue,
> the Great White World
> and the Black Bourgeosie
> have shoved the Negro Artist into
> the white and not-white dichotomy,
> the Afroamerican dilemma in the Arts—
> the dialectic of
> to be or not to be
> a Negro.

Notes

1. From *The M. B. Tolson Papers*, comp. by Ruth M. Tolson. Excerpts published in "Quotes or Unquotes on Poetry," *Kansas Quarterly* 7 (summer 1975): 37.

2. See Foreword to the first edition of *Libretto for the Republic of Liberia* (New York: Twayne, 1953).

3. Melvin B. Tolson, "A Poet's Odyssey," in *Anger, and Beyond: The Negro Writer in the United States*, ed. Herbert Hill (New York: Harper & Row, 1966), p. 184.

4. Ralph Ellison, "Richard Wright's Blues," in *Shadow and Act* (New York: Random House, 1964), pp. 78–79.

5. Joy Flasch, *Melvin B. Tolson* (New York: Twayne, 1972), pp. 44–45.

6. Ibid., pp. 22–38.

7. Ibid., p. 38; and p. 152, n. 25.

8. Gary Smith, "The Sonnets of Melvin B. Tolson," *College Language Association Journal* 29 (March 1986): 263–64.

9. *See* Arnold Rampersad, *The Life of Langston Hughes, Volume II* (New York: Oxford University Press, 1988), p. 234.

10. This discussion of *Harlem Gallery* has been excerpted, in a slightly altered form, from my essay "Telling It like It I-S *IS*: Narrative Techniques in Melvin Tolson's Harlem Gallery," which appeared in *New England Review/Bread Loaf Quarterly*, 8 (autumn 1985): 109–17.

11. Sarah Webster Fabio, "Who Speaks Negro?" *Negro Digest*, 16 (December 1966): 55–57.

12. Paul Breman, "Poetry into the Sixties," in *Poetry and Drama: The Black American Writer*, vol. 2, ed. C. W. E. Bigsby (Baltimore: Penguin Books, 1969), p. 101.

13. Geneva Smitherman, *Talkin and Testifyin: The Language of Black America* (New York: Houghton Mifflin, 1977), p. 159.

14. Ibid., pp. 147–48.

15. Ronald Walcott, "Ellison, Gordone and Tolson: Some Notes on the Blues, Style and Space," *Black World*, December 1972, p. 26.

Editorial Statement

Raymond Nelson

This edition of the poetry of Melvin B. Tolson collects the three books he published in his lifetime, *Rendezvous with America* (1944), *Libretto for the Republic of Liberia* (1953), and *Harlem Gallery* (1965), and five fugitive poems, "African China," "A Long Head to a Round Head," "The Man from Halicarnassus," "E. & O. E.," and "Abraham Lincoln of Rock Spring Farm," which were for the most part written and published during the interim between *Rendezvous* and *Libretto*. We have not attempted to collect fugitive poems written or published prior to 1944, on the principle that Tolson himself made a decision to exclude them from *Rendezvous*, so that our edition consists of the early poetry gathered in that volume and all subsequent poetry that Tolson saw through publication. Our purpose has been rather to make Tolson's important work available than to be exhaustive or definitive.

Without exception, the texts of the poems collected here are taken unmodified from their original publications in books or, for the fugitive poems, journals. Tolson was scrupulous about the accuracy of his texts and the appearance his verse made on the page. He seems also to have been fortunate in the cooperation he received from his publishers, and we have uncovered no substantive textual problems regarding any of his poems.

With the significant exception of *Harlem Gallery*, Tolson's poems have been left to stand on their own. The principle of letting the poet speak for himself through as little static as possible has been the primary but not the only reason for our decision to hold down the editorial voice. The poems of *Rendezvous with America* are genuinely straightforward; they can and should be read without supplements. After the publication of *Rendezvous* Tolson's poems became increasingly elliptical, ironic, and allusive in texture, but of those that can be difficult "A Long Head to a Round Head" and "The Man from Halicarnassus" are short enough to be accessible to anyone who will invest in them a little time and attention. For two other poems in his reinvention of the high style, "E. & O. E." and *Libretto for the Republic of Liberia*, Tolson himself supplied annotation. It is true that his notes are intended more to be part of these poems than a guide to them, but they do provide the agile reader with helpful handles and levers. For all of their bristling appearance, both "E. & O. E." and *Libretto* are focused on a single subject, and neither presents the kind of difficulty that is encountered in *Harlem Gallery*.

    Harlem Gallery is another kettle of fish. Our decision to provide extensive apparatus for it reflects not only a judgment that a reader would welcome such assistance but a judgment as well about its priority among Tolson's works. Of all the achievements of a distinguished career, *Harlem Gallery* seems the one most likely to find a place in humanity's great anthology. The need for an annotated edition of it was among the first motives that led to the collection presented here.

    One of the lessons *Harlem Gallery* teaches is about the responsibility of curators, critics, scholars, and other subalterns of art to facilitate and clarify. An editor should recognize an opening when he sees one.

"Harlem Gallery"
and Other Poems of
Melvin B. Tolson

RENDEZVOUS WITH
AMERICA

Rendezvous with America

I

Time unhinged the gates
Of Plymouth Rock and Jamestown and Ellis Island,
And worlds of men with hungers of body and soul
Hazarded the wilderness of waters,
Cadenced their destinies
With the potters'-wheeling miracles
Of mountain and valley, prairie and river.

> *These were the men*
> *Who bridged the ocean*
> *With arches of dreams*
> *And piers of devotion:*

Messiahs from the Sodoms and Gomorrahs of the Old World,
Searchers for Cathay and Cipango and El Dorado,
Mystics from Oubangui Chari and Uppsala,
Serfs from Perugia and Tonle Sap,
Jailbirds from Newgate and Danzig,
Patriots from Yokosuka and Stralsund,
Scholars from Oxford and Leyden,
Beggars from Bagdad and Montmartre,
Traders from the Tyrrhenian Sea and Mona Passage,
Sailors from the Skagerrak and Bosporus Strait,
Iconoclasts from Buteshire and Zermatt.

II

These were the men of many breeds
Who mixed their bloods and sowed their seeds.

Designed in gold and shaped of dross,
They raised the Sword beside the Cross.

These were the men who laughed at odds
And scoffed at dooms and diced with gods,
Who freed their souls from inner bars
And mused with forests and sang with stars.

These were the men of prose and rhyme
Who telescoped empires of time,
Who knew the feel of spinal verve
And walked the straight line of the curve.

These were the men of iron lips
Who challenged Dawn's apocalypse,
Who married Earth and Sea and Sky
And died to live and lived to die.

These were the men who dared to be
The sires of things they could not see,
Whose martyred and rejected bones
Became the States' foundation-stones.

III

Into the arteries of the Republic poured
    The babels of bloods,
    The omegas of peoples,
    The moods of continents,
    The melting-pots of seas,
    The flotsams of isms,

The flavors of tongues,
The yesterdays of martyrs,
The tomorrows of utopias.

Into the matrix of the Republic poured
White gulf streams of Europe,
Black tidal waves of Africa,
Yellow neap tides of Asia,
Niagaras of the little people.

America?
America is the Black Man's country,
The Red Man's, the Yellow Man's,
The Brown Man's, the White Man's.

America?
An international river with a legion of tributaries!
A magnificent cosmorama with myriad patterns and colors!
A giant forest with loin-roots in a hundred lands!
A cosmopolitan orchestra with a thousand instruments playing
America!

IV

I see America in Daniel Boone,
As he scouts in the Judas night of a forest aisle;
In big Paul Bunyan, as he guillotines
The timber avalanche that writhes a mile.

I see America in Jesse James,
As his legends match his horse's epic stride;

In big John Henry, as his hammer beats
The monster shovel that quakes the mountainside.

I see America in Casey Jones,
As he mounts No. 4 with the seal of death in his hand;
In Johnny Appleseed, as his miracles
Fruit the hills and valleys and plains of our Promised Land.

I see America in Joe DiMaggio,
As his bat cuts a vacuum in the paralyzed air;
In brown Joe Louis, surfed in white acclaim,
As he fights his country's cause in Madison Square.

I see America in Thomas Paine,
As he pinnacles the freedoms that tyrants ban;
In young Abe Lincoln, tanned by prairie suns,
As he splits his rails and thinks the Rights of Man.

V

A blind man said,
"Look at the kikes."
And I saw
Rosenwald sowing the seeds of culture in the Black Belt,
Michelson measuring the odysseys of invisible worlds,
Brandeis opening the eyes of the blind to the Constitution,
Boas translating the oneness in the Rosetta stone of mankind.

A blind man said,
"Look at the dagos."
And I saw

La Guardia shaping the cosmos of pyramided Manhattan,
Brumidi verving the Capitol frescoes of *Washington at York-
town,*
Caruso scaling the Alpine ranges of drama with the staff of song,
Toscanini enchanting earthward the music of the spheres.

A blind man said,
"Look at the chinks."
And I saw
Lin Yutang crying the World Charter in the white man's wilder-
ness,
Dr. Chen charting the voyages of bacteria in the Lilly Labora-
tories,
Lu Cong weaving plant-tapestries in the Department of Agri-
culture,
Madame Chiang Kai-shek interpreting the Orient and the
Occident.

A blind man said,
"Look at the bohunks."
And I saw
Sikorsky blue-printing the cabala of the airways,
Stokowski imprisoning the magic of symphonies with a baton,
Zvak erecting St. Patrick's Cathedral in a forest of skyscrapers,
Dvořák enwombing the multiple soul of the New World.

A blind man said,
"Look at the niggers."
And I saw
Black Samson mowing down Hessians with a scythe at Brandy-
wine,

Marian Anderson bewitching continents with the talisman of art,
Fred Douglass hurling from tombstones the philippics of free-
    dom,
Private Brooks dying at the feet of MacArthur in Bataan.

VI

America can sing a lullaby
When slippered dusk steals down the terraced sky;
Then in a voice to wake the Plymouth dead
Embattled hordes of tyranny defy.

America can join the riotous throng
And sell her virtues for a harlot song;
Then give the clothes that hide her nakedness
To help her sister nations carry on.

America can worship gods of brass
And bow before the strut of Breed and Class;
Then gather to her bosom refugees
Who champion the causes of the Mass.

America can loose a world of laughter
To shake the States from cornerstone to rafter;
Then gird her mighty loins with corded strength
In the volcanic nightmare of disaster.

America can knot her arms and brow
And guide across frontiers the untamed plow;
Then beat the plowshares into vengeful swords
To keep a rendezvous with Justice now.

VII

Sometimes
Uncle Sam
Pillows his head on the Statue of Liberty,
Tranquilizes himself on the soft couch of the Corn Belt,
Laves his feet in the Golden Gate,
And sinks into the nepenthe of slumber.

And the termites of anti-Semitism busy themselves
And the Ku Klux Klan marches with rope and faggot
And the money-changers plunder the Temple of
    Democracy
And the copperheads start boring from within
And the robber barons pillage the countryside
And the con men try to jimmy the Constitution
And the men of good will are hounded over the Land
And the People groan in the *tribulum* of tyranny.

Then
Comes the roar of cannon at Fort Sumter
Or the explosion of Teapot Dome
Or the Wall Street Crash of '29
Or the thunderclap of bombs at Pearl Harbor!

VIII

I have a rendezvous with America
At Plymouth Rock,
Where the *Mayflower* lies
Battered beam on beam
By titan-chested waves that heave and shock

And cold December winds
That in the riggings pound their fists and scream.
Here,
Now,
The Pilgrim Fathers draw
The New World's testament of faith and law:
A government of and by and for the People,
A pact of peers who share and bear and plan,
A government which leaves men free and equal
And yet knits men together as one man.

I have a rendezvous with America
At Valley Forge.
These are the times that try men's souls
And fetter cowards to their under goals.
Through yonder gorge
Hunger and Cold, Disease and Fear,
Advance with treasonous blows;
The bayonets of the wind stab through
Our winter soldiers' clothes,
And bloody footsteps stain the deep December snows.
Here,
Now,
Our winter soldiers keep the faith
And keep their powder dry . . .
To do or die!

I have a rendezvous with America
This Seventh of December.
The maiden freshness of Pearl Harbor's dawn,
The peace of seas that thieve the breath,

I shall remember.
  Then
Out of yonder Sunrise Land of Death
The fascist spawn
Strikes like the talons of the mad harpoon,
Strikes like the moccasin in the black lagoon,
Strikes like the fury of the raw typhoon.
            The traitor's ruse
            And the traitor's lie,
            Pearl Harbor's ruins
            Of sea and sky,
            Shall live with me
            Till the day I die.
Here,
Now,
At Pearl Harbor, I remember
I have a rendezvous at Plymouth Rock and Valley Forge
This Seventh of December.

IX

    In these midnight dawns
Of the Gethsemanes and the Golgothas of Peoples,
I put my ear to the common ground of America.
        From the brows of mountains
        And the breasts of rivers
        And the flanks of prairies
        And the wombs of valleys
    Swells the *Victory March* of the Republic,
    In the masculine allegro of factories
    And the blues rhapsody of express trains,

In the bass crescendo of power dams
And the nocturne adagio of river boats,
In the sound and fury of threshing machines
And the clarineting needles of textile mills,
In the fortissimo hammers of shipyards
And the diatonic picks of coal mines,
In the oboe rhythms of cotton gins
And the sharped notes of salmon traps,
In the belting harmonics of lumber camps
And the drumming derricks of oil fields.

X

In these midnight dawns
Of the vulture Philistines of the unquiet skies
And the rattlesnake Attilas of the uptorn seas . . .
In these midnight dawns
Of the Gethsemanes and the Golgothas of Peoples,
America stands
Granite-footed as the Rocky Mountains
Beaten by the whirlpool belts of wet winds,
Deep-chested as the Appalachians
Sunning valleys in the palms of their hands,
Tough-tendoned as the Cumberlands
Shouldering the truck caravans of US 40,
Clean-flanked as the lavender walls of Palo Duro
Washed by the living airs of canyon rivers,
Eagle-hearted as the Pacific redwoods
Uprearing their heads in the dawns and dusks of ages.

WOODCUTS FOR AMERICANA

The Mountain Climber

What whim of flesh, what quirk of soul,
  What cast of the Rubicon die
Fates him to the peaks that bayonet
  The winds and snows of the sky?

The pilgrimage withers the veins of him,
  Mirages plague the trail,
The yellow wasps of the sun swarm down,
  And rodent moods assail.

The funeral vultures hover: he sprawls
  Upon the commonplace
Of sharp quill grass and porcupine stones
  That beard the mountain's face.

A scabby rattle churns the weeds
  Beside a putrid log;
A skull, half buried, grimaces near
  The abyssal mouth of a bog.

What whim of flesh, what quirk of soul,
  What cast of the Rubicon die
Fates him to the peaks that bayonet
  The winds and snows of the sky?

Old Man Michael

One day I idled into the field of wheat
Where Old Man Michael, spectrally boned and quaint,
Stooped over the tares that prickled at his feet—
A Celtic prophet or a Coptic saint.

We folk laughed down at him: the quiz of surprise
In dress and talk, the way he jogged his head
In feeding snowbirds, and cocked books at his eyes,
And snored in church as if it were a bed.

And then he towered, nailed the chat in me:
And I felt the myth of what a man should be.

"You farmers mope around," he said, "complain
About the crops, about the stubborn sod.
You blame the sun, the moon, the stars, the rain,
The lack of rain, the crows, the insects . . . God!

"It's drudgery to weed tares out of wheat,
These devilish darnels that grain-roots stupefy.
Yet, if the one is many, we shall cheat
The marketplace and lay a harvest by.

"Yes, if the one is many, kinds in kind,
We shall not leave a world of tares behind."

When Great Dogs Fight

He came from a dead-end world of under breed,
A mongrel in his look and in his deed.

His head sagged lower than his spine, his jaws
Spooned wretchedly, his timid little claws
Were gnarls. A fear lurked in his rheumy eye
When dwarfing pedigrees paraded by.

Often he saw the bulldog, arrogant and grim,
Beside the formidable mastiff; and sight of them
Devouring chunks of meat with juices red
Needled pangs of hunger in his belly and head.

Sometimes he whimpered at the ponderous gate
Until the regal growls shook the estate;
Then he would scurry up the avenue,
Singeing the hedges with his buttercup hue.

The spool of luckless days unwound, and then
The izzard cur, accurst of dogs and men,
Heard yelps of rage beyond the iron fence
And saw the jaws and claws of violence.

He padded through the gate that leaned ajar,
Maneuvered toward the slashing arcs of war,
Then pounced upon the bone; and winging feet
Bore him into the refuge of the street.

A sphinx haunts every age and every zone:
When great dogs fight, the small dog gets a bone.

My Soul and I

(TO RUTH)

We sit alone on the pearl-dust couch of the shore,
        My Soul and I,
Nor watch the golden pyres tiered in the West,
        Where sunrays die.

The seagulls ski far down the crags of foam,
        Like arcs in flight;
But we are balmed in a shadowland of dreams
        That dusk the sight.

Though thick white pythons of the tide thresh in
        And ships crawl by
And night lets slip Venetian blinds . . . we dream,
        My Soul and I.

An Ex-Judge at the Bar

Bartender, make it straight and make it two—
One for the you in me and the me in you.
Now let us put our heads together: one
Is half enough for malice, sense, or fun.

I know, Bartender, yes, I know when the Law
Should wag its tail or rip with fang and claw.
When Pilate washed his hands, that neat event
Set for us judges a Caesarean precedent.

What I shall tell you now, as man is man,
You'll find in neither Bible nor Koran.
It happened after my return from France
At the bar in Tony's Lady of Romance.

We boys drank pros and cons, sang *Dixie*; and then,
The bar a Sahara, we pledged to meet again.
But lo, on the bar there stood in naked scorn
The Goddess Justice, like September Morn.

Who blindfolds Justice on the courthouse roof
While the lawyers weave the sleight-of-hand of proof?
I listened, Bartender, with my heart and head,
As the Goddess Justice unbandaged her eyes and said:

"To make the world safe for Democracy,
You lost a leg in Flanders fields—*oui, oui?*
To gain the judge's seat, you twined the noose
That swung the Negro higher than a goose."

Bartender, who has dotted every *i?*
Crossed every *t?* Put legs on every *y?*
Therefore, I challenged her: "Lay on, Macduff,
And damned be him who first cries, 'Hold, enough!' "

The boys guffawed, and Justice began to laugh
Like a maniac on a broken phonograph.
Bartender, make it straight and make it three—
One for the Negro . . . one for you and me.

Whence?

If the oar of the canoe
Shames your skill with flounce and flout,
Whence shall come the art to match
The snarl of riggings—
                    The riggings' clout?

If the valley's sunny path
Saps your muscle and bone and vein,
Whence shall come the strength to bear
The night of the crag—
                    The crag's terrain?

If the cry of the timber wolf
Gives your heart St. Vitus's dance,
Whence shall come the courage to face
The roar of the lion—
                    The lion's advance?

The Town Fathers

At the Courthouse Square
On the Fourth of July,
Beneath Old Glory's
Pyrotechnic sky,
The town fathers met,
Minus Bible and rye.

Against the statue
Of Confederate dead
The Mayor spat
His snuff and said,
"We need a slogan!"
And he palmed his head.

The Sheriff's idioms
Dynamited assent.
The Judge croaked a phrase
Latinistically bent.
And the Mayor pondered
With official intent.

On a neon billboard,
As high as a steeple,
The travelers puzzle
The amazing sequel:
The Blackest Land
And The Whitest People.

The Furlough

The worst can happen only in the brain:
  I gaze upon her silken loveliness,
She is a passion-flower of joy and pain
  On the golden bed I came back to possess.

I gaze upon her silken loveliness,
  I image the intimacies of eager lovers
On the golden bed I came back to possess.
  The eye of jealousy midnight uncovers.

I image the intimacies of eager lovers,
  As an artist, bit by bit, creates his dream.
The eye of jealousy midnight uncovers,
  No balm in Gilead heals one's hurt esteem.

As an artist, bit by bit, creates a dream,
  I stitched the gash of fate to serve my country.
No balm of Gilead heals one's hurt esteem,
  A soldier fights for Honor, Love, and Duty.

I stitched the gash of fate to serve my country,
  His treason stabbed the trinity in the back.
A soldier fights for Honor, Love, and Duty:
  A man's castle is a palace or a shack.

His treason stabbed the trinity in the back,
  His life was rubbish bargained in a fraud.
A man's castle is a palace or a shack:
  A victory lost at home is lost abroad.

His life was rubbish bargained in a fraud.
What yearnings torture a man in the tropic night!
A victory lost at home is lost abroad.
A furlough is an escalator to delight!

What yearnings torture a man in the tropic night!
I choked her just a little, and she is dead.
A furlough is an escalator to delight!
Her beauty gathers rot on the golden bed.

I choked her just a little, and she is dead,
    Tomorrow's sieve will sift the chaff and grain,
Her beauty gathers rot on the golden bed,
    The worst can happen only in the brain.

The Man Inside

(TO THE MEMORY OF V. F. CALVERTON)

They told me—the voices of hates in the land—
They told me that White is White and Black is Black;
That the children of Africa are scarred with a brand
Ineradicable as the spots on the leopard's back.

They told me that gulfs unbridgeable lie
In the no man's seascapes of unlike hues,
As wide as the vertical of earth and sky,
As ancient as the grief in the seagull's mews.

They told me that Black is an isle with a ban
Beyond the pilgrims' Continent of Man.

I yearned for the mainland where my brothers live.
The cancerous isolation behind, I swam
Into the deeps, a naked fugitive,
Defying tribal fetishes that maim and damn.

And when the typhoon of jeers smote me and hope
Died like a burnt-out world and on the shore
The hates beat savage breasts, you threw the rope
And drew me into the catholic Evermore.

We stood on common ground, in transfiguring light,
Where the man inside is neither Black nor White.

Old Houses

Aunt Martha bustles
From room to room
Between attic and basement,
With duster and broom.

Like an oven grenade,
In cobwebby corners
Her broom explodes
A babel of wonders.

Her summer crusade
Havocs the bugs.
Like an enfilade,
She rakes the rugs.

The sound and fury
Of table and bed
Whirs a panic of sparrows
To the oaks overhead.

Untenable grows
The vast of the house
For even the ghost
Of Lazarus' mouse.

The fogies convert
Back fences to staffs
And sow their gossip
With Pharisee laughs:

Aunt Martha's scowl
Is a lithograph's.

As the fogies watch
Her attic lairs
Jettison the junk
Of heirloom wares,
She shouts: "Old houses
Need cleaning upstairs!"

The Poet

The poet cheats us with humility.
Ignored by *Who's Who* among his peers
And *Job's News* also, yet this lapidary
Endures the wormwood of anonymous years:
He shapes and polishes chaos without a fee,
The bones of silence fat no pedigree.

His ego is not vain,
Stuffs not on caviar of smile and phrase.
He comes of nobler strain,
Is marrowed with racier ways:
The beggar Vanity feeds on the crumbs of praise.

He stands before the bar of pride,
Gives not a tinker's dam
For those who flatter or deride
His epic or epigram:
The potboy, not the connoisseur, toadies for a dram.

Peep through his judas-hole
And see the dogma of self at work,
The nerve and verve of soul
That in the sky-born lurk:
The eagle's heart abides not in the mole,
The poppy thrives not at the arctic pole.

A freebooter of lands and seas,
He plunders the dialects of the marketplace,
Thieves lexicons of Crown jewel discoveries,

Pillages the symbols and meccas of the race:
Of thefts the poet's magic leaves no trace.

An Ishmaelite,
He breaks the icons of the Old and New,
Devours your privacy like a parasite,
Parades the skeletons closeted with God and you:
The poet's lien exempts the Many nor the Few.

An anchoret,
He feeds on the raven's bread,
Candles worlds whose suns have set,
Leads Nature to the nuptial bed,
Bathes in pools that never mortals wet:
The poet unlocks the wilderness with an epithet.

A champion of the People versus Kings—
His only martyrdom is poetry;
A hater of the hierarchy of things—
Freedom's need is his necessity.
The poet flings upon the winds blueprints of Springs:
A bright new world where he alone will know work's menacings!

Esperanto

Neighbors in lands afar,
Our native bones and flesh,
Our means and ends bizarre,
The gods of the tribe enmesh
In nets and snares of war.

Our martyrdoms unequal,
The censor fogs ashore,
We, the little people,
Their shibboleths encore.
Often our eyes see not,
Beneath the sham wherefore,
Identity of plot.

Yellow and Black and White,
We mouth a Babel tongue;
But in Gehenna's blight,
When warps and woofs are wrung,
We speak the idioms of woe,
Speak from the morgues of night,
Our own, our Esperanto.

Many are we in one
Under the skull and skin:
Jesus, Judas, and Simpleton,
Hamlet, Babbitt, and Solomon—
Kith and kin.

Chinese and Arab and Jew,
Saxon and Eskimo,

Slav and Tartar and Kru,
Latin and Danakil and Crow—
In spite of tribal brand,
Our catholic tongue of woe
Speaks in every land
Our own, our Esperanto.

His heart is pitiless stone
Of unhewn monotone
Who hears one of us cry,
From the mesh,
Bone to bone,
Flesh to flesh,
And leaves his kith and kin to die.

Our fatherland is the earth,
Our race is humanity,
Our blood gave the freedoms birth
In the ward of history.

Our wealth is the universe
Of stars and seas and clods;
Our men of good will disperse
The icons of tribal gods.

Now put the freeman's ax
To the loins of the evil root,
Now cleave with the freeman's zax
The charnel-house of loot,
So that our children wax
On the freeman's fruit!

Views

He sees the Brussels lawn,
    The jasper seat,
The fountain, the chapel of shrubs,
    The aria street.

You see the alleyway yard
    With felon cans,
Sierras of rags and trash,
    And broken bans.

He looks at the front of the house,
    You look at the back:
He calls you a charlatan!
    You call him a quack!

The Unknown Soldier

I was a minuteman at Concord Bridge,
I was a frigate-gunner on Lake Erie,
I was a mortarman at Stony Ridge,
I fought at San Juan Hill and Château Thierry,
I braved Corregidor and the Arctic Sea:
The index finger brings democracy.

These States bred freedom in and in my bone—
Old as the new testament of Plymouth Bay.
When the Founding Fathers laid the Cornerstone
And rued the thirteen clocks that would not say
The hour on the hour, I nerved myself with them
Under the noose in the hand of the tyrant's whim.

I've seen the alien ships of destiny
Plow the sea mountains between the hemispheres.
I've seen the Gulf Stream of our history
Littered with derelicts of corsair careers.
I've heard the watchman cry, "The bars! The bars!"
When midnight held the funeral of stars.

I saw horizontal States grow vertical,
From Plymouth Harbor to the Golden Gate,
Till wedged against skyscapes empyreal
Their glories elbowed the decrees of fate.
These States bred freedom in and in my bone:
I hymn their virtues and their sins atone.

The tares and wheat grow in the self-same field,
The rose and thorn companion on the bush,

The gold and gravel cuddle in the yield,
The oil and grit and dirt together gush.
The Gordian knot *to be or not to be*
Snares not the free.

My faith props the tomorrows, for I know
The roots of liberty, tough-fibered, feed
On the blood of tyrants and martyrs; the judas blow
Tortures the branches till they twist and bleed:
And yet no Caesar, vitamined on loot,
Can liberty uproot!

I am the Unknown Soldier: I open doors
To the Rights of Man, letters incarnadine.
These shrines of freedom are mine as well as yours;
These ashes of freemen yours as well as mine.
My troubled ghost shall haunt These States, nor cease
Till the global war becomes a global peace.

DARK SYMPHONY

Dark Symphony

I

Allegro Moderato

Black Crispus Attucks taught
                    Us how to die
Before white Patrick Henry's bugle breath
Uttered the vertical
                    Transmitting cry:
"Yea, give me liberty or give me death."

Waifs of the auction block,
                    Men black and strong
The juggernauts of despotism withstood,
Loin-girt with faith that worms
                    Equate the wrong
And dust is purged to create brotherhood.

No Banquo's ghost can rise
                    Against us now,
Aver we hobnailed Man beneath the brute,
Squeezed down the thorns of greed
                    On Labor's brow,
Garroted lands and carted off the loot.

II

Lento Grave

The centuries-old pathos in our voices
Saddens the great white world,

And the wizardry of our dusky rhythms
Conjures up shadow-shapes of ante-bellum years:

Black slaves singing *One More River to Cross*
In the torture tombs of slave-ships,
Black slaves singing *Steal Away to Jesus*
In jungle swamps,
Black slaves singing *The Crucifixion*
In slave-pens at midnight,
Black slaves singing *Swing Low, Sweet Chariot*
In cabins of death,
Black slaves singing *Go Down, Moses*
In the canebrakes of the Southern Pharaohs.

III

Andante Sostenuto

They tell us to forget
The Golgotha we tread . . .
We who are scourged with hate,
A price upon our head.
They who have shackled us
Require of us a song,
They who have wasted us
Bid us condone the wrong.

They tell us to forget
Democracy is spurned.
They tell us to forget
The Bill of Rights is burned.
Three hundred years we slaved,

We slave and suffer yet:
Though flesh and bone rebel,
They tell us to forget!

Oh, how can we forget
Our human rights denied?
Oh, how can we forget
Our manhood crucified?
When Justice is profaned
And plea with curse is met,
When Freedom's gates are barred,
Oh, how can we forget?

IV

Tempo Primo

The New Negro strides upon the continent
In seven-league boots . . .
The New Negro
Who sprang from the vigor-stout loins
Of Nat Turner, gallows-martyr for Freedom,
Of Joseph Cinquez, Black Moses of the Amistad Mutiny,
Of Frederick Douglass, oracle of the Catholic Man,
Of Sojourner Truth, eye and ear of Lincoln's legions,
Of Harriet Tubman, Saint Bernard of the Underground Railroad.

The New Negro
Breaks the icons of his detractors,
Wipes out the conspiracy of silence,
Speaks to *his* America:

"My history-moulding ancestors
Planted the first crops of wheat on these shores,
Built ships to conquer the seven seas,
Erected the Cotton Empire,
Flung railroads across a hemisphere,
Disemboweled the earth's iron and coal,
Tunneled the mountains and bridged rivers,
Harvested the grain and hewed forests,
Sentineled the Thirteen Colonies,
Unfurled Old Glory at the North Pole,
Fought a hundred battles for the Republic."

The New Negro:
His giant hands fling murals upon high chambers,
His drama teaches a world to laugh and weep,
His music leads continents captive,
His voice thunders the Brotherhood of Labor,
His science creates seven wonders,
His Republic of Letters challenges the Negro-baiters.

The New Negro,
Hard-muscled, Fascist-hating, Democracy-ensouled,
Strides in seven-league boots
Along the Highway of Today
Toward the Promised Land of Tomorrow!

V

Larghetto

None in the Land can say
To us black men Today:

You send the tractors on their bloody path,
And create Okies for *The Grapes of Wrath*.
You breed the slum that breeds a *Native Son*
To damn the good earth Pilgrim Fathers won.

None in the Land can say
To us black men Today:
You dupe the poor with rags-to-riches tales,
And leave the workers empty dinner pails.
You stuff the ballot box, and honest men
Are muzzled by your demagogic din.

None in the Land can say
To us black men Today:
You smash stock markets with your coined blitzkriegs,
And make a hundred million guinea pigs.
You counterfeit our Christianity,
And bring contempt upon Democracy.

None in the Land can say
To us black men Today:
You prowl when citizens are fast asleep,
And hatch Fifth Column plots to blast the deep
Foundations of the State and leave the Land
A vast Sahara with a Fascist brand.

VI

Tempo di Marcia

Out of abysses of Illiteracy,
Through labyrinths of Lies,

Across waste lands of Disease . . .
We advance!

Out of dead-ends of Poverty,
Through wildernesses of Superstition,
Across barricades of Jim Crowism . . .
We advance!

With the Peoples of the World . . .
We advance!

A SONG FOR MYSELF

A Song for Myself

I judge
My soul
Eagle
Nor mole:
A man
Is what
He saves
From rot.

The corn
Will fat
A hog
Or rat:
Are these
Dry bones
A hut's
Or throne's?

Who filled
The moat
'Twixt sheep
And goat?
Let Death,
The twin
Of Life,
Slip in?

Prophets
Arise,

Mask-hid,
Unwise,
Divide
The earth
By class
And birth.

Caesars
Without,
The People
Shall rout;
Caesars
Within,
Crush flat
As tin.

Who makes
A noose
Envies
The goose.
Who digs
A pit
Dices
For it.

Shall tears
Be shed
For those
Whose bread
Is thieved
Headlong?

Tears right
No wrong.

Prophets
Shall teach
The meek
To reach.
Leave not
To God
The boot
And rod.

The straight
Lines curve?
Failure
Of nerve?
Blind-spots
Assail?
Times have
Their Braille.

If hue
Of skin
Trademark
A sin,
Blame not
The *make*
For God's
Mistake.

Since flesh
And bone

Turn dust
And stone,
With life
So brief,
Why add
To grief?

I sift
The chaff
From wheat
And laugh.
No curse
Can stop
The tick
Of clock.

Those who
Wall in
Themselves
And grin
Commit
Incest
And spawn
A pest.

What's writ
In vice
Is writ
In ice.
The truth
Is not

Of fruits
That rot.

A sponge,
The mind
Soaks in
The kind
Of stuff
That fate's
Milieu
Dictates.

Jesus,
Mozart,
Shakespeare,
Descartes,
Lenin,
Chladni,
Have lodged
With me.

I snatch
From hooks
The meat
Of books.
I seek
Frontiers,
Not worlds
On biers.

The snake
Entoils

The pig
With coils.
The pig's
Skewed wail
Does not
Prevail.

Old men
Grow worse
With prayer
Or curse:
Their staffs
Thwack youth
Starved thin
For truth.

Today
The Few
Yield poets
Their due;
Tomorrow
The Mass
Judgment
Shall pass.

I harbor
One fear
If death
Crouch near:
Does my
Creed span

The Gulf
Of Man?

And when
I go
In calm
Or blow
From mice
And men,
Selah!
What . . . then?

The Shift of Gears

The mechanic probes
The belly of the car,
And smears the jaw
With the zigzag scar,
And puckers his brow
As he wrenches a bar.

The driver curses,
And strikes a match,
And rams his hat,
And mops his thatch.
"What's wrong?" he taunts,
With lording dispatch.

The mechanic speaks
In the language of peers:
"A car or a man
Can outwear the years,
If horse sense handles
The shift of gears."

The Ballad of the Rattlesnake

The sharecroppers sat
In the Delta night;
Many were black,
And many were white.

And this is the tale
From the bearded mouth
Of the dreamer who saw
Green lands in the South:

The Apaches stake
On the desert sands
The blond man's feet
And the blond man's hands.

He curses and prays
And tugs apace.
The Apaches laugh
And spit in his face.

The blond man looks
With gibbering breath
At the diamond coils
And the fangs of death.

The chief ties a rock
To the rattler's tail.
The blond man's blood
Congeals like hail.

The diamond head
Hisses and pries.
The horny tail
The rock defies.

As custom wills,
Bent like a bow,
The red chief stoops
And taunts his foe.

A madness crawls
In the rattler's brain:
The naked white thing
Is the cause of its pain.

At every lurch,
The blond man dies.
Eternity ticks
Behind the eyes.

In the desert world
A scream tears space,
As the rattler strikes
The blond man's face.

Five miles away
The Apaches laugh
Like a frozen wind
In a crib of chaff.

The blond man lies
Like a bar of lead.

No hiss or laugh
Can vex the dead.

The desert holds
In its frying-pan
The bones of a snake
And the bones of a man.

And many a thing
With a rock on its tail
Kills the nearest thing
And dies by the trail.

*The sharecroppers sat
In the Delta night;
Many were black,
And many were white.*

*And this is the tale
From the bearded mouth
Of the dreamer who saw
Green lands in the South.*

A Scholar Looks at an Oak

Storms slug its head,
Its shoulders sag,
Its beard is shorn
Upon the crag.

In dawns and dusks
Its spine alone
Keeps it erect
Like Doric stone.

A squash grows up
At a summer's stroke;
An age wears out
To make an oak.

SONNETS

A *Primer* for *Today*

The great biologist said: "The semen of change
Crawls upward from the simple to the complex,
Through animal and plant, in kingdoms strange,
Whimmed by the drama of milieu and sex."

The great geologist said: "Nature disdains
Your gradualism. Islands retch and split,
Valleys swell up and mountains eddy to plains,
Cinder worlds vanish like comics in a skit."

The great economist said: "The species Man
Has spells of calm, too, spasms of devilment.
The fat years lull his nature for a span;
The lean years then midwife a malcontent."

The great historian said: "I want to know
Who knows when changes are too fast or slow."

The Gallows

He was my teacher a continent of years ago;
Yet bright as blood is the red-letter day he came
Into the drouth of the class, with his wits aflow,
To freshen the sesame in each alien name.

Month after month, the pan of his alchemy
Found nuggets of gold where others found alloy.
And the miracle of his integrity
Put bone and blood and soul into girl and boy.

He dumped the debris of customs on the refuse heap,
He tore down fences propped with a great Amen,
He set apart the huddling goats and sheep,
He let the oxygen of the freedoms in.

The lame, the halt, the blind—these struck him down;
Then the gallows of ignorance hanged the little town.

The Blindness of Scorn

The jungle huddled in like dungeon walls:
Green catacombs of shrubs, vague dinosaurs
Of sweating trunks, hanging gardens of palls,
And potter's fields of weeds and pollinars.

The Malay guide, in loin cloth, walked ahead
Along the corkscrew trail, with ear and eye
Alert; behind him, bronzed and helmeted,
The alien White came, cursing earth and sky.

"Sahib!" the Malay cried. "Sahib!" He bowed
And dropped his goatskin pack. "Stinkbug of hell!"
The master raged. The guide, with fear endowed,
Shoved violently the White. The python fell.

The Malay said, as the coils piled high and dense:
"Sahib, the blindness of scorn provokes offense."

If You Should Lie to Me

If you should lie to me and I should find
My soul webbed in the calculus of a lie,
Of snares in hell and earth the most unkind,
This snare would bleed the core of affection dry.

We vowed our constancy without ado
And let love's fiat merge the fiefs of heart.
If to this truth, then, you and I are true,
Nothing or none can rend our lives apart.

A fraud, a kiss of guile, a hidden knife—
These for Iago; but for you and me
A frankness that gives nakedness to life,
It matters not how aches reality.

The seven deadly sins I can abide:
A lie? That kills the *raison d'être* inside!

A *Hamlet Rives Us*

I saw him faltering toward me in the street:
His eyes emptied of living, his grief unshed.
Pain pitted my heart and meshed my doubtful feet,
As memory's alcove revealed his loved one dead.

Our sorrows mated then, for I had lost
The next of kin in the fogland of the year.
And yet a Hamlet rives us when the frost
Of death comes like a specter buccaneer.

I must console him in this awful hour:
It is the wise and decent thing to do.
Embarrassed, helpless, I was thieved of power
To utter the tags tragedy ordained untrue.

My friend passed by, unseeing in his grief;
And the lash of conscience gave me sweet relief.

The Traitor to France

This land is mine, for better or for worse:
Let no man put asunder sealed the pledge.
We who betrayed her freedoms cajole and curse
And drag her virtues through the marsh and sedge.

Mon Dieu! she is a bawling Magdalen,
A taxi-dancer and a cuckold's wench,
Seducing apaches and paillards and guttermen
Beyond the gaslights on a byway bench.

With robber barons in *flagrante delicto* caught,
No Jezebel is more whorish. Guillotine my name
Unmartyred, for the golden girls I sought
In Mammon's temple and the stalls of shame.

She was a virgin till my deception led
Her to the harlotry of Vichy's bed.

A Legend of Versailles

Lloyd George and Woodrow Wilson and Clemenceau—
The Big Three: England, America, and France—
Met at ,Versailles. The Tiger ached to know
About the myth to end war's dominance.

"One moment, gentlemen," the Tiger said,
"Do you really want a lasting peace?" And then
Lloyd George assented with his shaggy head
And Woodrow Wilson, nodding, chafed his chin.

"The price of such a peace is great. We must give
Up secret cartels, spheres of power and trade;
Tear down our tariff walls; let lesser breeds live
As equals; scrap the empires we have made."

The gentlemen protested, "You go too far."
The Tiger shouted, "You don't mean peace, but war!"

The Note

I saw her in a cluttered basement store,
Across a counter frivolous with toys.
Her alien face held griefs that haunt the poor,
As she wrapped up the trinkets for the boys.

I met her often, though I loved her not:
A soul compulsion drew me to her side.
On holidays in an untraveled spot,
We talked and dreamed and watched the combing tide.

This note is all she left to tell me why
She swam out to that fatal rendezvous.
Again I read . . . again: "It's best to die,
When there is nothing else for one to do."

And now I know that pity's worse than scorn
And love roots deepest when of pity born.

Inevitability

The mausoleum of a winter's day
Entombs a cosmic waste of hill and vale.
Yon cannibal pack of wolves tears at its prey,
Like villains fabled in a Norseman's tale.

He was their wily chief in years sped by;
He brought a reign of terror to man and beast.
Though fear of him had sucked their bones, his cry
Canceled by death, they on his carcass feast.

Thus decorated toadies ape the king,
Goosestep his thoughts and trumpet his success;
But when his toppled pomp goes glimmering,
The eunuched underlings deepen his distress.

They lick their chops and wag their foolish heads
And tear his counterfeit greatness into shreds.

The Braggart

His blond magnificence keyed his vanity,
As snowdrifts moored us at the cabined hearth.
His dog-eat-dog ethics appalled, and we
Were sea fish caught within the damming garth.

"The eagle kings the realm of birds," he said;
"The lion monarchs the jungle; the world of trees
Kneels to the redwood; Everest's imperial head
Outdazzles the peaks; the Pacific queens the seas.

"Elite and mongrel! That is Nature's plan,
A ladder-scheme and not a level-hood.
The Nordic is the zenith rung of Man,
And envy sires the lesser breeds no good."

The big game hunter said, "I saw a horde
Of ants unflesh a lion as he roared."

The Big Game Hunter

All day the Zulu hunters and their chief
Tracked in the bushland. Then a sudden roar
Cleaved forests, and with naked unbelief
The warriors watched the charging carnivore.

The giant chief saw that his rooted band
Would be wiped out. Though terror iced his heart,
He charged the jungle king; the fisted hand
Shot into the cavern mouth like an ebony dart.

The brave are blind to danger; the courageous see
And feel and know. Wise Latins placed the seat
Of courage in the heart, where it should be,
That naught may ape its grandeur, none may cheat.

The flower of sacrifice blooms the lunar year,
And conscience serves as pallbearer of fear.

The Dictionary of the Wolf

"We all declare for liberty," Lincoln said.
"We use the word and mean all sorts of things:
In the sweat of thy face shalt thou eat bread.
Rifle the basket that thy neighbor brings."

The grizzled axman squinted at Honest Abe,
The six feet four of him, gaunt, sad of face,
The hands to split a log or cradle a babe,
The cracked palm hat, the homespun of his race.

"The wolf tears at the sheep's throat: and the sheep
Extols the shepherd for cudgeling tyranny;
The wolf, convulsed with indignation deep,
Accuses the shepherd of murdering liberty.

"But the dictionary of the wolf is writ
In words the rats of time chew bit by bit."

OF MEN AND CITIES

Vesuvius

I

The galleon ages drift beyond the Beyond,
Fate's hobnails grind the hovel and the throne:
From bastion limestones of the Eocene Sea,
Vesuvius rears the pyramid of her cone.

Vesuvius sleeps: the bear in polar nights,
His huge paws limp, his vast head in repose.
Vesuvius sleeps: the Amazon boa sprawled,
Contemptuous of jungle ebbs and flows.

An heir of legends, the hillman tends his herd,
His crag-wise dog at ease on buffer paws;
And in the crater mouth the mammoth vines
Festoon the boulder teeth and splintered jaws.

The cattle graze along blue-yellow scarps,
In smug serenity the dumb things wear.
At crossbone terraces of black calcine,
The west wind combs the vineyard's purple hair.

The eagles brood on broken spars of cliffs,
Weary of heights imperial, like old kings
Scarred by the climb to fleshpot pinnacles,
Wit-blunted by the emptiness of things.

A chronic nightmare troubles Vesuvius,
As tides of flames and ashes fret below.
That lava beds their forebears' whited bones,
The placid sheep and cattle do not know.

II

The strong men counsel with the wise,
The strong who sow not what they reap.
The golden sandals strike the ruins,
The arrogant gray eyes outward sweep
Past scrofulous rocks. And miles away
Vesuvius lies asleep.

The hillman leaves his shaggy flock,
A specter bearded and warped and lame.
"A city here, my lords?" he cries.
"Yon mountain has a cursed name!"
The wise men wag. The strong men damn.
The shepherd's eyeballs flame.

The purple togas flaunt no more.
He speaks with earthborn dignity:
"Blacksmithing gods live in the cone.
Sometimes they sleep a century,
Then rouse and mighty forges roar
As if they madmen be.

"Is not Vesuvius like your Rome?
She gorges often and can't digest
The mass; and so the smithy gods
Must use the bellows; at their behest
The bloating lumps are vomited.
Vesuvius takes her rest.

"Beneath your very feet, my lords,
A city of the dead now lies.

You cannot change Vesuvius,
Nor yet the ways of fools and flies.
Who builds on the volcano's site
Is strong, nor good, nor wise."

III

The wise men cast Pompeii's die
And doom her to the lava bed.
The slaves sweat blood in apex suns,
And living bones bury the dead.

Their roofs embellished with lions' heads,
Black marble villas crest the hills;
Like hoarfrost, gleam the statues of gods
Along the marges of mirroring rills.

The sapphire domes of palaces
Dazzle the cypress and laurel and pine,
And odysseys of pearly stairs
End at the sea-foam's borderline.

The fame of Pompeii's gaieties
Sparkles like wine in faceted glass.
The boding tales of Vesuvius
Are ails forgot in hippocras.

The virgins view the carnivals
From cloistered balcony and façade;
But in the tapestried bazaars
Voluptuous courtesans promenade.

Perfumed eunuchs serve golden plates
To conquerors of Tyre and Es-Scham.
The statesmen stroll bronze-lettered flags
And seal fates with an epigram.

Numidian slaves in the marketplace
Barter for lords with lordly guile,
And Roman boys learn at the feet
Of hoary Greeks who never smile.

The rabbi pioneers his way
Past porticoed Apollo's shrine,
A prophet evangel of Elohim
With homing dreams of Palestine.

Old libertines in spicy baths
Rid waxing fat of bedevilment,
And senators slink down amethyst halls
Like waifs on curfew mischief bent.

The poets of the bellygods
Thieve nectars from the saber-men
Who forego beauty on the couch
To drag the captive princes in.

The world-wise scribble on frescoed walls
The scandals of the night before;
The odds and ends of bones and flesh
Shuffle beyond the palace door.

Patrician youths on Arabian steeds
Gallop across the lava plains,

And bacchants watch gladiators die
Like hapless flies in tropic rains.

Between the nobleman and plebe,
Between the saffron flags and dirt,
Between the peacock feast and gruel,
A dead world lies with wormwood girt.

Pompeii's vanities spit contempt
Into the beggars' rags and scars.
Pompeii worships the seven sins
As the seven wise men the seven stars.

IV

Vesuvius flings,
As an ox its yoke,
Huge beams of gas
And luminous smoke.
Like a beast in labor,
The pyramid cone
Rends the night land
With gasp and groan.

Prodigious columns
Of cinders rise:
Vast peacock fans
Plumage the skies.
With lightning fists
Sulphurous flashes
Lace and buffet
Monsters of ashes.

The sundered throat
Spews up the dead
Of seas in flames,
Yellow, blood-red.
The limestones churn
In mud and rain.
Convulsions tear
The bowels in twain.

Explosions hurl
Crag thunders out
And rivers of steam
In leviathan rout.
The storms of smoke
And lakes of sand
And seas of ashes
Deluge the land.

The blistering waves
Of heat descend,
Like gutting edges
Of torrid wind.
The lava gulf,
Glittering white,
Heaves to the sea
In the leprous night.

Three days, three ages,
The pumice stones
And jet-black mud
And vestige bones

And entrail lava
And squalls of doom
Pour from Vesuvius'
Stupendous womb!

The Shipwright

Down in the shipyard, day and night,
    The Galahads of the dock,
Hard as the sinews of basin rock,
    Build an ocean cosmopolite.

The rivets stab and the hammers bite
Into the beams and plates of steel
Of the Diesel heart and the belly keel.

We,
The workers of the world strike catholic notes
On woods and irons, wring from brassy throats
Epics of industry.

Day and night
The diapason puts
The bent-winged gulls to flight
And shakes the harbor and quakes the ground
And leaps at the suns like Prometheus bound.

Our matrix shapes our citizen of the world
To cross the churning mountains of the sea,
    Nor fashions a canoe to sail a lake
      In cool felicity.

The Triumph Aster

(FOR MADAME CHIANG)

Is it not strange
That East and West should meet
In the sanctum of this garden
Between skyscrapers of my native street?

The Triumph aster lifts
Its royal head
With reflex curling rays
Of brilliant red,
Like the gulfs of China's blood
The little people shed.

The Triumph aster wears
A diadem of quills,
Needles stitching the heart of a people
Daggered with myriad ills.

The Triumph aster dreams
Of the sesame of stars,
Beyond the skull-paved highroad
Of Burma's bolts and bars.

The Triumph aster stands
On the backbone of its stem,
Unbending as a martyr
Hymning a requiem.

Is it not strange
That East and West should meet
In the sanctum of this garden
Between skyscrapers of my native street?

The Bard of Addis Ababa

I

Out of the green glooms of Dambassa
Trots the massive yellow dog,
His prowlike jaws, his forehead
Scarred like an axman's log,
His growls presaging a menace
Like a fog-horn in a fog.

On the scrap pyres of Addis Ababa,
On the trash alps of Adowa,
He rips the hyena and jackal
With scimitar tooth and claw;
And he grinds the Bola boa
In the mill of his monster jaw.

Now the Bard of Addis Ababa
Looms, barefoot, on the height,
Thicket-bearded, cadaverous,
Black as the Gojjam night,
The gray eyes under tuft-ridges
Glowing like anthracite.

Barbaric splendor crowns him:
A busby of lion mane,
A London-born gift of the Negus
In the heyday of his domain,
A bejeweled corona befitting
A *ras* or a chamberlain.

With his black-gum staff of the shepherd
And his leopard traveling-bag,
He wanders from village to village
Under his forefathers' flag—
A hero of *grazmatch* and vendor,
Of *hakim* and beggar and wag.

A blooded Amharic scholar
With the lore of six thousand years—
Yet he wears a sackcloth *shamma*
From the looms of Tafwaiperes.
A Chinese dagger in his girdle
Ranks a pistol of English peers.

His name is an emblem of justice,
Greater than *lumot* of priest;
And outdoor courts invoke him
To sentence man or beast;
And debtors chained to their masters
Appeal to the Bard for release.

The battle-cry of his ballads,
The meters' blood-spurring pace,
The star-reach of his spearing forefinger,
The eloquence of his face,
The seven-league boots of his images—
Stir the palace and marketplace.

He chants of men fleshed in epics,
Of the freedoms that keep men free,
Of *negadis, ambas,* and *tuculs,*

Of Black Jew and Somali,
Of the burnt-faced little people,
And the Palaver House to be:

II

Rise up, ye warriors, do or die!
It's tooth for tooth and eye for eye!

Free are the rivers and mountains and plains,
    Proud are the backboned men
Who come from the forests of Dambassa
    And the lowlands of Ogaden.

The Fascist jackals shall die on the dunes,
    From Gambela to Danakil,
And the rain and the sun shall rot their thighs
    From Gojjam to Bodobo Hill.

The days of masters shall pass like the dust
    Of a westering caravan,
And the Palaver House shall feast and crown
    The kith and kin of Man.

Yea, the pit shall suck the masters down
    Like a dying ship at sea;
And a *ras*, a *dedjazmatch*, a king—yoho!—
    Each father's son shall be!

Rise up, ye warriors, do or die!
It's tooth for tooth and eye for eye!

III

Along the Imperial Highway
The heroes of Takkaze ride;
The silver-gilt shields and knife blades
Vie with the patriot's pride;
And the crowds in Addis Ababa
Swirl like a surfy tide.

The giant Galla captain,
Khaki-clad, nerveless, and straight,
Rides at the head of the column
On his richly-decked mule; the Great
Has brought his heroes and captives
Over crag and *amba* and *ait*.

The Black Shirts slump on the camels,
Haggard and granite-eyed;
No longer the gypsying Caesars
Who burnt-faced breeds deride:
In the river Takkaze their vanity
Lies with the Caesars who died.

On the steps of St. George's Cathedral
The golden Abuna stands,
And priests in purple togas
Wave censers with anointed hands,
And the eucalyptus cloisters
Echo with festive bands.

Princes and bishops and scholars
Pyramid to left and right

Of the Conquering Lion of Judah
And the Diadem of Light,
And the red-and-gold pavilion
Glitters with vassal and knight.

The Imperial Highway discovers
A great dog and a graybeard ahead.
"O Bard of Addis Ababa!"
Cry the heroes to wake up the dead.
And the Bard's face shines with a glory
No crown, no *lumot* can shed.

Damascus Blade

The craftsman of Es-Scham
Has finished his blade
For the Sunrise Sultan
Of the Bairam crusade.

Oh, the beauty of steel
With a watered face
Whose black and white veins
With gold interlace!

Oh, the grandeur of steel
In a scimitar
That cleaves in a trice
The black-iron bar!

Oh, the fineness of steel
That slits in twain
The floating gossamer
Of a chatelaine!

The ages shall envy,
And connoisseurs gape;
But the blade of Es-Scham,
What craftsman shall ape?

In the strength of beauty
And the beauty of strength,
It is oneness of width
And of height and of length.

The craftsman of Es-Scham
Has finished his blade
For the Sunrise Sultan
Of the Bairam crusade.

The Street Called Straight

In Damascus, the Pearl of the Desert,
  Near the pillars of Khan the Great
And dialed to sunrise and sunset,
  Lies the Street the wise call Straight.

Ah, the entrance hails the sunrise,
  As a babe greets the breast anew.
And the exit, like the lord of a tavern,
  Bids the setting sun adieu.

The sun nor the rain comes to vex one,
  For the roof is a sage's device;
And only the foolish dare puzzle
  The riddle of Paradise.

And only the pale-faced alien,
  By the legend of Judas bent,
Inquires for the house in Damascus
  The pieces of silver rent.

The synagogues lift their faces
  Like hermits from catacombs,
Who treasure the Tablets of Allah
  In the deeps of bats and gnomes.

The gray mud walls sequester
  The marble courts and towers,
The arabesques of fountains,
  And pools of rainbow flowers.

Ah, the pomegranates, figs, and citrons
   Importunate vendors have brought!
In Damascus, the Pearl of the Desert,
   The wanderer sups for naught.

But the fishhawk money-changers
Infest the khans and bazaars;
And the scented Magdalens beckon,
   Beckon like siren stars.

As I drain my mug dry in the tavern,
   Not far from the Judas gate,
I riddle: "What begets the crooked
   In the Street the wise call Straight?"

Babylon

I

Babylon, O Babylon,
Your wise men zone the zodiac and fret
The calendar of seven days to set.
Your myrrh-anointed Supermen gypsy forth
To loot the East and West, the South and North.
You twirl the roulette wheel of history
As nations chance and lose their liberty.
Your I-*ness* tiers the Tower of Babel high
        To tyrannize the sky.

The scimitar of the Euphrates splits in halves
The global city of the golden calves;
And Babylon's hundred gates of brass,
Like burnished waterfalls,
Arch the burnt skyscraper walls
Whereon four spans of chariots can pass.

Slaves unfreight the meccas of seas
Upon an empire's gluttonous quays.
Slaves each night take up the floor
Of the bridge stone-piered from shore to shore.

Slaves lock the gates to stairs that swerve
Down to the river's splinting curve.
Slaves shut out, with bolts and bars,
All but the *Marseillaise* of stars.

Babylon, O Babylon,
Here Nebuchadnezzar's sceptered sandals tread,

In godlike scorn that quakes the quick and dead,
The Hanging Gardens, miraculous with flowers
Terraced in Alps that shrink the skyscape towers.

Babylon, O Babylon,
Here Israel drinks the captive's scum of gall,
And here Belshazzar's soul knots with chagrin
As Daniel translates doom upon the wall:
Mene, mene, tekel upharsin.

II

Babylon, O Babylon,
Jezebel of the plains,
Shadow-shape of vanity,
Leech of fat domains,
Where the captive peoples
Ate the tyrant's chaff
Bats convene a diet
And hyenas laugh.

Drouths of Dust Bowl ages
Suck all glories dry.
Satrap, beast, and vassal
In the rubbish lie.
Babylon the harpy
Sits on charnel stones
Gnashing lamentations
From a throat of bones:

The looter of nations
Shall grovel and pass

Like the lizard's shadow
On the hoar morass.
Like the wandering leper
He shall cry in the night,
And the mockery of tongues
Shall double his plight.

As the silver is blasted
In the furnace heat,
As the hoofs of the storm
Trample the wheat,
As the bone of an ass
The Philistine clave,
The hand of vengeance
Shall smite from the grave.

A people divided
Against itself
By the Idols of Race
And Caste and Pelf
Writes its own epitaph
With the fingers of doom:
"Here lies a nation
In a suicide's tomb."

THE IDOLS OF THE TRIBE

The Idols of the Tribe

A State which, in the epoch of race poisoning, dedicates itself to the cherishing of its best racial elements, must some day be master of the world.

—*Mein Kampf*

I

The veldt men pray
Carved wood and stone
And tear their flesh
To vein and bone.

The idols scowl
In the brassy sun
Unmindful of
Appeasement done.

Yea, warriors cringe,
Whose tauntings dare
The regnant brute
In regal lair.

As tribal gods
The brave confound,
They bruise their heads
Against the ground.

Kennings of death
Encyst the square,
The mourners drool
And children scare.

Hyena laughs
Spear to the stars,
Dark bodies fall
Like ruptured spars.

Witch doctors whine
Edicts anew
And saint their mugs
Of chloral brew.

Fear grapples fear,
Crinkles the knife:
And life is death
And death is life.

And he who dies
Bequeaths the chief
His herd and flock,
But not his grief.

Who dares to mock,
Who dares to shove
The idols folk
Are schooled to love?

And graybeards croak
One fool alone
Reviled the *hakims*
Of wood and stone:

And headmen staked
The wretch to die

From dooms that crawl
And dooms that fly.

Ages fag out
In cyclic nights,
But sire and son
Repeat the rites.

II

The rule-or-ruin class, in idols of the tribe,
Creates narcissine images of itself;
Defends its fetishes from the merest gibe,
Like iron captains of the Guelf.

The black-veldt god
Behold, hair kinked and flat,
Against the sun's needling myriapod
A cooling mat.
The low wide nostrils ventilate
The long head in the incandescent air.
Insufferable sunrays cannot penetrate
Black tissues as the fair.
The python arm with reach to spare
Are at the beck of tribal law:
The black-veldt god is not aware
Of civilizations buried in the jungle's maw.

The yellow god
Behold, his mongoloid eye fold,
The color of his sod.

The cheekbones arched and bold,
The broad index of face,
The stoic mold
Herald the myth of race.
Lulled by the incense wisdom of repose,
Millenniums of candlelight,
The vegetarian god turns up his nose
At odors of the carnivorous white.

The Nordic god
Behold, his blue-gray eyes
Far-famed to conquer with a single prod
A people mazed in a hinterland of whys.
Hairy as the ape, of lip as thin,
With Mongol, one in blood, with African,
He makes a pseudo-science of his skin
And writes his autobiography *Superman.*

Race biases sow
Hemlocks to maim and blind,
Pile up Sinais of woe,
Jettison the freedoms of mind,
Breed the hydras of stealth,
Set kind razeeing kind,
Convert to potter's fields the commonwealth.

Drink, O Fool, the bias of the tribe,
Autograph the epitaph of pain,
Press to the heart the fangs of the moccasin bribe,
Rape beauty's flesh behind the crib of grain,
Let dust bowls blight the soul's topography,

Eat, O Fool, the racist shibboleth—
Damn the soul to sodomy!
Damn the soul to death!

III

How many times
Does a Southern town
Waste white genius
To keep the Blacks down?

How many times
Does progress stop
To find the maimed
A mythical prop?

How many times
Do a Führer's claws
Dig up dry bones
Of the gray Lost Cause?

How many times
Does the ermine class
Throw scraps of hate
To the starved white mass?

Five roads, the spokes of a county wheel,
Mortise the hub of our Courthouse Square:
Our graybeards fable our Daniel Boone,
Who brothered the red chiefs where
Five dark and bloody frontier paths,

Crossbones old as the skull of the moon,
Witnessed the sacrament pipe of peace,
Grim as the grin of a dead buffoon.

> *Gone are scalping-knives,*
> *Gone are red frontiers,*
> *Gone are homeborn chiefs,*
> *Gone are pioneers.*

> *Yet the town Five Points*
> *Worships myths of race;*
> *Like the veldt men, hates*
> *Alien norm and face.*

> *Sky the Jim Crow sign,*
> *Dam the ghetto's wrath,*
> *Gibbet freedom's sons—*
> *Tell it not in Gath!*

Out of the burial-crags of night
The felon winds hawk down;
Their devil claws riprap the roofs
That visor the town.

The stores on Main Street lean,
Tome to mummy tome;
The houses squat like smoking hulls
Half-convexed on a shoal of foam,
And glowworm windows in the deaf-dumb streets
Are greeting cards of home.

Idols of the tribe
Jail the spirit fast.
Scorn of lesser breeds
Flesh and bone outlast.

Vandal Z's of wind
Beggar vale and hill,
As the myths of race
Loot the people's will.

Upon the courthouse Justice stands,
Eyes fated not to see;
The town clock christens now the first-born hour
Of a day of hate to be.

Nor man nor beast prowls in his world,
But on the Courthouse Square
A statue of the Lost Cause bayonets
Contemporary air.

The skull and bones
Of yesterday
Haunts those who travel
The American Way.

Nobler to grope
In the dusk of dawn
Than to stumble back
In midnight's spawn.

Mein Kampf is not
A bible writ

With hand of gore
And heart of grit.

Mein Kampf is lepra
That whores the soul,
And the brothels of race
Nordic bawds control.

Yet thunderbolt hells
Of chastening rods
Smite ever Gomorrahs
Of tribal gods!

TAPESTRIES OF TIME

Tapestries of Time

I

The tugboat of the sun
Drags planet-laden barges
Past crags and shoals and marges,
Tomb worlds of vapor spun.
And harborless ships of stars,
Like whales with whited scars,
Steer through a universe
Naked of prayer and curse,
Along arc routes begun
Ere the Alpha of the Years
Axled the hemispheres.

The hoary druid Time
Leans upon his mace,
Discerns the odyssey of the tiny dace,
Sees the *raison d'être* worming from the slime,
Discovers the vigils of a soul-rived clod
In a rendezvous with God.

Time
Speaks in pantomime,
In spite of mimic clocks
And dirty voices on the soapless box.

Time
Saints the unity of blood and clime,
Martyred by Caesars of the Undersoul
Who rape the freedoms and their crimes extol.

Ere Pearl Harbor's red December
Burns out on the hearth of the Oversoul
Like an astral ember,
Ere Time the twin of Space
Shuts the door in my face . . .
I pause to remember
The warp and woof of the Whole.

II

Attila comes, the Scourge of God,
And his wormy flesh manures the sod
Like a Bactrian camel's rot.
Caesar ladders to the throne
And topples, daggered to the bone,
And the dustbroom of the wind sweeps clean the spot.

The sands of the Sahara shimmer white,
The peaks of Everest bastion the night,
    As the black ox ages go by.
The Amazon pyramids her catacomb bars,
The nightingale psalms the silver-casqued stars
    In the coroneted sky.

Alexander weeps and weeps because
No worlds uprear to give him pause,
And the maggots fat on his brain.
Napoleon ravages motherlands
And, cancer-eaten, walks the sands
God-damning in the oblivion of the rain.

The Atlantic crescendos its symphony,
The Mississippi swashbuckles to sea
        Like a tawny Captain Kidd.
The Alps bow their heads in cathedrals of snow,
The Tiber scoops out the valleys below,
        Where the sphinxes of Time are hid.

The puny tyrants who bullyrag
The People, as they strut and brag
Till the exodus of breath,
Are scythed like weeds by Prophet Time
And raked by irony sublime
Into the mute democracy of death.

III

I am the Undersoul of the quick and dead:
I speak of Man, the cosmic blunderhead,
Who mixes laughter with the crack of doom
And gives the hungry circuses for bread.

In the golden ages Man was quick to die
For truths and freedoms beyond the ear and eye;
But as his empires climbed on dead men's bones,
He duped the halt and blind with the Nietzschean lie.

The golden ages spermed the dreams of men,
For Science was a diapered infant then;
No *laissez faire* pimped in the marketplace,
And visions of hell were stumbling blocks to sin.

In a golden age Christ did His uttermost
To weld a brotherhood in the splintered host.
"Forgive them, for they know not what they do,"
The Messiah said, as He gave up the ghost.

Did irony from the Cross beset Man's soul
So that the Golden Rule christened his goal?
No, fleshpots soothed his conscience with lotus loves,
And the root of evil became his totem pole.

In the ashes of dawns he raked the worlds to find
The open sesame of the Master Mind.
His telescope discovered Paradise Lost
And left a biped for accidents to grind.

He leeched the whys that Faith had let alone
And stripped the human comedy to the bone.
His spade revealed the brim of no abyss
Whose worms of fire would make his foes atone.

He tinkered with Shakespeare's man, and with a flump
Its greatness fell upon the junkman's dump:
Its muscles the pulleys, its bowels the coils of pipe,
Its lungs the bellows, and its heart the pump.

And then Man's lording freedom of the will
Was a myth with Lidice and Yggdrasill.
He bellied downward to the crawling world:
To glut became the only good or ill.

He sucked the rinds of all forbidden fruits
And spliced his talents to the art of loot.

And hewed his morals to the deepest root.

He diademed the blond Neanderthal
His cynics laughed the curfews out of date,
And stop-watch patriots seized the helms of State:
In ten stunned years the little peoples quailed
Like lambs before the *tribulum* of fate.

The Nazi knave paraded the Quisling clown,
As quicksands sucked eons of freedoms down.
Man sits like Rodin's Thinker in the ruins,
But still he wears the fool's rag-tattered crown.

When X grinds in its mill Man's golden ware,
He shakes the very Pleiades with his prayer.
When bored Chance deigns to curtsy, the ego-ass
Demotes his God and tries the circle to square.

His missionaries psalm and catechize,
While traders hawk their bags of rum and lies.
His lazars fleece the pockets of the huts,
While the natives dream of mansions in the skies.

Hypocrisy guts the nation at a stride,
And Belials take the freedoms for a ride.
The sword of empire murders the weak and small:
The same sword dooms the strong to suicide.

Like snake magicians of the Singhalese,
His pacifists play the foolish pipes of peace
To lull the hooded cobras of Caesarism
And bring the nation a moment of surcease.

His tonguesters wedge the White against the Black;
His bellygods muster the Palace against the Shack;
His ostrichmen island the people and wall them in
And dagger his catholic charters in the back.

To escape the waste land of the Doomsday hour,
His poets scurry into the ivory tower.
The ghosts of Milton and Whitman grieve without,
While the moderns sonnetize a hothouse flower.

His saviors, strong of muscle and of gland,
Drown all the issues in a big brass band.
"The Home! The Church! Democracy!" they yell.
"God called us from the plow to save the land!"

His Tories in the money-palace sit
And chew the snuff of words and plot and spit;
The seven-league boots of Revolution kick
The tills and money-changers into the pit.

His scholars prowl in leprous Gothic stalls
And document their deadwood rituals.
"We must not stoop to vulgar pros and cons,"
They mumble as the shell-quakes topple walls.

His public servants wave the Bible and flag
And kiss the babies and sweat and bullyrag
And mouth the dusty phrases of the dead
And guzzle liquor till their bellies sag.

His holy men bow the knee in chancels dim,
Their far-away voices intoning Elohim:

The skying Golden Rule collides with the bombs
Of Man, a little lower than Seraphim.

A battle royal surges day and night,
As myriad sects lend fist and voice to Right;
And isms break into isms, like chandeliers
A simpleton shatters in a crook of spite.

While neither-nor liberals, wise and overwise,
Carve epigrams bejeweled with surprise,
The earthy Caesar corrals the *hoi polloi*
And leads them down the Appian Way of Lies.

Through lexicons the dialecticians plod
To find the cathedra of the Delphian god;
Then like a midnight felon, the Caesar comes
To drag the doctors before the firing squad.

And now about Man magna chartas lie,
Whose bones the jackals of cynicism licked dry.
The parliament of ants decrees to live,
But Man can only legislate to die.

IV

I am the Oversoul of the brothered dead
Who tie no more the knots and needle the thread.
Pity the blind who bathed in the fabulous Nile
And prattled about a mud hole in its bed.

Honor the sage who purged his tongue of pride
And drank the elixir of the Great Divide.

Pity the fool who neighbored the poets' Alps
And marveled at the cracks in the mountainside!

Myriads of prophets, ascetic of face and girth,
Have hymned the Judgment Day of Man and earth.
The vampire winds pillaged their graves, and now
New prophets haunt the bema and the hearth.

Defeatists whittle martyrdoms that adorn,
And cynics scissor utopias forlorn:
The sea yet boils and stars in ellipses spin
And Man reduces his debits to peppercorn.

Jailed by the peaks, shackled by the salt Red Sea,
Pursued by chariots geared with tyranny,
Age after age, Man works his miracles
To reach the Promised Land ordained to be.

While poets wail jeremiads and forfeit their hair
And dialecticians syllogize despair
And diplomats lacerate their covenants,
Man climbs the cosmic epochs, stair by stair.

In all the worlds, who pockets power and pelf
And foxes his Ten Commandments on the shelf
And yet is verved with such nobility
His conscience digs a hell to damn itself?

In all the worlds, who dovetails yesteryears
With the tomorrows of the hemispheres
And understands the tragedy of laughter
And comprehends the comedy of tears?

In all the worlds, who murals a symphony
As armies grapple in scarlet anarchy
And knows oases in the Saharas thrive
And sinews a Jesus with immortality?

The bearded Saxons applaud with spear and cup
As the hoary bard at the mead board waxes up
To quake the rafters with ballads. He does not dream
A Shakespeare and his cronies thus will sup.

In Timbuctoo, the ebony craftsman, untaught,
Hammers his iron into the pattern of thought.
He does not dream the Diesel-powered *Zephyr*
Will hurdle the hours as if the miles were naught.

The dark age doctor mixes his galling brew
And leeches the patient's veins till they dry askew.
He does not dream his wit's-end arrow points
To vistas of medicine pinnacled from his view.

The Malayan artist dips his stick in sapan
And limns his cubist forms, though the tribal ban
Corks him in secrecy. He does not dream
The Florentine will fresco the Vatican.

The Angle judge convenes his petty court,
Bulwarked by spears imperiling spite or sport.
He does not dream his droits of common law
The tribunals of mighty peoples will import.

The Arab sage with the scalpel of his eye
Probes unknowns in the groins of the roofing sky.

He does not dream the Balboas of upper worlds
Will index stars that primitives deify.

The Viking hews his vessel from a tree
To dare the fog and foam of mystery.
He does not dream Homeric ships will scan
The heaving hexameters of the epic sea.

The Zulu thuds his rubadubs on a drum
And stirs the distant warriors like *geshu* rum.
He does not dream the wireless telegraph
Will ape the messenger of heathendom.

The Hellenist teaches youths the wisdom-ways
With word and cudgel in the sweating days.
He does not dream, in the arts and sciences,
The learned moderns will his learning praise.

The traveler fights across ramparts of snow,
Harried by dynasties of sleet and blow.
He does not dream that hordes of embattled seeds
Await the reveille of spring below.

A moment of truth kernels the husk of this:
At the apex hang the grapes of loveliness,
But he who travels the short hypotenuse
Instead of the long right angle goes amiss.

If the compass fall beneath a Caesar's wheel,
Lose not your mecca of the commonweal.
The hour of sackcloth comes when the Compass-God
Is caught in the skewing knives of the gibbet-wheel.

Damn those who think below their navels and plan
The Lidice of the Parliament of Man:
Our caveman sires witchhunted utopians
Who dreamed the warring families into a clan.

The daylight ages come, night ages go,
On sunset hearths the embers of Waterloos glow;
And he who tries to stop earth's *Limited*
Reaps the oblivion that know-nothings sow.

The Diogenic myth is a vacuole
That gives a peep at the unraveling Whole:
A failure of nerve can make a glowing match
A conflagration or a fumarole.

Todays postponed until tomorrows break
The dams of custom, like a deluging lake;
And suns shall dawn on the ruins of Babylons
The tides left stinking in their crimson wake.

No freedoms came on gold plates to your sires
Whose rebeldom all but the ass inspires.
The valley of dry bones breathes the faith in Man
And cities gather flesh in the ashes of pyres.

Stand not like foolish prophets round the biers
Of worlds embalmed, and grieve away the years.
Man strides the Atlas of Red-Letter Days
To hail the Apocalypse of Hemispheres!

V

The will to live dooms tyranny to die.
The spinal cord of life is quick and raw,
And he who dares to vex the nerve must lie
Beneath the axing sanction of the Law.

The oak, root-fisted, slugs the rock-chinned soil,
The hog uptears the pen in spite of scars,
The eagle lashes the steel wires that entoil,
The tiger rips against the Bessemer bars.

The tyrant is a fool with a lighted match
Who walks into a powder-freighted room,
A blindman poised to lift the pivoting latch
Of a door that sentinels a pit of doom.

The tyrant is a dwarf bedeviled to prop
An avalanche that rives the bastile of night,
An imbecile muscled with the whim to stop
The blade of the guillotine in naked flight.

The tyrant strives to change the lunar tide
Of human nature, make the rivers run
Like rabbits up the vertical mountainside,
And shift the axis of the thundering sun.

VI

Death I have seen:
A sheep pulped in a boa's rhythms of steel,

A cuckold dirked in a dead-end maze of spleen,
A glowworm canceled by a careless heel,
A hobo minced like beef in an engine wheel.

Death I have seen:
An awful grandeur dying in a moose,
A rebel enhaloed by the guillotine,
A stallion razed by lightning bolted loose,
A pawn of demagogy kicking from a noose.

Death I have seen:
A lava gulf embowel the corpse of a town,
A desert custom saber the fellaheen,
A bomber rend a flame-embroidered gown,
A tentacled ocean suck a vessel down.

Death I have seen
In beggar's sackcloth, in priest's armozeen;
But I, nor Prophet Time, shall ever see
The death of Liberty.

VII

Shall the mad dog bite
From the goad of heat
And go free to fang
The child in the street?

The Chinese rivet the Burma Road and Valley Forge,
The Greeks fight again with teeth at Thermopylae's gorge.

The Ethiops duel tanks with Danakil spears,
The Dutch and Belgians dynamite trains and piers.

> *Shall the cobra prod*
> *The housewife's face*
> *And coil in a corner*
> *To menace the place?*

The Fortresses drop their Magna Charta shells,
The Atlantic convoys plow through seaquake hells.

The Yugoslavs raze bastiles with oven grenades,
The Serbs and Poles mete vengeance on suicide raids.

> *Shall the tiger gut*
> *A man in strips*
> *And clock to routine*
> *The gore of his trips?*

The Norwegians snipe for Tomorrow from fiord and scree,
The Hindus die for the shape of a world to be.

The South Americans brother at Trinidad,
The Russians miracle a world at Stalingrad.

> *Shall the rats infest*
> *The house of grain*
> *And starve the lord*
> *Of the domain?*

The French set the Day of Judgment underground,
The Lavals and Quislings quake at a Banquo sound.

The Anglo-Americans bridge the Middle Sea,
The continents paean the V for V*ictory.*

VIII

Cities crunch in the python coils of tanks,
Stukas grind into bonedust patriot ranks.

Bellies of oceans bloat with men and ships,
Maelstroms redden the Axis apocalypse.

The things men live by suffer blow on blow
At Munich, Shanghai, Oslo, Prague, Bataan.
In many a midnight Freedom has buckled low
And walked in togaed victory at dawn.

Already legends gear the brave and free
From Dunkirk, Sevastopol, and the Coral Sea.

The New World Charter banners the Peoples' fight,
A cloud by day and a pillar of fire by night.

From the gates of Chungking to the Potomac quays,
From the zenith zone to the nadir zone of the poles,
On the five continents and the isles of seven seas,
The Four Freedoms symphonize a billion souls.

O Hammers of Justice, hark to the mothers of men:
Beat into plowshares Tokio, Rome, and Berlin!

The Swastika Terror cannot conjure a plan
To stop the calendared March of the Global Man!

FUGITIVE POEMS

African China

I   A connoisseur of pearl
necklace phrases,
Wu Shang disdains
his laundry, lazes
among his bric-a-brac
metaphysical;
and yet dark customers,
on Harlem's rack
quizzical,
sweat and pack
the forked caldera of
his Stygian shop:
some worship God,
and some Be-Bop.

Wu Shang discovers
the diademed word to be,
on the sly,
a masterkey
to Harlem pocketbooks,
outjockeyed by
policy
and brimstone
theology.
alone!

II   As bust and hips
her corset burst,
An Amazonian fantasy,
a Witness of Jehovah
by job and husband curst,
lumbers in.
A yellow mummy in a mummery
a tip-toe,
Wu Shang unsheathes a grin,

and then, his fingers sleeved,
gulps an ugh and eats his crow,
disarmed by ugliness disbelieved!

At last he takes his wits
from balls of moth,
salaams, "Dear Lady, I, for you,
wear goats' sackcloth
to mark this hour and place;
cursed be the shadow of delay
that for a trice conceals a trace
of beauty in thy face!"

Her jug of anger emptied, now he sighs:
"Her kind cannot play euchre.
The master trick belongs to him
who holds the joker."
His mind's eye sees a black hand drop
a red white poker.

III   The gingered gigolo,
vexed by the harrow of a date
and vanity torn,
goddamns the yellow sage,
four million yellow born,
and yellow fate!

The gigolo
a wayward bronco
seen but unheard,
Wu Shang applies the curb-bit word:
"Wise lovers know
that in their lottery success
belongs to him who plays a woman
with titbits of a guess."

The sweet man's sportive whack
Paralyzes Wu Shang's back.

"Say, Yellah Boy, I call yo' stuff
the hottest dope in town!
That red hot mama'll never know
she got her daddy down."

IV   Sometimes the living dead
stalk in and sue for grace,
the tragic uncommon
in the comic commonplace,
the evil that the good
begets in love's embrace,
a Harlem melodrama
like that in Big John's face

as Wu Shang peers at him
and cudgels a theorem.
The sage says in a voice ilang-ilang,
"Do you direct the weathercock?"
And then his lash, a rackarock,
descends with a bang,
"Show me the man who has not thrown
a boomerang!"

. . . words, no longer pearls
but drops of Gilead's balm.
Later, late, Wu Shang remarks,
"Siroccos mar the toughest palm."
The bigger thing, as always, goes unsaid:
the look behind the door of Big John's eyes,
awareness of the steps of *Is*,
the freedom of the wise.

V   When Dixie Dixon breaks a leg
on arctic Lenox Avenue
and Wu Shang homes her, pays her fees,
old kismet knots the two
unraveled destinies.

The unperfumed
wag foot, forefinger, head;
and belly laughter waifs ghost rats
foxed by the smells of meat and bread;
and black walls blab, "Good Gawd,
China and Africa gits wed!"

VI   Wu Shang, whom nothing sears,
says Dixie is a dusky passion flower
unsoiled by envious years.

And Dixie says
her Wu Shang is a Mandarin
with seven times seven ways of love,
her very own oasis in
the desert
of Harlem men.

In dignity, Wu Shang and Dixie walk
the gantlet, Lenox Avenue;
their son has Wu Shang's cast
and Dixie's hue.

The dusky children roll
their oyster eyes
at Wu Shang, Junior, flash
a premature surmise,
as if afraid:
in accents Carolina
on the streets they never made,
the dusky children tease,
"African China!"

A Long Head to a Round Head

I   A camel, vain
in the pitch-and-toss
of 'Ibhri yesteryears,
sought horns
and lost
its ears.

The timid, athwart
the Sophoclean edge,
see an ocelot
sabre-toothed till flesh redeems the pledge
change signeted in blood for change
that changes not.

The timorous,
medieval as an Evpatorian rood,
see Ticino, perilous
on a platitude,
switch the jewels in the razor's rings
to match his mood.

II   Since polysyllabic pomp
is but crude rubber in a roller
marathon, your face
turns to frozen whey as nose and shoulder
vilipend the race.

Although the sun of fate's high C
peacocks in the wentletrap door,
your shadow is no longer
than before.

Although you glut the wretches
who take nor give
the purgative

whatever is, is,
before your dilettante sketches
only the phrases in the glasses
of werewolves fiz.

None calls the folds of Caesar's toga back:
before your vanity
westers to the maggots' feast,
your izzard thought shall be
of trousers creased.

III   The needle's eye impedes the camel less
than the narcissist's pate
the **Vox** proverb Alcuin's letter quotes
to Charles the Great.

Levite caesuras on the road to Jericho
heed not the arses of the widow Scorn
in travail; so
the Caesarean ictus of irony romantic
delivers the torn aristocratic
particle **de**
stillborn.

Salons may cheep
Odi profanum vulgus et arceo,
remembering not
anonymous thumbs and index fingers keep
the candelabra of the ermined aglow,
remembering not

the nameless tier
the ultimate Thule of a name,
just as a hundred thousand hands
pyramided Cheops' fame.

A despot is to the people as
a dangling participle to a noun:
a sceptre's seal is an iota's scribble
upon the testament of a crown.

The Man from Halicarnassus

The poet in Herodotus takes possession of the historian.   H. G. WELLS

O Togas of the Yeas on Ares Hill,
for Clio's sake, you laurel
my talent with ten talents, in spite of birth, and wise
me to the ways, in Typhon's shop, by which the shekel
decores the vase to dull the Just's surmise:
the trochilus is safe
in crocodile jaws; so conjure up
no Hippias of the Scroll. When gnomon fails
its shadow, my integrity shall be a beggar's cup
outside the banking-house of Egibi
or, Cheops-like, send Clio to the stew;
and if the tongue of tongues should die,
tomorrow's tomorrows will do
what I have done to yesterdays in Cabiri.

Across Aegean whitecaps, see the flaxen-dyed
hetaera that Darius stript adown
and then . . . and then—O Infamy!—
charged the *Pornilon Telos*; yet, my native town,
with ciphers in her womb,
esteemed as Heliopolitan spit
the Aes Corinthiacum of History:
soul split
from body, is it *i* or *you* or *it*?

I saw an Ethiop eunuch stretch his hand
toward Athens. Yea, I heard his Phrygian cry

of "Becos" climb the vapor-stairs from the climax of land.
I was as he, an iota of the Man to be, and he as I,
lonely as the only
peak's disintegrated rock.
I am no pigeon homing from a dialectic shock,
I am no ox-hoof treading ugh upon a scroll;
intone, therefore, O Sons of Athens, say in stone,
for me and Man: "The soul of Tresas equals Tresas' sole."

Cyrus, who conquered gold with camel smell,
when coaxed to shift his capital to earth
less churlish, slit cajolery
as teeth cut necks in the gum: "Soft lands give birth
to soft men." Stud this dogma with Hippocrates'
aphorism, "Race is geography."

Between Musaeus' amphibrach and Aha's scrawl,
the Pygmy's grunt and Osirtasen's consonant,
Erythraean sea-deserts of ages sprawl:
see the Lybian ex-king, O Words of Mouth,
scabby with mange mites; see the tawny crag
slandered by black-letter scars, the snaggleteeth
to shame a Scythian gutter-hag;
his abyssal portents as impotent as the vocables
hallowing Xerxes' pyramid of pebbles,
the dogs of oblivion lap them up without a wag.

The *gabbalah* syllabled in Etruscan caves
and vauntings tesselated in Persian halls,
the prayer wheels frescoed in Byzantine shrines

and recipes engraved in Magnesian stalls,
the conquests molded in Chaldaic bas-relief
and laws embellishing Euboean walls,
the lesser great memorialized on Lesbian goats
of brass—these are the soul's upsurge to fetter change
that changes not . . . to smash the vial
of Tartarean hemlock that Time, the while he gloats,
pours down the throats
of the triumvirs, Mineral and Vegetable and Animal

Oh, that we had a Petalá to link the lands
of Sunrise and Sunset! World feuds ferment like yeast
in Parthian malts and rob the senses. I
fear the thunder in the West, the lightning in the East.

A trireme sage from Heliopolis, by way of Meroë,
the minds of scribes bobbing sea biscuits round
his prow and stern, sanded scrolls for Elephantiné
and mused: "A people can be bat serpents flying
black abises dying,
or gods outwearing
Calpe and Abila, tearing
Ne plus ultra asunder!"

E. & O. E.

Ya mi talle se ha quebrado como caña de maíz.   LORCA

I

If,
eyeless in irony,
to be
is Scylla
and not to be
Charybdis,
where is the dilemma?

Is it not, oh,
is it not because of my
taste for *beccafico*
my vassalage to an Act of *Poietes*,   10
that I
let this pleonastic red
ink *bêche-de-mer* of the Dane —
a Fysshstrete tinker's dam
in zero's shadow —
drain and drain and drain
the spinal marrow
of nth *comédie*
from the *tragédie humaine?*   20

II

Though
I dot my *i* in this
and rend the horns
of tribal ecbasis,

the Great White World's
uncrossed *t*
pockets the skeleton key
to doors beyond
black chrysalis.

∴ I think ∴   30
I am what I am not:
if Nazarene
by lot,
if no Hellene
in the Old Gadfly's sense,
I am, perhaps, a Roman and no Roman, save
among the dense.

In defense
of Madame de Civilis,
a zombi slut who came to preen   40
in Fornix Square,
I toppled the guillotine
into the moat
dug by the *adola mentis*.

III

Tick, tock,
knock, knock:
no hand
can stop
the tick
of clock: 50
tick, tock,
Knock, KNOCK!

O forty days
of rain and night,
who's there?
O sight—
less listeners on
Abraxa's storm
cellar stair,
is it   60
Everyman
from the no man's land
of Everywhere?

O brave new world
begotten by despair
in Tom Thumb's tomb,
is it, is it,
the cradle womb
of Alpha
rocking   70

Evil and Good?
Is it, is it,
Omega
knocking
on gopher wood?

IV

O adage ox,
is it
the hyssop of the haunted
that symbols red
the lintel and the side-posts   80
at the door
of the undaunted?

Is it
the encore
of Bellerium's
Mysterious Stranger?
Is it, is it,
the doubleganger
of Nevermore?

O too   90
too solid flesh,
who's there?
Is it
Mammon's cook to tickle afresh
the palate with the béchamel sauce
of an august event
to alchemize substance in-
to accident?

O Passage back
to Genesis   100
of scarf-skins
like yours and mine and his,
O proud A.-S.
wild with surmising,
is it, is it,
the whited sepulcher's
dike capsizing
in the dolor
of the rising
tide of color?   110

O pulses of the world,
is it, is it,
the land of lands'
king of kings'
hand of hands'

decree
of earth and water?
O Kali Yuga,
is it, is it,
the ghost of the iron-   120
monger's son
to barter
his *Ilande* sermon
for the key
to the Bastille
at Mt. Vernon?

Open, locks,
whoever knocks!

V

Inside the bowl
the marble sped   130
against the rhythms of the wheel
and round the numbered black and red
compartments, till
the pursy times'
Tartufean shill
hazarded:

"Why place
an empty pail
before a well
of dry bones?   140
Why go to Ninevah to tell
the ailing that they ail?
Why lose the Golden Fleece
to gain the Holy Grail?"

VI

Why should I go
to Ninevah between
death-rattles out of Nowhere
into Nothing?
                    I have seen
the unlaid ghosts   150
of twenty sex-o'-clock cities along
the White Whale's Acheron
freeze the dog
days, make
the crow's-nest hog
like the spine of a dated truth:
hawk eyes
unspectacled by ruth
are not hawk-eyed enough
to pierce the winding sheet of fog   160
that turns hawk into quail . . .
to pierce the seascape's brambly night,
lopped rough,
sheared white,
by arc blades of the gale.

VII

'Sdeath!
The tail
of doomsday struck

I-*ness* in me
between parentheses   170
of my eternity:
ere one could do the five steps of a phrase,
my Tarshish odyssey

died in the scarlet viva of
a geyser: flung,
from perigee
to apogee,
to the crackling of thorns
under a pot, I,
a Momus scarecrow   180
with crossbones and horns,
dapped to Mt. Aetna's harpooned flesh below.

Death?
It's a jot less
than iota.
Dying
is the ogress
lying
in penumbra
wrying   190
identity to the dregs
with tentacles of
the seven plagues.

VIII

I am no ape
of Benares. I have won
no Monthyon
prize. Though I
have cut a G clef and a belletristic S,
naked on
roller skates in Butte Montmartre,   200
sweated palm to palm
to down beats of
the tom tom,
in Sorgue's studio

with the Black Venus,
and, a leaning question mark upon
a blue white metal bar, drunk piccolo
with Salmon, Apollinaire,
MacOrlan, and Picasso–
yet, out of square,   210
I have not said,
"Hippoclides doesn't care."

I have not kept
barb and Arab
in my stable,
nor had a cherub
in a garb
of sable
serve guests
a death's   220
head at my table.

Until
my skin
was blister copper,
I have not stood within
the free-soil gate,
pole in hand,
to knock off monkey hats
exported to the hinterland.

My yes, no Louis de Béchamel's   230
with kissing-crust,
failed to mix the penalties
of Dives
and of Lazarus,
and burned no vigils at the gates
of King Ahasuerus,
and blew on this tainted ball

neither cold nor hot
at sight of black plume tokens
of Agathocles' pot.   240

O procul este,
profani!
Micawber-like, a tide-
waiter, I
have thewed myself
to wait like *Osorio*
on Pople's shelf:
no true Propontic, I
have glimpsed no Sea
of Marmara between   250
illusion and reality;
between
finesse and *géométrie*
no green
green desert where
years come to me.

IX

Nor have I heard
a voice in Ramah:
I, from Dan
to Beersheba,   260
have been a stone
skipping over water;
to atone,
my solar plexus sought the navel cord
in vain. I have grown
as empty as a cenotaph set

among deaf-mutes without
a one-hand alphabet.

I have not, with a face
card, introduced   270
into the marketplace
cos-lettuce from an aerie,
and munched with rabbit glee
beneath the *du-haut-en-bas* grimace
of a dozen marble Caesars, as
the sulky pike
mocked the impertinent friskings of the dace
against a Teverean dike.

When owls scream
and crickets cry   280
and painted devils say,
Sleep no more!"
not yet have I
plucked from the sanguine flower
the petals inscribed with *Ai!*

X

I sought no Golden Fleece,
no Holy Grail,
as tonic spasms behind me locked
the Black Hole gate of teeth
to the *Weltschmerz* intervale   290
between sierras of quivering flesh . . .
blinded by vomitings of scabby shale
and spume and incrustations, sucked
in by Atlases of gravity,
and thereby hid
from the Iliad

of elephantine lesser deaths in gale and sea,
I slid like a sliver of ice through the gullet, I slid
like the wraith of scintilla,
between the jaws   300
of Calpe and Abila,
pursued by no apocalyptic Hound
but by the *Lasche* of God . . .
no Prometheus unbound,
but a *jod*,
a *jod* uncircumcised, adrift
on the glassy tongue
of Obsidian Cliff,
I cried, or I,
across the Hanging Gardens of fat,   310
seemed to cry,
"Let this cup pass from me!"
as I glimpsed, through the ankh of habit, the red
red Place of the Skull and the Way of All
Flesh . . .then *le mal du siècle* plummeted
me, like the ignis fatuus
of a bedeviled thunderhead,
over and over and over
the tissue cataracts of Widows' Tears
and across the plateaus of fishes dead . . .   320
eternities later, by Fear set free of fears,
though churned by entrail-dooms volcanic,
the *Weltschmerz* twisted me like the neck of a torticollis
in enzymatic juices oceanic,
and swirled me down and down and down
the fabulous fathomless fatty-tumorous canyon of the whale
with the grind and the drag
of the millstone
sphinx of Why
on my wry   330
head and neck . . .alone . . .alone . . .alone . . .

                              to die
                gyrating into the wide, wide privacy
                of the Valley of Hinnom's By-and-By . . .
                              down
                              down
                              down
        untouched by the witches' Sabbath of any wall
    until the maelstrom womb of the underworld swallowed my
                         Adamic fall!   340

        XI

        Ecce homo!
                Pero
                    yo ya no
                        soy yo:
        behold a micro-all-in-all
        ashen as the ashes of saltwort
        in Aguazall:
        no Captain Ahab,
        but a Jonah—
        a jonah shrunk   350
        by a paraclete
        Malebolgean,
        in funk
        Tartarean
        and heat
        Gehennan,
        from his scalp to the balls of his feet!

                    I sought
                    in a Tarshish nook
                    neither the Golden Fleece   360
                    nor the Holy Grail
                    but a pruning-hook.

XII

Beneath
> the albatross,
> the skull-and-bones,
> the Skull and Cross,
> the Seven Sins Dialectical,
>> I do not shake
>> the Wailing Wall
>>> of Earth,
>> nor quake
>> the Gethsemane
>>> of Sea,
>> nor tear
>> the Big Top
>>> of Sky
>> with Lear's prayer,
>>> or Barabas' curse,
>>> or Job's cry!

370

Notes to "E. & O. E."

The man in the poem takes the title from the phrase "errors and omissions ex-
cepted." The abbreviation is doubtless an *apologia pro vita sua* as well as a bow to
custom in Webster's appendix. The epigraph, itself an image of the abbreviated,
will obviously call to mind Lorca's two ballads on Antoñito the Camborio and also
the ways of two men in two ways of life—the sophisticated and the primitive.

1–20. Cf. *Hamlet*, III, i. In sections I and II and VI, the protagonist weighs Ham-
let's False Stress, "an Act of *Poietes*," in order to avoid the Dane's formal fallacy in in-
formal reasoning. V. Shaw, *Logic*, 205. Cf. Hibben: "To be is not to be, and not to
be is to be."

30–31. In an attempt to establish his *I-ness* as a Negro—a concept in itself a
unity of opposites—the man combines the Cartesian definition with a variant of
the Law of Synthetic Identity. This is the key to his allusions in the poem.

34. This *soi-disant* nickname grew out of the maieutic *"Tò ti?"* The protago-
nist's words have frequently an ethnic twist.

35. This line from Paul, "debtor both to Greeks and Barbarians," illustrates the
synecdochic thinking in minority groups, which often leads to Rome, Highgate,
Tarshish, or Golgotha.

37. The figure of Madame de Civilis in Fornix Square, "an old bitch gone in
the teeth"—Maran and Tagore pictured her unforgettably—was suggested by a
generic word. V. Sanger, *The History of Prostitution*, 72–73. Also the footnotes on
Horace and Martial and Plautus in the chapter on Rome. Cf. Maran, *Batouala*, the
preface.

44. V. Bacon, *Novum Organum*, Sections, 38–44.

46. Cf. *Macbeth*, II, iii. Cf. De Quincey, *On the Knocking at the Gate in Mac-
beth*. Cf. Eliot, *Fragment of an Agon*.

57. V. De la Mare, *The Listeners*.

61. Cf. *Everyman*.

75. Cf. Genesis, VI, ix–xxv.

76. V. Aeschylus, *Agamennon*, 43–44.

80. V. Exodus, XII, xxii.

86. V. Twain, *The Mysterious Stranger*.

94. Cf. Chaucer, *The Pardoner's Tale*, 206–212. V. Philippians, III, xviii–ix:
"For many walk . . . whose god is the belly." Cf. an African proverb: "The belly is
the foremost of the gods."

99. Cf. Whitman, *Passage to India*.

106. V. Matthew XXIII, xxvii.

109–10. Cf. Stoddard, *The Rising Tide of Color*. The theme of this book led to
the famous Stoddard-Du Bois debate in Chicago—a concrete example of the tridi-
mensionality in note 35.

114. Cf. Shelley, *Ozymandias*.

117. The symbol of submission among the Indo-Aryans was earth and water. Some African tribes still use this symbol.

129. In this section, confronted by the knocker, "the Tartufean shill," the man faces the dilemma of the bowls—the roulette wheel and the Holy Grail. The latter was derived from the Low Latin *gradale*, and this in turn from *cratella*, a bowl. Here as in the *Parzival* of Wolffram von Escenbach, the Grail is not merely the bowl that caught the blood of Christ at the Last Supper, but it is also

"a light to guide, a rod
To check the erring,"

a portent to those who find "a ship going to Tarshish." A shill is hired by a gambling house to draw customers to the table and create "a fine spirit"; yet the biggest problem of a casino is to protect itself from a crooked shill.

145. As the man echoes the shill's rhetorical question, he is unaware of the irony of reaching a point—as Kafka pointed out—beyond which, there is no turning back. Cf. Father Mapple's sermon in Melville's *Moby Dick*, IX, 33–41. Also Pfeiffer, *The Old Testament*, Part IX, iv, "Jonah," 589.

148. V. Anderson, *Out of Nowhere into Nothing*.

151. V. Toynbee, *A Study of History*.

178. Cf. Ecclesiates, XII, vi. Also Hardy, *The Three Strangers*.

182. The man realizes that "Mt. Aetna's harpooned flesh" is the White Whale encountered by the *Jereboam*, the *Samuel Enderby*, the *Rachel*, the *Delight*, and the *Pequod*.

183. Adrift, he makes a last effort to strip Hamlet's dilemma of its False Stress— its equivocation and ethos—by contrasting the noun *death* and the gerund *dying*.

194. In the interlude before the act of extinction, he has the remembrance of things past. V. Schopenhauer, *On Women*, the account of the Monkey Temple.

196. V. Gautier, *Preface to Mademoiselle de Maupin*, the Monthyon prize.

205. V. Salmon, *La Négresse de Sacre-Coeur*. This was the period of the expatriates in Paris, when the Continent felt the impact of Benin art and Harlem jazz. V. McKay, *A Long Way from Home*. Also Hughes, *The Big Sea*.

212. Herodotus tells the story of Hippoclides. Cf. Newman, *Apologia pro Vita Sua*, Part III, "History of My Religious Opinions."

214. V. Pycraft, *Animals of the World*, 1941.

228. Ataturk stationed guards at the gates of Istanbul, to knock these symbols of submission to Europeans from the heads of his subjects.

231. Kissing-crust is the soft part of the crust, where the loaves touch one another in baking.

241. Cf. Virgil, *Aeneid*, VI, 258.

246. Lamb wrote to Coleridge, August 26, 1814:"There is a stock of 'Remorse' on hand, as Pople conjectures, for seven years consumption."

248. Cf. *Othello*, III, iii, 453.

255. Middleton. *The Mayor of Quinborough*, I, i, 102–3.

273-77. Cf. Lamb, *Dream-Children: A Reverie*. Also Dreiser, *The Financier*, 5.

280. Cf. *Lycidas*, 106.

282. Cf. *Macbeth*, II, ii. Also De Quincey, *Preliminary Confessions*: "And I awoke in struggles, and I cried aloud—'I will sleep no more!'"

289. Cf. Father Mapple: ". . . and the whale shoots—to all his ivory teeth, like so many white bolts, upon his prison."

296. Cf. Homer, *Iliad*, the opening lines. Also De Quincey: "I am now arrived at an iliad of woes . . ." This section is indebted to the experiences of James Bartley, who was swallowed by a cachalot whale on a February afternoon in 1891 while the whaler *Star of the East* was cruising off the Falkland Islands. The flensers rescued him. Later, he accepted the offer of a carnival proprietor and toured the British Isles and Europe for five years—up to the time of his premature death in 1896. V. Allen and Unwin, *Whaling: Its Perils and Profits*, London, 1900. Cf. the symbolism of descent in Virgil's *Aeneid*, Dante's *Inferno*, Milton's *Paradise Lost*, Nietzsche's *Also sprach Zarathustra*, and Thompson's *Hound of Heaven*. The Darwinian descent of man, of course, has multiple signification. The faceted symbolism of Zarathustra's "down-going," as seen in the verb *untergehen* and the noun *Untergang*, has been noted by A. Tille and M. Bozman. In the case of the protagonist, then, descent and ascent are synchronous, as in that of Jonah, who, "dying downwards" in the belly of the fish, composed and recited a poem.

312. Cf. Matthew, XXVI, xxxix.

313. The whale is bleeding internally from the harpoons in its bulk, and this fact evokes the blood image.

341. V. John, XIX, vi. Cf. Nietzsche, *Ecco Homo*. Also Durant: "*Ecco homo!*—alas, we behold the man here only too well!"

342-44. Cf. Lorca, *Romance sonámbulo*:

> "*Pero yo ya no soy yo,*
> *ni mi casa es ya mi casa.*"

348. Cf. *Moby Dick*, CXXXV, "The Chase—Third Day."

362. V. Isiah, II, iv.37.

Abraham Lincoln of Rock Spring Farm

I

Along the Wilderness Road, through Cumberland Gap,
The black ox hours limped toward Sunday's sun,
Across a buff clay belt with scrawls of stone,
Where bird and beast quailed in the bosom brush
From February's fang and claw; the stars,
Blue white, like sheer icicles, spired aglow
As if the three wise men barged in the East
Or priests in sackcloth balked the Scourge of God.

Foursquare by the rite of arm and heart and law,
The scrubby log cabin dared the compass points
Of Rock Spring farm, man's world, God's universe,
The babel of the circumstance and era.
The frozen socket of its window stared
Beyond the spayed crabapple trees, to where
The skulls of hills, the skeletons of barrens,
Lay quiet as time without the watch's tick.

Not knowing muck and star would vie for him,
The man Tom sank upon an ax-split stool,
Hands fisted, feet set wide to brace the spirit,
Big shoulders shoved, dark hazel eyes glazed by
Grotesqueries of flame that yawled and danced
Up, up, the stick-clay chimney. While fire imps combed
The black and bristling hair, the acids of thoughts
Made of the orby face an etching-plate.

II

Near pyrotechnic logs, the purling kettle,
Aunt Peggy puffed her pipe on God's rich time:
A granny at a childbed on the border,
Where head and backbone answered the tomahawk
Her wise old eyes had seen a hundred Nancys
In travail tread the dark winepress alone;
Her wise old hands had plucked a stubborn breed
Into the outer world of pitch and toss.

The cabin that her myth and mission entered
Became a castle in which Aunt Peggy throned
A dynasty of grunts and nods and glances.
The nest, the barn, the hovel had schooled her in
The ABC of motherhood, and somehow
She'd lost her ego in the commonweal:
She sensed so accurately a coming child
That rakes dubbed her the St. Bernard of Sex!

And now her keyhole look explored Tom Lincoln
Beneath the patched homespun, the hue and cry
Of malice, until she touched his loneliness,
The taproot that his fiber gave no tongue.
Then, lulling the wife, troubled in flesh and mind,
She eased the sack quilts higher and mused the while:
There's but one way of coming into the world,
And seven times seventy ways of leaving it!

III

The woman Nancy, like a voyager sucked
Into the sea's whale belly by a wreck,
Buoyed to the surface air of consciousness

And clutched the solace of her corn-husk bed.
Her dark face, sharped in forehead, cheekbone, chin,
Cuddled in dark brown hair; her eyes waxed grayer
With wonder of the interlude: her beauty
And courage choked Aunt Peggy's hyperbole!

Out of the fog of pain, the bog of bygones,
The bag of cabin cant and tavern tattle,
She picked the squares to piece tomorrow's quilt:
She puzzled now, as then, about her father
Who let wild Lucy Hanks bundle and carry
Flesh of his flesh beyond the Cumberland Gap:
A strange roof is no roof when imps of fear
Pilfer the fatherless in blossom time.

Year in, year out, the daughter tinkered with
The riddle of her birth; the mother chided
The woman Nancy as she had the child,
"Hush thee, hush thee, thy father's a gentleman."
The butt of bawd, grand jury, Sunday bonnet,
Lucy, driven, taught her daughter the Word,
And Nancy, driven, taught her son the Word,
And Abraham, driven, taught his people the Word!

IV

The man Tom bit his fingernails, then rammed
His pockets with the hector hands that gave
Raw timber the shape of cabinet and coffin,
And in his lame speech said: "Aunt Peggy, listen.
Now that our Nancy's time is come, I'm haunted
By my own nothingness. Why breed nobodies?"
He tapped the dirt floor with the iron-capped boot
That aided fist and skull in border fights.

Aunt Peggy counseled: "Tom, you say the say
Poor Joseph probably said in that low stable
Ere Jesus came into this mishmash world."
She paused, then boxed the ears of cynicism:
"It's true, down in the barnyard, blood speaks loud,
Among the hogs, the chickens, the cows, the horses;
But, when it comes to Man, who knows, who knows
What greatness feeds down in the lowliest mother?"

The man Tom turned and spat: his naked surmise
Ranged out and out. Aunt Peggy's innermost said:
"Your father Abraham, bred like Daniel Boone,
Conquered a land with gun and ax and plow,
Baptized it in his blood! I say, I've said,
What's in a baby is God Almighty's business;
How the elders wring it out is worry enough!
The best, the worst—it's all, all human nature."

V

The tavern, Tom remembered, the New Year's Eve,
The clubfoot scholar bagged in Old World clothes,
With arrowy eyes and a hoary mushroom beard.
An Oxford don, he hymned the Bastille's fall
In spite of the hair-hung sword; his betters set
Him free to hail new truths in new lands, where
He seined with slave and master, knave and priest,
And out of all fished up the rights of man:

"As Citizen Lincoln asks, 'What's human nature?'
His full mug says a clear mind puts the question
Which ties the fogey scholar in a knot!
My new idea fed to his new baby
Would fetch the New World and the New Year peace!
The sum of anything unriddles the riddle:

The child whose wet nurse is the mother-of-all
Grows like a pine unmarked by rock or wind.

"To make a New World and a New Year, Plato
And Jesus begged the boon of little children!
Now Citizen Lincoln asks, 'What's human nature?'
It's what we elders have: no baby has it.
It's what our good and bad graft on the neutral.
It's what our rulers feed the boy and girl.
It's what society garbs nature in.
It's a misnomer: call it *human nurture!*"

VI

Aunt Peggy hovered closer, with flawless rites
Grown lyrical from habit: muffled pain sounds
Dragged from the bed of cleated poles; she hawed
Tom Lincoln, as one turns a nag aside,
Then swooped her way, even as a setting hen
Carves a dictatorship from yard to nest.
And Tom again was squeezed into a cell
Whose inmates were the ghosts of unsuccess.

Later his memories climbed a gala peak,
His Nancy's infare that ran riotous:
The bear meat, venison, wild turkey, duck,
The maple sugar hanging for the whiskey,
The red ham, gourds of syrup, bowls of honey,
The wood coal pit with brown and juicy sheep,
The guzzling, fiddling, guttling, monkeyshining:
A continent sprawled between that day and this!

A havenot on the frontier is no havenot;
A Crusoe without Friday has no conscience:
Yet Tom's grub living gnawed him like the teeth

Of slavery, land titles, melancholy.
He, like his forebears, visioned a Promised Land
And tidied ways and means to fly the barrens
That doomed the flesh to peck, to patch, to pinch,
And wrung the soul of joy and beauty dry.

VII

The black ox hours limped by, and day crawled after.
White prongs of ice, like dinosaur fangs, gleamed in
The cavernous mouth of Rock Spring; snowbirds shivered
And chirped rebellion; a cow with jags and gaps
Chewed emptily; hogs squealed in hunger fits;
And scrags of dogs huddled against the chimney,
Which shoveled smoke dust into the throats and noses
Of ragged winds kicking up snow in the desert.

Nancy lay white, serene, like virgin milk
After the udder's fury in the pail.
Beneath the sack quilts and the bearskin robe,
In yellow petticoat and linsey shirt,
The baby snuggled at her breast and gurgled—
An anonymity of soft red wrinkles.
Aunt Peggy, hovering, grinned, "He's Sabbath-born.
Remember . . .Sunday—it's red-letter day!"

Like ax and helve, like scythe and snath, the bond
Held Tom and Nancy: she smiled at his halt smile,
His titan's muss in picking up the baby.
Tom frowned and spat, then gulped, "He's legs! All legs!"
Aunt Peggy beamed, "Long legs can eat up miles."
Tom gloomed, "The hands—look at the axman's hands!"
And Nancy mused, "The Hankses' dream, the Lincolns',
Needs such a man to hew and blaze the way."

LIBRETTO FOR THE
REPUBLIC OF LIBERIA

DO

Liberia?
No micro-footnote in a bunioned book
Homed by a pedant
With a gelded look:
You are
The ladder of survival dawn men saw
In the quicksilver sparrow that slips
The eagle's claw!

Liberia?
No side-show barker's bio-accident, 10
No corpse of a soul's errand
To the Dark Continent:
You are
The lightning rod of Europe, Canaan's key,
The rope across the abyss,
Mehr licht for the Africa-To-Be!

Liberia?
No haply black man's X
Fixed to a Magna Charta without a magic-square
By Helon's leprous hand, to haunt and vex: 20
You are
The Orient of Colors everywhere,
The oasis of Tahoua, the salt bar of Harrar,
To trekkers in saharas, in sierras, with Despair!

Liberia?
No oil-boiled Barabas,
No Darwin's bulldog for ermined flesh,
No braggart Lamech, no bema's Ananias:
You are
Libertas flayed and naked by the road   30
To Jericho, for a people's five score years
Of bones for manna, for balm an alien goad!

Liberia?
No pimple on the chin of Africa,
No brass-lipped cicerone of Big Top democracy,
No lamb to tame a lion with a baa:
You are
Black Lazarus risen from the White Man's grave,
Without a road to Downing Street,
Without a hemidemisemiquaver in an Oxford stave!   40

Liberia?
No Cobra Pirate of the Question Mark,
No caricature with a mimic flag
And golden joys to fat the shark:
You are
American genius uncrowned in Europe's charnel-house.
Leave fleshpots for the dogs and apes; for Man
The books whose head is golden espouse!

Liberia?
No waste land yet, nor yet a destooled elite,   50
No merry-andrew, an Ed-dehebi at heart,
With St. Paul's root and Breughel's cheat:
You are
The iron nerve of lame and halt and blind,
Liberia and not Liberia,
A moment of the conscience of mankind!

RE

The Good Gray Bard in Timbuktu chanted:
"Brow tron lo — eta ne a ne won oh gike!"

Before Liberia was, Songhai was: before
America set the raw foundling on Africa's   60
Doorstep, before the Genoese diced west,
Burnt warriors and watermen of Songhai
Tore into *bizarreries* the uniforms of Portugal
And sewed an imperial quilt of tribes.

In Milan and Mecca, in Balkh and Bombay,
Sea lawyers in the eyeservice of sea kings
Mixed liquors with hyperboles to cure deafness.
Europe bartered Africa crucifixes for red ivory,
Gewgaws for black pearls, *pierres d'aigris* for green gold:
Soon the rivers and roads became clog almanacs!   70

The Good Gray Bard in Timbuktu chanted:
"Wanawake wanazaa ovyo! Kazi yenu wazungu!"

Black Askia's fetish was his people's health:
The world his world, he gave the Bengal light
Of Books the Inn of Court in Songhai. *Beba mzigo!*
The law of empathy set the market price,
Scaled the word and deed: the gravel-blind saw
Deserts give up the ghost to green pastures!

Solomon in all his glory had no Oxford,
Alfred the Great no University of Sankoré: 80
Footloose professors, chimney sweeps of the skull,
From Europe and Asia; youths, souls in one skin,
Under white scholars like El-Akit, under
Black humanists like Bagayogo. *Karibu wee!*

The Good Gray Bard in Timbuktu chanted:
"Europe is an empty python in hiding grass!"

Lia! Lia! The river Wagadu, the river Bagana,
Became dusty metaphors where white ants ate canoes,
And the locust Portuguese raped the maiden crops,
And the sirocco Spaniard razed the city-states,   90
And the leopard Saracen bolted his scimitar into
The jugular vein of Timbuktu. *Dieu seul est grand!*

And now the hyenas whine among the barren bones
Of the seventeen sun sultans of Songhai,
And hooded cobras, hoodless mambas, hiss
In the gold caverns of Falémé and Bambuk,
And puff adders, hook scorpions, whisper
In the weedy corridors of Sankoré. *Lia! Lia!*

The Good Gray Bard chants no longer in Timbuktu:
"The maggots fat on yeas and nays of nut empires!"   100

MI

Before the bells of Yankee capital
Tolled for the feudal glory of the South
And Frederick Douglass's Vesuvian mouth
Erupted amens crushing Copperheads,

Old Robert Finley, Jehovah's Damasias,
Swooped into Pennsylvania Avenue
To pinion Henry Clay, the shuttlecock,
And Bushrod Washington, whose family name

Dwarfed signatures of blood: his magnet Yea
Drew Lawyer Key, the hymnist primed to match   110
A frigate's guns, and Bishop Meade, God's purse,
And Doctor Torrey, the People's clock: they eagled

The gospel for the wren Republic in
Supreme Court chambers. That decision's cash
And credit bought a balm for conscience, verved
Black Pilgrim Fathers to Cape Mesurado,

Where sun and fever, brute and vulture, spelled
The idioms of their faith in whited bones.
No linguist of the Braille of prophecy ventured:
The rubber from Liberia shall arm   120

Free peoples and her airport hinterlands
Let loose the winging grapes of wrath upon
The Desert Fox's cocained nietzscheans
A goosestep from the Gateway of the East!

FA

A fabulous mosaic log,
    the Bola boa lies
        gorged to the hinges of his jaws,
      eyeless, yet with eyes . . .

in the interlude of peace.

The beaked and pouched assassin sags   130
    on to his corsair rock,
    and from his talons swim the blood-
    red feathers of a cock . . .

in the interlude of peace.

The tawny typhoon striped with black
    torpors in grasses tan:
    a doomsday cross, his paws uprear
    the leveled skull of a man . . .

in the interlude of peace

SOL

White Pilgrims, turn your trumpets west!   140
Black Pilgrims, *shule, agrah,* nor tread
The Skull of another's stairs!

This is the horned American
Dilemma: yet, this too, O Christ,
This too, O Christ, will pass!

The brig *Elizabeth* flaunts her stern
At auction blocks with the eyes of Cain
And down-the-river sjamboks.

This is the Middle Passage: here
Gehenna hatchways vomit up   150
The debits of pounds of flesh.

This is the Middle Passage: here
The sharks wax fattest and the stench
Goads God to hold His nose!

Elijah Johnson, his *Tygers heart*
In the whale's belly, flenses midnight:
"How long? How long? How long?"

A dark age later the answer dawns
When whitecap pythons thrash upon
The molar teeth of reefs   160

And hallelujahs quake the brig
From keel to crow's-nest and tomtoms gibber
In cosmic *deepi-talki.*

Elijah feels the Forty Nights'
Octopus reach up to drag his mind
Into man's genesis.

He hears the skulls plowed under cry:
"*Griots,* the quick owe the quick and dead.
A man owes man to man!"

"*Seule de tous les continents,*" the parrots   170
chatter, "*l'Afrique n'a pas d'histoire!*"
Mon petit doigt me l'a dit:

"Africa is a rubber ball;
the harder you dash it to the ground,
the higher it will rise.

"A lie betrays its mother tongue.
The Eye said, 'Ear, the Belly is
the foremost of the gods.'

"Fear makes a gnarl a cobra's head.
One finger cannot kill a louse.   180
The seed waits for the lily.

"No fence's legs are long enough.
The lackey licks the guinea's boot
till holes wear in the tongue.

"A camel on its knees solicits
the ass's load. Potbellies cook
no meals for empty maws.

"When skins are dry the flies go home.
Repentance is a peacock's tail.
The cock is yolk and feed.   190

"Three steps put man one step ahead.
The rich man's weights are not the poor
man's scales. To each his coole.

"A stinkbug should not peddle perfume.
The tide that ebbs will flow again.
A louse that bites is in

"the inner shirt. An open door
sees both inside and out. The saw
that severs the topmost limb

"comes from the ground. God saves the black   200
man's soul but not his buttocks from
the white man's lash. The mouse

"as artist paints a mouse that chases
a cat. The diplomat's lie is fat
at home and lean abroad.

"It is the grass that suffers when
two elephants fight. The white man solves
between white sheets his black

"problem. Where would the rich cream be
without skim milk? The eye can cross   210
the river in a flood.

"Law is a rotten tree; black man, rest
thy weight elsewhere, or like the goat
outrun the white man's stink!"

Elijah broods: "The fevers hoed
Us under at Sherbro. Leopard saints
Puked us from Bushrod Beach

"To Providence Island, where John Mill,
The mulatto trader, fended off
The odds that bait the hook.   220

"The foxes have holes, the birds have nests,
And I have found a place to lay
My head, Lord of Farewells!"

And every ark awaits its raven,
Its vesper dove with an olive-leaf,
Its rainbow over Ararat.

LA

Glaciers had shouldered down
The cis-Saharan snows,
Shoved antelope and lion
Past *Uaz-Oîriet* floes.   230

Leopard, elephant, ape,
Rhinoceros and giraffe
Jostled in odysseys
To Africa: siamang laugh

And curse impaled the frost
As Northmen brandished paws
And shambled Europe-ward,
Gnashing Cerberean jaws.

After *netami lennowak*,
A white man spined with dreams   240
Came to cudgel parrot scholars
And slay philistine schemes.

"The lion's teeth, the eagle's
Talons, shall break!" declared
Prophet Jehudi Ashmun,
Christening the bones that dared.

When the black bat's ultima smote
His mate in the yoke, he felt
The seven swords' *pis aller*
Twist in his heart at the hilt.   250

He said: "My Negro kinsmen,
America is my mother,
Liberia is my wife,
And Africa my brother."

TI

O Calendar of the Century,
red-letter the Republic's birth!
O Hallelujah,
oh, let no *Miserere*
venom the spinal cord of Afric earth!
Selah!   260

"Ecce homo!"
the blind men cowled in azure rant
before the Capitol,
between the Whale and Elephant,
where no longer stands Diogenes' hearse
readied for the ebony mendicant,
nor weeping widow Europe with her hands
making the multitudinous seas incarnadine
or earth's *massebôth* worse:
O Great White World, thou boy of tears, omega hounds   270
lap up the alpha laugh and *du-haut-en-bas* curse.
Selah!

O Africa, Mother of Science
. . . *lachen mit yastchekes* . . .
What dread hand,
to make tripartite one august event,
sundered Gondwanaland?
What dread grasp crushed your biceps and
back upon the rack
chaos of chance and change   280
fouled in Malebolgean isolation?
What dread *elboga* shoved your soul
into the *tribulum* of retardation?
melamin or melanin dies to the world and dies:
Rome casketed herself in Homeric hymns.
Man's culture in barb and Arab lies:
The Jordan flows into the Tiber,
the Yangtze into the Thames,
the Ganges into the Mississippi, the Niger
into the Seine.   290
Judge of the Nations, spare us: yet,
fool latins, alumni of one school,
on Clochan-na-n'all, say *Phew*
. . . *Lest we forget! Lest we forget!* . . .
to dusky peers of Roman, Greek, and Jew.
Selah!

Elders of Agâ's House, keening
at the Eagles' feast, cringing
before the Red Slayer, shrinking
from the blood on Hubris' pall—   300
carked by cracks of myriad curbs,
hitherto, against the Wailing Wall
of Ch'in, the blind men cried:
All cultures crawl
walk hard
fall,
flout
under classes under
Lout,
enmesh in ethos, in *masôreth,* the poet's flesh,   310
intone the Mass of the class as the requiem of the mass,
serve *adola mentis* till the crack of will,
castle divorcee Art in a blue-blood moat,
read the flesh of grass
into bulls and bears,
let Brahmin pens kill
Everyman the Goat,
write Culture's epitaph in *Notes* upstairs.
O *Cordon Sanitaire,*
thy brain's tapeworm, extract, thy eyeball's mote!   320
Selah!

Between pavilions
small and great
sentineled from capital to stylobate
by crossbow, harquebus, cannon, or Pegasus' bomb
. . . *and none went in and none went out* . . .
hitherto the State,
in spite of Sicilian Vespers, stout
from slave, feudal, bourgeois, or soviet grout,
has hung its curtain — scrim, foulard, pongee,   330
silk, lace, or iron — helled in by Sancho's fears
of the bitter hug of the Great Fear, Not-To-Be —
oscuro Luzbel,
with no bowels of mercy,
in the starlight
de las canteras sin auroras.
Behind the curtain, aeon after aeon,
he who doubts the white book's colophon
is Truth's, if not Laodicean, wears
the black flower T of doomed Laocoön.   340
Before hammer and sickle or swastika, two
worlds existed: the Many, the Few.
They sat at Delos', at Vienna's, at Yalta's, ado:
Macbeth, without three rings, as host
to Banquo's ghost.
Selah!

Like some gray ghoul from Alcatraz,
old Profit, the bald rake *paseq*, wipes the bar,
polishes the goblet vanity,
leers at the tigress Avarice   350
as
she harlots roués from afar:
swallowtails unsaved by loincloths,
famed enterprises prophesying war,
hearts of rags (*Hanorish tharah sharinas*) souls of chalk,
laureates with sugary grace in zinc buckets of verse,
myths rattled by the blueprint's talk,
ists potted and pitted by a feast,
Red Ruin's skeleton horsemen, four abreast
. . . galloping . . .   360
Marx, the exalter, would not know his East
. . . galloping . . .
nor Christ, the Leveler, His West.
Selah!

O Age of Tartuffe
. . . *a lighthouse with no light atop* . . .
O Age, *pesiq*, O Age,
kinks internal and global stinks
fog the bitter black estates of Buzzard and Og.
A Dog, I'd rather be, o sage, a Monkey or a Hog.   370
O Peoples of the Brinks,
come with the hawk's resolve,
the skeptic's optic nerve, the prophet's *tele* verve
and Oedipus' guess, to solve
the riddle of
the Red Enigma and the White Sphinx.
Selah!

O East . . . *el grito de Dolores* . . . O West,
  pacts, disemboweled, crawl off to die;
white books, *fiers instants promis à la faux,*   380
in sick bay choke on mulligan truth and lie;
  the knife of Rousseau hacks the anatomy
      of the fowl necessity;
    dead eyes accuse red Desfourneau,
whose sit-down strike gives High-Heels vertigo;
    the wind blows through the keyhole
  and the fettered pull down the shades;
while *il santo* and *pero* hone phillipics,
  Realpolitik explodes the hand grenades
        faits accomplis   390
      in the peace of parades;
  caught in the blizzard *divide et impera,*
    the little gray cattle cower
    before the Siamese wolves,
      pomp and power;
  Esperanto trips the heels of Greek;
in brain-sick lands, the pearls too rich for swine
  the claws of the anonymous seek;
  the case Caesarean, Lethean brew
  nor instruments obstetrical at hand,   400
the midwife of the old disenwombs the new.
      Selah!

The *Höhere* of Gaea's children
is beyond the *dérèglement de tous les sens,* is beyond
  gold fished from cesspools, the *galerie des rois,*
the seeking of cows, *apartheid,* Sisyphus' despond,
the Ilande intire of itselfe with *die Schweine* in mud,
  the potter's wheel that stocks the potter's field,
Kchesinskaja's balcony with epitaphs in blood,
  deeds hostile all, O Caton, to hostile eyes,   410
  the breaking of foreheads against the walls,
  gazing at navels, thinking with thighs

        . . .

The *Höhere* of God's stepchildren
is beyond the sabotaged world, is beyond
das Diktat der Menschenverachtung,
la muerte sobre el esqueleto de la nada,
the pelican's breast rent red to feed the young,
summer's third-class ticket, the *Revue des morts,*
the skulls trepanned to hold ideas plucked from dung,
Dives' crumbs in the church of the unchurched,   420
absurd life shaking its ass's ears among
the colors of vowels and Harrar blacks
with Nessus shirts from Europe on their backs

. . .

The *Höhere* of X's children
is beyond Heralds' College, the *filets d'Arachné,* is beyond
maggot democracy, the *Mal éternel,* the Bells of Ys,
the doddering old brigades with aorist medicines of poetry,
the *Orizaba* with its Bridge of Sighs,
the *oasis d'horreur dans un déserte d'ennui,*
the girasol rocks of Secunderabad,   430
Yofan's studio and *Shkola Nenavisti,*
the *otototoi* — in Crimson Tapestries — of the *hoi polloi,*
Euboean defeats
in the Sausage Makers' bout
the fool himself himself finds out
and in the cosmos of his chaos
repeats.
Selah!

The *Höhere* of one's pores *En Masse*
. . . Christians, Jews, *ta ethne* . . .   440
            makes as apishly
brazen as the brag and brabble of brass
            the flea's fiddling
            on the popinjay,
            the pollack's pout
            in the net's hurray,
            the jerboa's feat
        in the fawn and the flout
                of
            Quai d'Orsay,   450
            White House,
            Kremlin,
            Downing Street.
Again black Aethiop reaches at the sun, O Greek.
Things-as-they-are-for-us, *nullius in verba,*
                speak!
            O East, O West,
            on tenotomy bent,
            Chang's tissue is
            Eng's ligament!   460
                Selah!

Between Yesterday's wars
now hot now cold
the grief-in-grain of Man
dripping dripping dripping
from the Cross of Iron
dripping
drew jet vampires
of the Skull;
Between Yesterday's wills of Tanaka, between   470
golden goblet and truckling trull
and the ires
of rivers red with the reflexes of fires,
the ferris wheel
of race, of caste, of class
dumped and alped cadavers till the ground
fogged the Pleiades with Gila rot: Today the mass,
the Beast with a Maginot Line in its Brain,
the staircase Avengers of base alloy,
the *vile canaille* — *Gorii!* — the *Bastard-rasse*,   480
the *uomo qualyque*, the *hoi barbaroi*,
the *raya* in the *Oeil de Boeuf*,
the *vsechelovek*, the *descamisados*, the *hoi polloi*,
the Raw from the Coliseum of the Cooked,
Il Duce's Whore, Vardaman's Hound —
unparadised nobodies with maps of Nowhere
ride the merry-go-round!
Selah!

DO

a *pelageya* in *as seccas* the old she-fox today
eyes dead letters mouth a hole in a privy　　　　　　　　　490
　　taschunt a corpse's in a mud-walled troy of *jagunços*
　　　(*naze naze desu ka servant de dakar*) (*el grito de yara*)
　　　　cackles among the garbage cans of mummy truths
　　　　o frontier saints bring out your dead

the aria of the old *sookin sin* breaks my shoulders
lasciatemi morire o africa (*maneno matupu*)
　　the fat of fame didn't outlast a night in hog's wash
　　nor geneva's church nor the savage's ten pounds
　　　for stratford's poor (bles be ye man for jesvs sake)
　　　here one singeth *per me si va nella città dolente*　　　500

below the triumvirate flag & tongue & mammon
while *blut und boden* play the anthemn *iron masters gold*
　　ruble shilling franc yen lira baht and dime
　　brass-knuckled (*la légalité nous tue*) and iron-toed
　　　wage armageddon in the temple of *dieu et l'état*
　　　o earl of queensberry o last christian on the cross

vexilla regis prodeunt inferni what is man f.r.a.i. *tò tí*
(a professor of metaphysicotheologicocosmonigology
　　a tooth puller a pataphysicist in a cloaca of error
　　a belly's wolf a skull's tabernacle a #13 with stars　　　510
　　　a muses' darling a busie bee *de sac et de corde*
　　　a neighbor's bed-shaker a walking hospital on the walk)

lincoln walks the midnight epoch of the ant-hill
and barbaric yawps shatter the shoulder-knots of white peace
    jai hind (dawn comes up like thunder) *pakinstan zindabad*
    britannia rules the waves *my pokazhem meeru*
        the world is my parish *muhammad rasulu 'llah*
        hara ga hette iru oh yeah *higashi no kazeame*

naïfs pray for a guido's scale of good and evil to match
worldmusic's sol-fa syllables (*o do de do de do de*)   520
    worldmathematics' arabic and roman figures
    worldscience's greek and latin symbols
        the letter killeth five hundred global tongues
        before esperanto garrotes voläpuk *vanitas vanitatum*

o majesty-dwarf'd brothers *en un solo espasmo sexual*
ye have mock'd the golden rules of eleven sons of god
    smitten to rubble *ein feste burg* for a few acres of snow
    buried the open sesame *satya bol gat hai* among dry bones
        wasted the balm *assalamu aleykum* on lice and maggots
        snarled the long spoon for the scaly horror   530

pin-pricks precede blitzkriegs *mala' oun el yom yomek*
idiots carol happy dashes in st. innocent's little acre
    of rags and bones without brasses black and red
    booby mouths looted of the irritating parenthesis
        patrol skulls unhonored by a cromwell's pike
        snaggleteeth glutted *in sudori vultus alieni*

o sweet chariot these aesop's flies without mirth
these *oh-mono* without music in greed's akeldama
    are one with the great auk of the north star
    mouldy rolls of noah's ark and wall street   540
        nuclei fed to demogorgon's mill
        alms for oblivion raindrops minus h_2o

o's without figures on ice the sun licks
pebbles let fall in the race of a night sea
    jockeyed by beaufort no. 12
      iotas of the *yod* of god in a rolls royce
        the seven trumpets of today's baby boys summon peace
        and the walls come tumblin' down (christ sleeps)

and no mourners go crying *dam-bid-dam*
about the ex-streets of scarlet letters   550
    only the souls of hyenas whining *teneo te africa*
    only the blind men gibbering *mboagan* in greek
      against sodom's pillars of salt
      below the mountain of rodinsmashedstatues *aleppe*

        .   .   .   .

Tomorrow . . . O . . . Tomorrow,
Where is the glory of the *mestizo* Pharaoh?
The Mahdi's tomb of the foul deed?
Black Clitus of the fatal verse and Hamlet's arras?
The cesspool of the reef of gold?
Der Schwarze Teufel, Napoleon's savior?   560
The Black Virgin of Creation's Hell Hole?
Tomorrow . . . O . . . Tomorrow,
Where is Jugurtha the dark Iago?
The witches' Sabbath of sleeping sickness?
The *Nye ke mi* eyeless in the River of Blood?
The Tagus that imitates the Congo?
The *Mein Kampf* of *kitab al sudan wa'lbidan?*
The black albatross about the white man's neck?
O Tomorrow,
Where is the graven image *pehleh* of *Nash Barin?*   570
Their white age of their finest black hour?
The forged minute book of ebony Hirsch?
The chattel whose Rock vies with the Rime of the upstart Crow?
Ppt. knows.

. . . .

The Futurafrique, the *chef d'oeuvre* of Liberian
          Motors slips through the traffic
          swirl of axial Parsifal-Feirefiz
          Square, slithers past the golden
          statues of the half-brothers as
          brothers, with *cest prace* . . .   580
The Futurafrique, the accent on youth and speed
          and beauty, escalades the Mount
          Sinai of Tubman University, the
          vistas of which bloom with co-
          eds from seven times seven lands . . .
The Futurafrique, windows periscopic, idles past
          the entrance to the 70A subway
          station, volplanes into the aria
          of Swynnerton Avenue, zooms
          by the Zorzor Monument, zigzags   590
          between the factory hierarchies,
          rockets upcountry and backcoun-
          try, arcs the ad-libbing soapy
          blue harbor crossroads of Wal-
          dorf Astorias at anchor, atom-
          fueled and burnished in ports
          of the six seagirt worlds . . .
The Futurafrique strokes the thigh of Mount Bar-
          clay and skis toward the Good-
          lowe Straightaway, whose colo-   600
          ratura sunset is the alpenglow
          of cultures in the Shovelhead Era
          of the Common Man . . .
The Futurafrique glitters past bronze Chomolungma, odic
          memorial to Matilda Newport—
          on and on and on, outracing the
          supercoach of the Momolu Bu-
          kere Black-Hound winging along
          the seven-lane Equatorial High-
          way toward Khopirû . . .   610

The Futurafrique, flight-furbished ebony astride
velvet-paved miles, vies with the
sunflower magnificence of the
Oriens, challenges the snow-lily
diadem of the Europa . . .
The Futurafrique, with but a scintilla of its Niagara
power, slices Laubach Park,
eclipses the Silver Age Gibbet
of Shikata-gai-nai, beyond the
ars of Phidias; on and on, herds   620
only blears of rotor masts roulet-
ting, estates only rococo decks
and sails swirling, the Futur-
afrique, the Oriens, the Auster,
the Americus, the Europa, rend
space, gut time, arrowing past
tiering Nidaba, glissading side
by side, into the cosmopolis of
Höhere — the bygone habitat of
mumbo jumbo and blue tongue,   630
of sasswood-bark jury and tsetse
fly, aeons and aeons before the
Unhappie Wight of the Ques-
tion Mark crossed the Al Sirat!

The United Nations Limited volts over the unten-
anted, untitled grave of Black
Simoom, the red Chaka of *ruse
de guerre*, the Cheops of pyra-
mids with the skulls of Pygmy
and Britisher, Boer and Arab . . .   640

The United Nations Limited careers across Seretse
        Khama's Bechuanaland, yester-
        day and yesterday and yester-
        day after the body of Living-
        stone knelled its trek in dry salt
        from Lake Bangeula to the sab-
        bath of Westminster Abbey . . .
The United Nations Limited horseshoe-curves Stan-
        ley Falls, sheens the surrealistic
        harlotry of the mirage-veiled   650
        Sahara, quakes the dinosaurian
        teeth bolted in the jaws of Ti-
        besti, zoom-zooms through the
        Ptolemaic Subterane like a silver
        sirocco . . .
The United Nations Limited, stream-phrased and air-
        chamoised and sponge-cush-
        ioned, telescopes the polyge-
        netic metropolises polychro-
        matic between Casablanco and   660
        Mafeking, Freetown and Addis
        Ababa!

The Bula Matadi, diesel-engined, fourfold-decked,
        swan-sleek, glides like an ice-
        ballet skater out of the Bight of
        Benin, the lily lyricism of whose
        ivory and gold figurines larked
        space oneness on the shelf ice
        of avant-garde Art . . .
The Bula Matadi swivels past isled Ribat, where, in   670
        a leaden age's iliads, the Black
        Messiah and his Black Puritans,
        exsected by Sodoms and Go-
        morrahs, daunted doxy doubts
        with skeletons of dharna . . .

The Bula Matadi skirrs up the Niger, with her Khufu
        cargo from Tel Aviv and Hiro-
        shima, Peiping and San Salva-
        dor, Monrovia and Picayune!

Le Premier des Noirs, of Pan-African Airways, whirs   680
        beyond the copper cordilleran
        climaxes of glass skyscrapers on
        pavonine Cape Mesurado . . .
Le Premier des Noirs meteors beyond the Great White
        Way of Kpandemai, aglitter
        with the ebony *beau monde* . . .
Le Premier des Noirs waltzes across Lake Chad, curv-
        ets above the Fifth Cataract,
        wantons with the friar stars of
        the Marra Mountains, eagles its   690
        steeple-nosed prow toward the
        Very Black and the iron cur-
        tainless Kremlin!

The Parliament of African Peoples plants the winged
        lex scripta of its New Order on
        Roberts Avenue, in Bunker Hill,
        Liberia . . .
The Parliament of African Peoples pinnacles *Novus
        Homo* in the Ashmun Interna-
        tional House, where, free and   700
        joyful again, all mankind unites,
        without heralds of earth and
        water . . .
The Parliament of African Peoples churns with magic
        potions, monsoon spirits, zonal
        oscillations, kinetic credenda,
        apocalyptic projects — shudder-
        ing at its own depth, shudder-
        ing as if Shakespeare terrified
        Shakespeare . . .   710

The Parliament of African Peoples, chains riven in
    an age luminous with alpha ray
    ideas, rives the cycle of years
    lean and fat, poises the scales
    of Head and Hand, gives Sci-
    ence dominion over Why and
    Art over How, bids Man cross
    the bridge of Bifrost and drink
    draughts of rases from verved
    and loined apes of God with   720
    leaves of grass and great audi-
    ences . . .
The Parliament of African Peoples, After the Deluge,
    wipes out the zymotic zombi
    cult of God's wounds, exscinds
    the fetid fetish Zu'lkadah, bans
    the genocidal *Siyáfa,* enroots
    the Kiowa anthemn *Geh Tai*
    Gea . . .
The Parliament of African Peoples pedestals a new   730
    golden calendar of Höhere and
    quickens the death-in-life of the
    unparadised with the olive al-
    penstocks of the Violent Men . . .
The Parliament of African Peoples decrees the Zu'l-
    hijyah of Everyman and eter-
    nizes *Afrika sikeléľ iAfrika* . . .

The Parliament of African Peoples hormones the Iscariot-
      cuckolded Four Freedoms, up-
      holsters warehoused *unto each*   740
      according as any one has need,
      keystones italics ushered in by
      epee Pros and Cons Incorrup-
      tible, banishes cicerones of the
      witch hunt under the aegis of
      Flag and Cross, while the tiered
      galleries and television conti-
      nents hosanna the Black Jews
      from the cis-Danakil Desert,
      the Ashantis from the Great   750
      Sierra Nile, the Hottentots from
      Bushland, the Mpongwes from
      the Cameroon Peoples' Repub-
      lic, the Pygmies from the United
      States of Outer Ubangi ...
The Parliament of African Peoples signets forever
      the *Recessional of Europe* and
      trumpets the abolition of itself:
      and no nation uses *Felis leo* or
      Aquila heliaca as the emblem of   760
      blut und boden; and the hyenas
      whine no more among the bar-
      ren bones of the seventeen sun-
      set sultans of Songhai; and the
      deserts that gave up the ghost
      to green pastures chant in the
      ears and teeth of the Dog, in
      the Rosh Hashana of the Afric
      calends: *"Honi soit qui mal y*
      pense!"   770

Notes to
Libretto for the Republic of Liberia

LINE

7. Cf. Dryden, *All for Love*, II, i:
   ". . . upon my eagle's wings
   I bore this wren, till I was tired of soaring,
   and now he mounts above me."

11. Cf. Raleigh, *The Soul's Errand.*

15. V. Nietzsche, *Thus Spake Zarathustra.*

18. Cf. Shakespeare, *Othello*, III, iii:
    "Haply, for I am black . . ."

19. *Magic-square:* a symbol of equality. The diagram consists of a number of small squares each containing a number. The numbers are so arranged that the sum of those in each of the various rows is the same. Cf. Thomson, *The City of Dreadful Night*, XXI, 1061.

20. Cf. Willis, *The Leper.*

30. The motto of Liberia: "The love of liberty brought us here."

32. Cf. Carlyle: "God has put into every white man's hand a whip to flog a black man."

38. Cf. the tavern scenes in Boulton's comic opera, *The Sailor's Farewell.*

42. *Cobra Pirate.* V. Hardy, *Les Grands Etapes de l'Histoire du Maroc*, 50-54. *The Question Mark.* The shape of the map of Africa dramatizes two schools of thought among native African scholars. To the Christian educator, Dr. James E. Kwegyir Aggrey, it is a moral interrogation point that challenges the white world. According to Dr. Nnamdi Azikiwe, the leader of the nationalistic movement on the West Coast, foreigners consider it "a ham-bone designed by destiny for the carving-knife of European imperialism." I have found very fruitful the suggestions and criticisms of Professor Diana Pierson, the Liberian, and Dr. Akiki Nyabongo, the Ugandian. I now know that the Question Mark is rough water between Scylla and Charybdis.

43. Cf. Bismarck: "They [Negroes] appear to me to be a caricature of the white man."

44. Cf. Shakespeare, *Henry IV*, III, i:
    "A foutra for the world and worldlings base!
    I speak of Africa and golden joys."

46. Cf. Emerson: "While European genius is symbolized by some majestic Corinne crowned in the capitol at Rome, American genius finds its true type in the poor negro soldier lying in the

trenches by the Potomac with his spelling book in one hand and his musket in the other." V. Maran, *Batouala*, 9: "Civilization, civilization, pride of the Europeans and charnel-house of innocents, Rabindranath Tagore, the Hindu poet, once, at Tokio, told what you are! You have built your kingdom on corpses."

48. *The books whose head is golden*. Cf. Rossetti, *Mary's Girlhood*.

50. *Destooled*. On the Gold Coast the "Stool" is the symbol of the soul of the nation, its Magna Charta. In 1900, Sir Frederick Hodgson, Governor of the Gold Coast, demanded that the Ashantis surrender their "Stool." They immediately declared war. "Destooling" is a veto exercised by the sovereign people over unpopular rulers.

51. *Ed-dehebi:* "The Master of Gold." He was the conqueror of Songhai, with its fabulous gold mines.

54. *The iron nerve*. Cf. Tennyson, *Ode on the Death of the Duke of Wellington*.

56. V. the address of Anatole France at the bier of Emile Zola.

57. Cf. *A Memoir of Tennyson*, Vol. I, 46, the letter of Arthur Hallam to William Gladstone on the Timbuktu prize poem: "I consider Tennyson as promising fair to be the greatest poet of our generation, perhaps of our century." V. Delafosse, *Les Noirs de L'Afrique*. The Schomburg Collection, in Harlem, contains many rare items on the civilization at Timbuktu. Dr. Lorenzo Turner's *Africanism in the Gullah Dialects*, by tracing West Coast derivatives to their Arabic and Moslem and Portuguese cultural roots, has revealed the catholicity and sophistication of African antiquity and exploded the theory of the Old English origin of the Gullah dialects.

58. I am informed that variations of this *eironeia* or mockery may be found in scores of African languages. It means here: "The world is too large—that's why we do not hear everything." Cf. Pliny, *Historia Naturalis*, II: "There is always something new from Africa." Also Swift:

> "So geographers, in Afric maps,
> With savage pictures fill their gaps . . ."

69. *Black pearls*. V. Shakespeare, *Two Gentlemen of Verona*, V, i. Also *Othello*, II, i:

> "Well prais'd! How if she be black and witty?"

Mr. J. A. Rogers treats the subject and time and place adequately in *Sex and Race*.

LINE

72. *Wanawake wanazaa ovyo:* "The women keep having children right and left." *Kazi yenu wazungu:* "It's the work of you white men."

75. *Beba mzigo:* "Lift the loads." This repetend is tacked on *ex tempore* to ballads growing out of a diversity of physical and spiritual experiences.

80. V. Du Bois, *The World and Africa*, a book to which I am deeply indebted for facts.

81. The nomadic pedagogues gathered at Timbuktu are not to be confused with the *vagantes* of the *Carmina Burana*.

82. *Souls in one skin.* V. Firdousi, *The Dream of Dakiki*, I, A.

84. *Karibu wee.* Among primitives hospitality is a thing poetic— and apostolic. *Jogoo linawika: Karibu wee.* "The rooster crows: Welcome!" *Mbuzi wanalia: Karibu wee.* "The goats bleat: Welcome."

87. *Lia.* The word means "weep" and seems to follow the patterns of *"otototoi"* in the Aeschylean chorus.

92. *Dieu seul est grand.* These first words of Massillon's exordium, delivered at the magnificent funeral of Louis XIV, brought the congregation to its feet in the cathedral. For an account of the destruction of Timbuktu, see the *Tarikh el-Fettach*. The *askia* Issahak, in a vain attempt to stop the Spanish renegades at Tondibi, used cows as Darius had used elephants against the Macedonian phalanx.

100. *Nut empires.* Cf. Sagittarius, *New Statesman and Nation*, May 1, 1948, the poem entitled "Pea-Nuts":
> "The sun of Empire will not set
> While Empire nuts abound."

122. The airfields of Liberia sent 17,0000 bombers a month against Rommel's *Afrika Korps*.

141. *Shule, agrah:* "Move, my heart." Cf. Sharp, *Shule, Shule, Shule, Agrah.* It is a refrain from old Gaelic ballads.

142. *Skull: "gulgoleth,"* a place of torment and martyrdom. *Another's stairs.* Cf. Rossetti, *Dante at Verona*, the epigraph from *Paradiso*, XVII:
> "Yea, thou shalt learn how salt his food who fares
> Upon another's bread—how steep his path
> Who treadeth up and down another's stairs."

143. V. Myrdal, *An American Dilemma.* Cf. Aptheker, *The Negro People in America.* Also Cox, *Race, Caste and Class.*

147. *Auction blocks.* Cf. Rolfe, *Diary, 1619:* "About the last of August came a Dutch man of warre that sold us twenty negars." Also Field, *Freedom Is More than a Word:* "And the Negroes have been in this country longer, on the average, than their white neighbors; they first came to this country on a ship called the 'Jesus' one year before the 'Mayflower' . . ." *With the eyes of Cain.* Cf. Watson, *The World in Armor.*

148. Cf. John Davis, *Travels,* the chapter on a slave hanging alive on a gibbet in South Carolina: ". . . the negur lolled out his tongue, his eyes starting from their sockets, and for three long days his only cry was Water! Water! Water!" *Sjamboks.* Cf. Padmore, *Africa:* "The Africans are housed like cattle in a compound . . . they are guarded by foremen armed with the sjambok, a hide whip—the symbol of South African civilization."

155. *Tygers heart:* Greene's allusion to "the onely Shake-scene."

163. Cf. LaVarre: "My black companions had two languages: *deepitalki,* a secret language no white man understands; and *talkitalki,* a concoction of many languages and idioms which I understood."

167. *Skulls plowed under.* Cf. Sharp, *The Last Aboriginal.*

168. *Griots:* "living encyclopedias." Giryama, Bantu, Amharic, Swahili, Yoruba, Vai, Thonga, Zulu, Jaba, Sudanese—these tribal scholars speak, with no basic change in idea and image, from line 173 to 214. The Africans have their *avant garde* in oral literature. Sometimes one of these bards becomes esoteric and sneers in a council of chiefs a line like this: "The snake walks on its belly." And thus elder statesmen are often puzzled by more than the seven ambiguities. Delafosse feared that the mass production technics introduced by missionaries and traders would contaminate art for art's sake in Africa.

170. These words of Guernier are no longer *ex cathedra:* the scope of a native culture is vertical—not horizontal.

194. *A stinkbug.* Cf. Kipling, *The White Man's Burden.*

221. Cf. Matthew VIII, xx.

226. V. *New York Times,* "Journey to Ararat," April 17, 1949. Cf. Maill's translation of a poem by an officer in the hospital at Erivan:

> "Here is Mount Ararat. It has a brooding look . . .
> One would think it was waiting to be set free."

LINE

230. *Uaz-Oîrit.* "The Very Green," the ancient Egyptian name for the Mediterranean.

239. *Netami lennowak*: "the first men."

240. Cf. Virgil, *Aeneid,* IV, 625: "*Exoriare aliquis!*"

245. *Prophet Jehudi Ashmun.* Lincoln University, the oldest Negro institution of its kind in the world, was founded as Ashmun Institute. The memory of the white pilgrim survives in old Ashmun Hall and in the Greek and Latin inscriptions cut in stones sacred to Lincoln men. The annual Lincoln-Liberian dinner is traditional, and two of the graduates have been ministers to Liberia.

249. V. Apollinaire, *La Chanson du Mal-Aimé,* the fifth and sixth sections.

258. *Miserere.* Cf. Newman, *The Definition of a Gentleman*: ". . . we attended the Tenebrae, at the Sestine, for the sake of the Miserere . . ."

262. *Cowled in azure*: the cloak of deceit and false humility. Cf. Hafiz, *The Divan (Odes)*, V, translated by Bicknell.

264. *Whale and Elephant*: the symbols Jefferson used to designate Great Britain with her navy under Nelson and France with her army under Napoleon. V. Anderson, *Liberia,* X.

269. *Masseboth*: "sacred pillars." Cf. Genesis, XXVIII, xviii. Also the J author.

270. *Thou boy of tears.* Cf. Shakespeare, *Coriolanus,* V, v.

274. *Lachen mit vastchekes*: "laughing with needles being stuck in you"; ghetto laughter.

275. Cf. Blake, *The Tiger.*

276. Cf. Hardy, *The Convergence of the Twain.*

286. V. Pycraft, *Animals of the World,* 1941-1942. *A fortiori,* the American trotter is "a combination of barb and Arab on English stock."

287. V. Christy, *The Asian Legacy and American Life.* This book contains vital facts on Oriental influences in the New Poetry. What I owe the late Professor Arthur E. Christy, a favorite teacher, is not limited to the concept of "the shuttle ceaselessly weaving the warp and weft of the world's cultural fabric."

293. *Clochan-na-n'all*: "the blind men's stepping-stones." Cf. Ferguson, *The Welshmen of Tirawley.*

297. V. Aeschylus, *Agamemnon.*

LINE

301. Cf. Shakespeare, *Coriolanus,* I, i, 67-76. See also Mr. Traversi's essay on this phase of the play.

303. I came across these words somewhere: "The Ch'in emperor built the Great Wall to keep out Mongolian enemies from the north and burned the books of China to destroy intellectual enemies from within."

310. Cf. Akiba: "*Masôreth* is a fence for the sayings of the fathers."

312. *Adola mentis.* V. Bacon, *Novum Organum.*

313. *Divorcee Art.* Cf. Gourmont: "*Car je crois que l'art est par essence, absolument inintelligible au peuple.*"

325. *Pegasus' bomb.* Cf. Dobson, *On the Future of Poetry.*

326. V. Joshua VI, i.

327. Cf. Treitschke: "The State is Power. Of so unusual a type is its power, that it has no power to limit its power. Hence no treaty, when it becomes inconvenient, can be binding; hence the very notion of arbitration is absurd; hence war is a part of the Divine order." Contrast this idea with Lincoln's premise that the people can establish either a republic of wolves or a democracy of lambs, as instanced in the poem *The Dictionary of the Wolf.* Cf. Bismarck: "The clause *rebus sic stantis* is understood in all treaties."

330. *Curtain.* Cf. Crile, *A Mechanistic View of War and Peace, 1915*: "France [is] a nation of forty million with a deep-rooted grievance and an iron curtain at its frontier."

331. *Sancho's fears.* V. Cervantes, *Don Quixote de la Mancha,* Part II, translated by Peter Motteux, the episode of the letter: "To Don Sancho Pança, Governor of the Island of Barataria, to be delivered into his own hands, or those of his secretary."

332. *The Great Fear.* V. Madelin, *French Revolution,* 69.

333. Alberti, *Sobre los Angeles.*

334. Cf. the aphorism: "*La politique n'a pas d'entrailles.*"

335. Cf. Meredith, *Lucifer in Starlight.*

340. Cf. Hawthorne, *The Scarlet Letter*: "The black flower of civilized society, a prison."

344. V. Boccaccio, *The Three Rings.* Cf. Lessing, *Nathan the Wise.*

348. *Paseq*: "divider." This is a vertical line that occurs about 480 times in our Hebrew Bible. Although first mentioned in the *Midrash Rabba* in the eleventh century, it is still the most mysterious sign in the literature.

LINE

353.   Cf. Cavafy, *Waiting for the Barbarians.*

354.   *Famed enterprises.* V. Erasmus, *The Praise of Folly,* "Soldiers and Philosophers," *in toto,* the revised translation by John Wilson.

355.   *Hearts of rags . . . souls of chalk*: Whitman's epithets for the "floating mass" that vote early and often for bread and circuses. *Hanorish tharah sharinas*: "Man is a being of varied, manifold, and inconstant nature." V. Della Mirandola, *Oration on the Dignity of Man.* Cf. Cunha: "The fantasy of universal suffrage [is] the Hercules' club of our dignity."

356.   *Zinc buckets of verse.* V. Pasternak, *Definition of Poetry. Sugary grace.* Cf. Martial, *To a Rival Poet.*

359.   Cf. Tennyson, *Idylls of the King:*
           "Red Ruin, and the breaking up of laws."
       V. Revelation VI. Cf. Jouve, *La Resurrection des Morts.* See the White Horse, the Red Horse, the Black Horse, and the fourth horse, the worst:
           "Tu es jaune et ta forme coule à ta charpente
           Sur le tonneau ajouré de tes côtes
           Les lambeaux verts tombent plus transparents
           La queue est chauve et le bassin a des béquilles
           Pour le stérile va-et-vient de la violence . . ."

363.   *The Leveler.* V. The Acts V, xxxii-xxxvi.

367.   *Pesiq:* "divided." V. Fuchs, *Pesiq ein Glossenzeichen.* It seems to me that this linguistic symbol gives us a concrete example of the teleological—perhaps the only one. By an accident of *a priori* probability, the sign in itself indicates both cause and effect, and the index of the relationship is served synchronously by either *paseq* or *pasiq.* Of course the protagonist of the poem uses them for his own purpose on another level.

369.   *Bitter black estates.* Cf. Petrarca, *The Spring Returns, but Not to Him Returns,* translated by Auslander. *Buzzard.* V. Dryden, *The Hind and the Panther. Og.* V. Tate, *Second Part of Absalom and Achitophel,* the passage inserted by Dryden.

370.   V. Rochester, *Satyr against Mankind.* Cf. Cocteau, *Le Cap de Bonne Espérance:* "*J'ai mal d'être homme.*"

378.   The watchword of Hidalgo, "Captain General of America."

380.   Cf. Muselli, *Ballade de Contradiction:*
           "Fiers instants promis à la faux,
           Eclairs sombres au noir domaine!"

384. Cf. Camus, *The Artist as Witness of Freedom*: M. Desfour-neau's ". . . demands were clear. He naturally wanted a bonus for each execution, which is customary in any enterprise. But, more important, he vigorously demanded that he be given . . . an administrative status. Thus came to an end, beneath the weight of history, one of the last of our liberal professions. . . . Almost everywhere else in the world, executioners have already been installed in ministerial chairs. They have merely substi-tuted the rubber stamp for the axe."

386. Cf. Nietzsche, *Thus Spoke Zarathustra*, 232.

388. *Il Santo and Pero*: respectively, the nicknames of Nietzsche and Trotsky—the first innocently ironical, the second ironically innocent.

393. Cf. the remark of Nicholas I to a harassed minister of war: "We have plenty of little gray cattle." The Czar had in mind the Russian peasant.

397. *Brain-sick lands.* V. Meredith, *On the Danger of War.*

398. In the fable of Antisthenes, when the hares demanded equality for all, the lions said: "Where are your claws?" Cf. Martial, *Epigram XII*, 93: *"Dic mihi, si fias tu leo, qualis eris?"*

403. *Höhere.* Cf. Petronius: *"Proecipitandus est liber spiritus."*

405. In the Gilded Era, cynics said of Babcock: "He fished for gold in every stinking cesspool." *Galerie des rois.* Cf. Verlaine, *Nocturne Parisien*, the reference to the twenty-eight statues of French kings.

406. *The seeking of cows*: this is the literal meaning of the word "battle" among the ancient Aryans who ravaged the Indo-Gangetic plains. The backwardness of their culture is attested by their failure to fumigate and euphemize their war aims. *Apartheid*: the South African system of multi-layered segre-gation.

410. *Deeds hostile all*: these words are from the *Chorus to Ajax,* by Sophocles, which Mr. Forrestal apparently read just before his death. *O Caton*: Cato the Younger committed suicide in 46 B. C. He had spent the previous night reading Plato's *Phaedo.* Cf. Lamartine, *Le Désespoir.*

411. *The walls*: "economic doctrines." The figure is Blok's.

414. *Sabotaged world.* Cf. Salmon, *Age de l'Humanité.*

LINE

415. V. Mitscherlich and Mielke, *Doctors of Infamy*, translated by Norden. Cf. Grotius, *De Jure Belli et Pacis*, "Prolegomena," XVIII: ". . . a people which violates the Laws of Nature and Nations, beats down the bulwark of its own tranquillity for future time." ·

417. Cf. Ronsard, *Le Bocage*. Also Musset, *La Nuit de mai*.

418. V. Gautier, *Vieux de la vieille*, the reference to Raffet's *nocturne* showing Napoleon's spirit reviewing spectral troops.

419. Plekhanov had Alexander II in mind when he used the trepan figure.

421. V. Cendrars, *Eloge de la vie dangereuse*.

422. Rimbaud, in a town near the Red Sea, looked toward Khartoum and wrote: *"Leur Gordon est un idiot, leur Wolseley un âne, et toutés leurs entreprises une suite insensée d'absurdités et de déprédations."* But fifty years later, when the Black Shirts entered Harrar, the ex-poet who plotted with Menelik against Italy was not there to hear Vittorio Mussolini's poetic account: "I still remember the effect produced on a small group of Galla tribesmen massed around a man in black clothes. I dropped an aerial bomb right in the center, and the group opened up like a flowering rose. It was most entertaining."

425. *Filets d'Arachné*. Cf. Chénier, *Qui? moi? de Phébus te dicter les leçons?*

426. *Mal éternel*. Cf. Lisle, *Dies irae*.

429. Cf. Baudelaire, *Le Voyage*.

430. V. Robinson, the Preface to *The Story of Medicine*.

431. *Yofan's studio*: Napoleon's old residence by the Kremlin wall. *Shkola Nenavisti*: a Berlin film on a Dublin subject in a Moscow theater.

432. *Otototoi*. See Gilbert Murray's Notes to *Aeschylus*.

433. Cf. Ovid, *Tristia*, quoted by Montaigne in *Of Three Commerces*. "Whoever of the Grecian fleet has escaped the Capharean rocks ever takes care to steer clear from those of the Euboean sea."

439. Cf. Lamartine: *"Il faut . . . Avec l'humanité t'unir par chaque pore."* Cf. Hugo, the Preface to *Les Contemplations*: "When I speak to you of myself, I am speaking to you of you." And again, Romains: *"Il faut bien qu'un jour on soit l'humanité!"*

454. *Black Aethiop.* Cf. Shakespeare, *Pericles,* II, ii:
   "A knight of Sparta, my renowned father,
   And the device he bears upon his shield
   Is a black Aethiop, reaching at the sun;
   The word, '*Lux tua vita mihi*'."

455. *Nullius in verba.* V. Lyons, *The Royal Society.*

464. *Grief-in-grain.* The "grain" I have in mind in this figure consists of the dried female bodies of a scale insect found on cacti in Mexico and Central America. The dye is red and unfading. Cf. Henley, *To James McNeill Whistler, in toto.*

479. Cf. Cavafy, *The Footsteps.*

480. *Gorii.* The voyage of the Carthaginian general Hanno carried him as far as what is now Liberia. The aborigines he saw were called *Gorii,* which later Greek and Latin scholars turned into "gorilla." However, to Hanno's interpreter and in the Wolof language today, the expression means "These too are men."

482. *Raya.* In the Turkish conquest of the Southern Slavs, the maltreated people became *raya* or cattle. Conquest salves its conscience with contempt. Among the *raya* for five hundred years, the ballads of the wandering *guslars* kept freedom alive. *Oeil de Boeuf*: a waiting room at Versailles. Cf. Dobson, *On a Fan That Belonged to the Marquise de Pompadour.*

483. *Vsechelovek*: "universal man." In spite of its global image, this concept has a taint of *blut und boden.* Ever since Dostoevski, in a eulogy on Pushkin, identified the latter's genius with *vsechelovek,* the term has created pros and cons. Cf. the Latin: "Paul is a Roman and not a Roman." *Descamisados*: "the shirtless ones."

484. The line was suggested by the history of the *Crudes* and *Asados* of Uruguay.

485. *Il Duce's Whore.* V. *Ciano Diaries 1939-43,* edited by Gibson. This is one of the "many instances of the vast contempt in which Il Duce held his people."

486. Cf. Milton, the outline of *Adam Unparadised.*

489. *Pelageya*: the wench of the Draft Constitution. V. Gogol, *Dead Souls.* As *seccas*: the devastating periodic droughts of Brazil.

491. *Taschunt.* Cf. Frobenius, *African Genesis,* 47 (Faber & Faber, Ltd.): "He felt that he had a thabuscht." A *mudwalled troy of jaguncos*: the home of Maciel's fanatics.

492. *Naze naze desu ka.* V. Mailer, *The Naked and the Dead,* the

LINE

diary of Major Ishimara, 247. Also Apollinaire, *Les Soupirs du Servant de Dakar*. *El grito de yara*: the watchword at Manzanillo, October 16, 1869.

494. Cf. Francia: ". . . now I know that bullets are the best saints you can have on the frontiers." *Bring out your dead*: the cry of the bellman walking by night in front of the deadcart. V. Defoe, *Journal of the Plague Year*.

495. *Aria*. Cf. Ludwig: "Dictatorship is always an aria, never an opera." *Sookin sin*. V. Duranty, *One Life, One Kopeck*, 3. *Breaks my shoulders*. Cf. Baudelaire: "*Pour ne pas sentir l'horrible fardeau du temps qui brise vos épaules et vous penche vers terre, il faut vous enivrer sans trêve*."

496. *Lasciatemi morire*. V. Monteverdi, *Lament of Arianna*. Cf. Mendelssohn, *Aria from Elijah*: "O Lord, take away my life, for I am not better than my fathers." See also Mecaenas:

"*Debilem, facito manu,*
Debilem pede, coxâ;
Lubricos quate dentes:
Vita dum superset, bene est . . ."

Maneno matupu: "empty words," an epithet used in *deepitalki*—not *talki-talki*.

497. *Hog's Wash*: a London newspaper edited by Daniel Isaac Eaton during the "Anti-Jacobin Terror." Its name was an ironical allusion to Burke's epithet, "the swinish multitude."

498. *Savage's ten pounds*. Cf. Voltaire, *Irene*, the preliminary letter: "Shakespeare is a savage with sparks of genius in a dreadful darkness of night." See Shakespeare's will and epitaph.

500. *Here one singeth*. Cf. *Aucassin and Nocolete*, translated by Andrew Lang, the warning *aubade*, or "dawn song," of the sentinel on the tower above the trysting place.

502. When Croesus showed Solon his gold, the sage said: "Sir, if any other come that hath better iron than you, he will be master of all this gold."

504. *La légalité nous tue*. Muraviev, the Hangman, when he was governor-general of Poland, wrung this cry from the people.

507. *Vexilla regis prodeunt inferni*. Cf. Dante, *Inferno*, Canto XXXIV. *Tò tí*: "What is it?" This was the old gadfly's everlasting question.

508. Cf. Boileau, *Satires*, IV, 5-10.

509. *Tooth Puller*: "*Tiradentes*," the nickname of the first martyr of

LINE

Brazilian independence. *A cloaca of error.* See Pascal's doctrine of the Thinking Reed. Cf. Jarry, *Gestes et Opinions du Dr. Pataphysicien.*

510. *A belly's wolf.* Cf. Beaumont and Fletcher, *Woman Pleased.* Also Malley: "Religion is a process of turning your skull into a tabernacle, not of going up to Jerusalem once a year." *#13 with stars*: James Wilkinson, American general and secret Spanish agent, who sought to establish an empire in the Southwest under his own sword and sceptre.

511. Orlov in a letter to Golonin branded Muraviev as *"un homme de sac et de corde."*

512. *The Walk*: the *Peripatos* of the Lyceum.

513. *Epoch of the ant-hill.* V. Amiel, *Journal*: "The age of great men is going . . ."

514. *Shoulder-knots.* Cf. Swift, *A Tale of the Tub*, II.

515. *Dawn comes up like thunder.* Cf. Kipling, *Mandalay.*

516. *My pokazhem meeru*: "We'll show the whole world."

517. *The world is my parish*: Wesley's announcement of his mission.

518. *Hara ga hette iru*: "The belly has shrunken." *Higashi no kazeame*: the code words all Japanese embassies had received by mid-November, 1941. This phrase—"East wind rain"—was to be repeated in a short-wave news broadcast in case of a rupture in Japanese-American relations.

520. *O do de do de do de.* V. Shakespeare, *King Lear*, III, iv.

525. V. Newman, *The Dream of Gerontius.* Cf. Silva:

> "*Juan lanas, el mozo de esquina,*
> *Es absolutamente igual*
> *Al Emperador de la China;*
> *Los dos son un mismo animal.*"

527. V. Luther:

> "*Ein feste Burg ist unser Gott*
> *Ein gute Wehr und Waffen.*"

Voltaire looked upon the Seven Years' War as the devastation of Europe to settle whether England or France should win "a few acres of snow" in Canada.

528. *Satya bol gat hai*: "In truth lies salvation."

529. *Assalamu aleykum*: "Peace to you."

531. Cf. Napoleon's words to Czar Alexander at Tilsit, June 22, 1807: "If they want peace, nations should avoid the pin-pricks

LINE

that precede cannon-shots." *Mala' oun el yom yomek.* It is said that Taha Shanin, the Dongolawi, as he plunged his spear into General Gordon, cried: "O cursèd one, your time has come!"

532. *St. Innocent's.* Cf. Browne, *Hydriotaphia or Urn Burial.* Also Job XIV, vii. The hag Today in the poem says the idiots have a word for it. In China it means "Kong Hi Sing Yen"; in Africa, "Happy Dashes"; in America, "Merry Christmas." Cf. F.P.A., *For the Other 364 Days*: "Christmas is over and Business is Business."

533. *Brasses black and red.* Cf. Newbolt, *He Fell among Thieves.* Also his *Clifton Chapel,* the inscription which gives an epitome of two or three brasses in the Chapel:

> " 'Qui procul hinc,' the legend's writ—
> The frontier-grave is far away—
> 'Qui ante diem periit:
> Sed miles, sed pro patria'."

534. *Irritating parenthesis*: Cunha's figure for the problem of miscegenation. V. Cunha, *Os Sertoes,* II, ii, 108-110.

537. *O sweet chariot*: I have in mind the Negro spiritual.

538. *Oh-mono*: "high-muck-a-mucks." *Greed's akeldama.* V. The Acts I, xv-xxi.

541. *Demogorgon's mill.* Cf. Shelley, *Prometheus Unbound.*

546. *God in a rolls royce*: Father Divine. Some years ago in a jeremiad issued from one of his "heavens" he announced that he had reduced the Mayor of New York City "to a tittle of a jot" during the Harlem riot.

547. *The seven trumpets.* Cf. Joshua VI, viii. *Today's baby boys*: the code words for the A-bombs. The day after it was proved at Alamagordo, New Mexico, that the weapon worked, the late Henry L. Stimson, then secretary of war, received the message: "Baby boy born today mother and child doing well."

548. In the days of the Norman King Stephen, men cried out that "Christ and His saints slept."

549. *Dam-bid-dam*: "blood for blood." This was the way the Saadists phrased the idea of talion at the Abbasiya mausoleum of Nokrashy Pasha. Cf. Leviticus XXIV, xvii-xxi.

551. *Souls of hyenas*: another reference to the bloody Muraview, "this loathsome figure with a bulldog's face and a hyena's soul." The phrase is from Kucharzewski. *Teneo te Africa*: the words

uttered by Caesar when he stumbled and fell on touching the shore of Africa. Cf. Suetonius, *Lives of the Caesars*.

552. *Mboagan:* "death."

554. *Rodinsmashedstatues.* The twisted version of the hag Today keeps her from seeing that only the hands of the statues have been chopped off; and thus she misses the apocalypse in the Rodin image, the magnetic needle of whose compass pivots toward the Africa-To-Be (*Höhere* and *Khopirû*), set as the goal, by the protagonist, in the first section. For an elucidation of this transitional Janus-faced image, see Lajos Egri, *The Art of Dramatic Writing*, 30-31. *Aleppe.* Cf. Dante, *Inferno*, Canto VII: "*Pape Satan! pape, aleppe!*"

555. *Tomorrow.* V. Blake, *The Bard.* Cf. Rimbaud: "*Je vais dévoiler tous les mystères . . . mort, naissance, avenir, passé, cosmogonie, néant.*" Also Goethe, *Faust*, 7433:
"Enough, the poet is not bound by time."

558. *The fatal verse.* Alexander the Great made Black Clitus, "his best beloved," King of Bactria and commander of his celebrated cavalry, which synchronized with the Macedonian phalanx to deliver a battle's one-two punch. Dropsica, Clitus' mother, was Alexander's nurse. During the Persian campaign, a furious argument broke out at the king's supper table. He snatched a spear from a soldier and ran it through Clitus as he came from behind a curtain shouting a verse from Euripides' *Andromache*:
"In Greece, alas, how ill things ordered are!"
V. Plutarch, *Lives*, "Alexander." Cf. Shakespeare, *Hamlet*, III, iv.

559. The epithet African intellectuals give to Johánnesburg.

560. The German army's nickname for General Dumas, who rescued Napoleon from the Mamelukes by riding a stallion into a mosque in Cairo. The general's astounding feats kept him from getting a marshal's baton. He never recovered from the blow.

561. Cf. Xenophanes: "Men have always made their gods in their own images—the Greeks like Greeks, the Ethiopians like Ethiopians." Again Professor Christy's figure of "the world's cultural fabric" is evidenced in the statues of the Black Virgin Mary and Negro saints which were common in Germany and Latin Europe, as well as northern Africa, during the Middle Ages. The stained glass of the Cathedral at Chartres has portraits in

LINE

ebony. *Creation's Hell Hole*: the name the Italians gave the Danakil Desert.

566. Cf. Moog, *Um Rio imita o Rheno*. Moog created his symbol to suggest the heavy German settlement in Rio Grande do Sul. The line indicates a historical parallel when 10,000 Negroes gathered in Lisbon and threatened to outnumber the whites.

567. *Kitab al sudan wa'lbidan*: "the superiority of the black race over the white." Before the swastika gave Nordicism the Stuka, an Arab scholar, Al-Jahiz, issued his racist theory in reverse: another instance of similarity in dissimilarity.

570. *Pehleh*: "money." *Nash Barin*: before the October Revolution, this expression meant "Our Master" or God. I don't know its present meaning. Cf. I Timothy VI, v. Also Milton, *Paradise Lost*, 678.

573. *The chattel*: "Tariq." *Rock*: Gibraltar was named for this black general and ex-slave. *The Rime of the upstart Crow*. Cf. Shakespeare, *Sonnet LV*:
> "Not marble, nor the gilded monuments
> Of princes, shall outlive this powerful rime."

574. *Ppt. knows*. V. Swift, *Journal to Stella*, March 15, 1712.

577. *Parsifal-Feirefiz*. Cf. Eschenbach, *Parsifal*. Also Du Bois, *The World and Africa*, X.

580. *C'est prace*: "all honor to labor."

587. *70A subway*. V. Wilson, *Liberia*, for many of these references.

590. The Zorzor twins were miracle-workers in iron, see line 273.

610. *Khopirû*: "To Be." The concept embraces the Eternity of Thence, which, free from blind necessity, contains the good life.

619. *Shikata-gai-nai*: "It cannot be helped." This is the stoicism with which Japanese villagers meet the earth convulsions of sacred Fujiyama. In other lands it is fate, kismet, predestination, artistries of Circumstance, economic determinism, necessitarianism—from Aeschylus' Nemesis to Chénier's *filets d'Arachné*. Sometimes it takes the form of the sophistry, *human nature does not change*. As a hidden premise it blocks the kinetic; it confuses the feral with the societal and leads to *petitio principii*. History, then, remains a Heraclitean continuum of a world flaring up and dying down as "it always was, is, and shall be." Some moderns have turned this ancient seesaw figure of a crude

dialectics into a locomotive of history. In the poem, however, the flux of men and things is set forth in symbols whose motions are vertical-circular, horizontal-circular, and rectilinear. In spite of the diversity of phenomena, the underlying unity of the past is represented by the ferris wheel; the present by the merry-go-round; and the future by the automobile, the train, the ship, and the aeroplane. I placed the ship image in the middle of the images of swifter vehicles to indicate the contradiction in the essence of things, the struggle of opposites, which mankind will face even in *Khopirû* and *Höhere*. By the Law of Relativity, history will always have its silver age as well as its golden, and each age will contain some of the other's metal. Because of these upward and onward lags and leaps, it is not an accident that Liberia reaches her destination, the Parliament of African Peoples, after the aerial symbol. Cf. Meredith, *The World's Advance*, the figure of the reeling spiral.

620.   *Ars of Phidias*. Cf. Rodin: "Beyond Phidias sculpture will never advance." Also Shakespeare, *Troilus and Cressida*:
        "The baby figure of the giant mass
        Of things to come.

627.   *Nidaba*. Cf. Dr. Samuel Noah Kramer's translation of a Sumerian tablet in the Museum of the Ancient Orient: "You have exalted Nidaba, the queen of the places of learning."

680.   *Le Premier des Noirs*. When Napoleon became First Consul, Toussaint L'Ouverture addressed him in this manner: "From the First of the Blacks to the First of the Whites."

691-692.   *The Very Black:"Qim-Oîrit,"* or the Red Sea. V. Maspero, *The Dawn of Civilization*, I.

699-700.   Cf. Beethoven, *Ninth Symphony*, "Finale."

702-703.   *Heralds of earth and water*: ancient symbols of submission.

707.   In this phrase Hugo was describing Hugo.

727.   *Siyáfa*: "We Die."

728-729.   *Geh Tai Gea*: "All Is Well."

734.   *The Violent Men*: the stigmatized advocates of the Declaration of Independence in the First and Second Continental Congresses. V. Meigs, *The Violent Men*.

737.   *Afrika sikeléľ iAfrika*: "Africa save Africa."

HARLEM GALLERY
Book I, The Curator

ALPHA

The Harlem Gallery, an Afric pepper bird,
        awakes me at a people's dusk of dawn.
The age altars its image, a dog's hind leg,
and hazards the moment of truth in pawn.
        The Lord of the House of Flies,
        jaundice-eyed, synapses purled,
    wries before the tumultuous canvas,
                The Second of May—
                    by Goya:
            the dagger of Madrid
                    vs.
            the scimitar of Murat.
    In Africa, in Asia, on the Day
of Barricades, alarm birds bedevil the Great White World,
a Buridan's ass—not Balaam's—between no oats and hay.

    Sometimes a Roscius as tragedian,
        sometimes a Kean as clown,
    without Sir Henry's flap to shield my neck,
I travel, from oasis to oasis, man's Saharic up-and-down.

    As a Hambletonian gathers his legs for a leap,
            dead wool and fleece wool
        I have mustered up from hands
            now warm or cold: a full
            rich Indies' cargo;

but often I hear a dry husk-of-locust blues
descend the tone ladder of a laughing goose,
        syncopating between
        the faggot and the noose:
        "Black Boy, O Black Boy,
        is the port worth the cruise?"

Like the lice and maggots of the apples of Cain
        on a strawberry tree,
        the myth of the Afroamerican past
        exacts the parasite's fee.

        Sometimes the spirit wears away
        in the dust bowl of abuse,
like the candied flesh of the barrel cactus which
        the unpitying pitch
        of a Panhandle wind
        leaves with unpalatable juice.

Although the gaffing *"Tò tí?"* of the Gadfly girds
        the I-ness of my humanness and Negroness,
                the clockbird's
                jackass laughter
                in sun, in rain,
                at dusk of dawn,
mixes with the pepper bird's reveille in my brain,
where the plain is twilled and the twilled is plain.

BETA

O Tempora,
what is man?
(Pull down the ladder of sophistry!)
O Mores,
what *manner* of man is this?
(Guy the ologists in effigy!)

Who knows, *without no,*
the archimedean pit and pith of a man?
(Ask the Throttler at Gîza!)
But if one seeks the nth verisimilar,
go to Ars by the way of Pisgah:
as the telescope of Galileo
deserted the clod to read the engirdling idioms of the star,
to the ape of God,
go!

But if one, a lotus eater, seeks
the umbrella of the green bay tree,
go to Solomon's seal—
to the ant's synecdoche.
To explore the troubled Virgin Pool *in* and *out* of man,
one needs the clarity
the comma gives the eye,
not the head of the hawk
swollen with rye.

O Heroics, O Pathetics,
what gives a figure in the fresco *Life* its stance?
Should my head escape a Herod's charger
after the Salomean dance,
let it go
(*non astutia, animo*)
with a frown nor a smile,
beyond the dust and ashes of tartufish guile.

The great god Biosis begets
the taste that sets apart
the pearls and olivets.

In *The Dialogue of Lees,*
a lee said, "The higher altitudes produce
the better teas."

As we, in a strange land, strangers, walked
beyond the Black Stone's colonnade,
the Amharic eunuch's voice
was hushed
like the embrace in an accolade:
"Great minds require of us a reading glass;
great souls, a hearing aid."
But I,
in the shuttlebox world,
again and again,
have both mislaid.

In the drama *Art,*
with eye and tongue,
I play a minor vocative part,
like the O
of St. Bridget when it is rent
by the basso profundo
in the abysmal D
of his fortissimo
descent.

So none shall ever censure me
because my emptiness grew as hard
as the tartar *g* in go,
nor, with a *beau geste* as white as a chard,
speed hyacinths to me
because, with a rival boast
(like that of the Thracian bard),
I lost my sight and voice
to the vanity of the Uppermost.

Among husks
in the crib of the psyche,
among chaff,
the jumping mice of anxiety, unable to stand the gaff,
tattle
a secret that knocks
no Lilliputian off his pegs:
"Hunter, O hunter,
let winter yellowlegs

strut and brattle—
in the if-of-things nothing is final
but the death rattle."

Like ironstone in its bed
or a fixed idea in the head
spin of a Ph. D.,
I am pegged as an ex-professor of Art:
from the start,
routine gored my identity—
a fore-
and-
aft
hat
tusked by a boar.
Ex sets me in my status: *formerly*
but not now;
and quoth the Raven, "Nevermore!"
In the Harlem Gallery,
not even a godling ism of Art rises up to bow to,
nor a horseshoe bias perches above the door.

My heart
nor
my head
turns a wheel of prayer
when certified Yeas and Nays are said
by pilgrim academics in the Babel of Art,
for the death of the quick
or the breath of the dead;

but within the flame is a core
of gas as yet unburnt
and undetected like an uninflected spoor.

Caviar I've eaten in many a vantage,
mulligan stew in many a retreat,
with Young Men labeled by their decades
The Lost, The Bright, The Angry, The Beat.

I was not gilded, like them,
with the gift of tongues.
Absent like shadow in Byzantine painting,
the upper rungs
of my ladder are zeros.

As a shoemaker
translates a second-hand boot,
each decade reshaped the dialects of
the owl's hoot,
the lamb's bleat,
the wolf's cry,
the hyena's laugh.
As serpents, sly,
The Lost, The Bright, The Angry, The Beat
(tongues that tanged bees in the head around the clock)
did not stoop the neck to die
like a dunghill cock.

GAMMA

The mecca Art is a babel city in the people's Shinar
with a hundred gates
and busybody roads
that stretch beyond all dates,
where sweating pilgrims fleshed in hallelujahs
jostle like cars in a bumping race;
and apostates
(sour chunks of fat
in a leviathan churning vat)
bob up and down,
bob to and fro,
to dodge, in a rain forest of phews,
the cobra's spit and the tiger's blow
apostles arrow at the face
in the name of dusty messiahs of the bethel place.

Like Caesar's Gaul,
like the papal tiara, tripartite,
the revolving stage of Experience,
at our midnight
show, downstages Heart and Hand and Soul—
each memorable in his immemorial role
in Veridic's *Human Comedy*,
where anther's nectar mixes with ox's gall.
We who are we
discover *altérité* in the actors on
the boards of the Théâtre Vie.

No catharsis homes:
no empathy calls:
synapses of the thinking reed snap
from too little reality
when the heavy dark curtain falls.

As the Utrillo of the Holy Hill *trans*figured
a *dis*figured Montmartre street
into a thing of beauty, to haunt
the unhaunted and the undaunted,
no Atropos said, "No-side"—so,
on the curve of a parallel detour,
nostalgia changes the fat and the gaunt
plug-uglies of our bygone selves,
shadowed and shadowing,
where
two fatheads and four flat feet
patrol the night watchman's beat.

Before he deserted the streets of Harlem,
and the fuel in his furnace died at curfew,
my Afroirishjewish Grandpa said:
"Between the dead sea Hitherto
and the promised land Hence
looms the wilderness Now:
although his confidence
is often a boar bailed up
on a ridge, *somehow,*

the Attic salt in man survives the blow
of Attila, Croesus, Iscariot,
and the Witches' Sabbath in the Catacombs of Bosio."

In salon, café, and studio,
from Greenwich Village to Montparnasse,
across the dialectic Alps from Dō to Dō,
my eyes and ears have shadowed the pros and cons
punctured with hot needles.
The *Closerie des Lilas!*
The *Café Voltaire!*
A magicked pageant beetles
along the horizon! Art is a harbor of colors
(with a hundred mosaic sail)
like Joseph's coat.

O hail
Paolo's doomsday *Sodom* that brasses
caricatures of patterns and colors and masses
fluxing away from the cruxing incandescence convulsing
the engouled town!
O hail
Tintoretto's *Paradise,*
lustrous and pulsing
with blue and silver,
red and ivory and brown!

DELTA

Doubt not
the artist and his age
(though bald as the pilled head of garlic),
married or divorced
and even vying downstage,
are both aware
that God or Caesar is the handle
to the camel's hair.

Ye weeping monkeys of the Critics' Circus
(colorless as malic acid in a Black Hamburg grape),
what profit it to argue at the wake
(a hurrah's nest of food and wine
with Auld Lang Syne
to cheer the dead),
if the artist wrought
(contrary to what the black sanders said)
for Ars',
the Cathedra's, or the Agora's sake?
No critic a Gran Galeoto
between the Art-lover and the work of art,
the world-self of the make-
believe becomes the swimming pool of a class,
the balsam apple
of the soul and by the soul and for the soul,
or silvered Scarahaeus glass
in which Necessity's *figuranti* of innocence and guilt
mirror themselves as they pass.

If brass,
in the name
of Id or Sinai or Helicon, wakes up the trumpet,
is it to blame?

Although
the moment's mistone
and the milieu's groan
sharp an unbearable ache
in the f of the age's bone,
this pain is only the ghost of the pain
the artist endures,
endures
—like Everyman—
alone.

The artist
is
a zinnia
no
first frost
blackens with a cloven hoof;
an eyeglass
—in the eye of a dusty wind—
to study the crosses and tangles in warp and woof;
an evergreen cherry
parasitic upon a winter sun;
a paltry thing with varicose veins
when the twelve fatigues are done.

Under the Lesbian rule of the seeress Nix,
blood and black bile
mix:
in the second of a bestiary-goat's caprice,
Élan,
the artist's undivorceable spouse
becomes
a Delilah of Délice
or
a Xanthippe bereft
of sonnets from the Portuguese.

In Chronos Park
the Ars-powered Ferris wheel revolves
through golden age and dark
as historied isms rise and fall
and the purple of the doctor's robe
(ephemeral as the flesh color of the fame flower)
is translated into the coffin's pall.

The St. John's agony
of the artist
in his gethsemane
without a St. John's fire—
the Vedic god of the snaky noose discovers;
his far far cry,
like the noise of block tin,
crackles the sky:

"Wayfaring man
unneighbored by
a wayfaring tree
(though one may rue
this bark of the Moreton Bay laurel),
it is true
a something *trans*-Brow or *cis*-Brow
—or both—
wills one to the wings of the eagle,
or to the teats of the sow.
Yet, no lip need sneer to the beard of an ape of God,
'Thou thing of no bowels, thou!'
So I say as the Sire
who chastens and rewards,
'Let thy blue eyes
resist white stars of red desire.' "

Like the shape of Africa,
the *raison d'être* of Art is a question mark:
without the true flight of the bat,
it is a hanker in the dark.
Not as face answers face in water,
but as windows answer each other,
one viewer,
lyrical as Hafiz in his cups,
discovers a lark;
his companion,
flat as an open Gladstone bag,
spies out an ark.

The blow of a fist on the nape,
this question came from a Dog,
"What color can escape
the fluky flues in the cosmic flux?"
Perhaps the high-C answer lies
in the wreck the sea sucks
back into her bowels. Let
the *Say* be said:
"In Philae the color is blue;
in Deir-el-Baheri, red;
in Abydos, yellow—
and these are by the ravens fed."

Art
is not barrel copper easily separated
from the matrix;
it is not fresh tissues
—for microscopic study—
one may *fix*:
unique as the white tiger's
pink paws and blue eyes,
Art
leaves her lover as a Komitas
deciphering intricate Armenian neums,
with a wild surmise.

EPSILON

The idols of the tribe,
in voices as puissant as the rutting calls
of a bull crocodile, bellow:
"We
have heroes! Celebrate them upon our walls!"

The frond of the walking leaf bends back,
discovers that (in the vanity
of Deir-el-Baheri frieze
and Savonnerie tapestry)
the spoors in the vein
of Art, indicative as uterine souffles, tail out a snide:
"From Dutch canals, not Siloam, came
the water in Rembrandt's pool
(as laughing Dogs confide);
and Milton's Lucifer was a Cavalier—
his God, a Roundhead
(in full career,
without an egghead to gibe):
dramatis personae of the ethos
miracled to befool
the hubris of the tribe."

O Lord of the House of Flies,
thy graven images of blood and class,
wise as the great horned owl of evil is wise,
infix the heart of an Ishmael
with the cold and yellow eyes

of the elite of serpent complexity:
the split-hair instant
that fear and blind choice verticalize
the venom fangs,
the ponderous coils bolting the cuneiforms
paralyze
(with the nonesuch of Pre-Cambrian artistry)
even a Michelangelesque imagination,
for its eternity.

O bulls of Bashan,
a nod from you is worse than a brief
from Diable Boiteux.
Just as a reef
at the head of a square sail
taken in or shaken out,
without fail,
regulates the size of the canvas,
a belief
shifted pro or shifted con,
as even the Dogs dare say,
fixes the four dimensions of A-is-A—
the center of gravity of the man inside.

A mute swan not at Coole, Beaufort's scale,
with the eerie mood of Bizan ware,
indicates a gale:
strange weather—strange
for a man or a mouse to make a change.

Again
by the waters of Babylon we sit down and weep,
for the pomp and power
of the bulls of Bashan
serve Belshazzarian tables to artists and poets who
serve the hour,
torn between two masters,
God and Caesar—
this (for Conscience),
the Chomolungma of disasters.

Again
we hang our harps upon the willows,
for the Ichabod and Sir Toby Belch of the olive leaf,
who,
lacking vitamin B,
lose an appetite for even grief.

Sicilian Bull and Sicilian Vespers
non obstante,
Art's
yen to beard in the den
deep down under root and stone
fossick gold and fossil ivory
stands out
like a whale's
backbone.

ZETA

My thoughts tilted at the corners like long Nepalese eyes,
I entered, under the Bear, a catacomb Harlem flat
(grotesquely vivisected like microscoped maggots)
where the caricature of a rat
weathercocked in squeals
to be or not to be
and a snaggle-toothed toilet
grumbled its obscenity.
The half-blind painter,
spoon-shaped like an aged parrot-fish,
hauled up out of the ruin of his bed
and growled a proverb in Yiddish.

His smiting stare
was a Carib's forefinger prizing
Vuelta tobacco leaves in the butt of a pipe.
No half-man disguising,
he wore his odds and ends
like a mandarin's worked gold
and seated image nodding in silk,
as his bold
thumb motioned me to an expendable chair.
His sheaf of merino hair
an agitated ambush,
he bottomed upon the hazard of a bed—sighing:
"The eagle's wings,
as well as the wren's,
grow weary of flying."

His vanity was a fast-day soup—thin, cold.
Through a glass darkly I saw the face
of a fantast, heard the undated voice of a poet crying,
among scattered bones in a stony place,
"No man cares for my soul!"

Perhaps the isle of Patmos
was like this.
Here emerges the imago
from the impotence of the chrysalis
in the dusk of a people's dawn—
this, this,
thought I as I gazed at his *Black Bourgeoisie*:
colors detonating
fog signals on a railroad track,
lights and shadows rhythming
fog images in a negative pack:
this, somehow, a synthesis
(savage—sanative)
of Daumier and Gropper and Picasso.
As a Californian, I thought *Eureka;*
but as Ulfilas to the dusky Philistines I said,
"Oh!"

Although
the Regents of the Harlem Gallery are as eye-
less as knitting needles, *Black Bourgeoisie*
(retching foulness like Goya's etching,
She Says Yes to Anyone)
will wring from their babbitted souls a Jeremian cry!

John Laugart,
alive beyond the bull of brass,
measured my interior—and said:
"A work of art
is an everlasting flower
in kind or unkind hands;
dried out,
it does not lose its form and color
in native or in alien lands."

Was he a radical leaf
created upon an under stem
at the behest
of the uncreated Diadem?
A fish of passage,
by hook unseen or crook unheard?
My curious art tried to gull his face,
the mug of a male umbrella bird,
haply black and mute.

This castaway talent
and I,
bent by paths coincident
on the lunar day
of Saint Crispin
(no matter how, by the heels, the land lay)
were fated to be
the Castor and Pollux of St. Elmo's fire,
on Harlem's Coalsack Way.

The Regents of the Harlem Gallery
suffer the carbon monoxide of ignorance
which—undetected in the
conference chamber—
leaves my budget as the
corpse of a chance.

John Laugart
—a Jacob that wrestles Tribus and sunders bonds—
discovers, in the art of the issues
of Art, our pros, as well as our cons,
fused like silver nitrate used
to destroy dead tissues.

Derisive ha-has of the half-alive
may gird the loins of the soul,
or rive
the ribs of the mind.
Yet, in the
grime and the sublime
of illusion and reality
(among olivets and pearls),
sometimes irony
bends back the cues,
like a reflexive verb,
and gives the Gomorrhean blues
to the bulls of Bashan
that loose the full
butt of the bull
of blurb.

Again and again
huddled into a *cul-de-sac*
and skewed into sticks-in-the-mud
as to what shade of black
the villain Ultra should wear,
the dogs in the Harlem manger fret away their nails,
rake their hair,
initiate a game of pitch-and-toss;
then (wried by the seventh facial nerve) confuse
the T-shape of the gibbet with the T-shape of the cross.

Laugart's epitaphic words,
permanent as terre verte, are cooped
in my psyche.
A Bleak House grotesque,
his lower lip a drooped
whispering bell,
he wove—impressionistically,
like a Degas weaver,
and in a manner Gallic, *dégagé*—
coral stitches of the signature of an Apelles
in his *pièce d'identité*:

"Since dish on dish of tripe often put
our master Rodin under a spell,
perhaps this bootleg liquor eclipses my will
as dram steps on the heels of dram;
yet, I shall never sell
mohair for alpaca
to ring the bell!"

At once the ebony of his face
became moodless—bare
as the marked-off space
between the feathered areas of a cock;
then, his
spoon-shape straightened.
His glance
as sharp as a lance-
olate leaf, he said:
"It matters not a tinker's dam
on the hither or thither side of the Acheron
how many rivers you cross
if you fail to cross the Rubicon!"

Postscript:
He was robbed and murdered in his flat,
and the only witness was a Hamletian rat.
But out of *Black Bourgeoisie* came—
for John Laugart—
a bottle of Schiedam gin
and Charon's grin
and infamy,
the Siamese twin
of fame.

ETA

Her neon sign blared two Harlem blocks.
In Aunt Grindle's
Elite Chitterling Shop
the variegated dinoceras of a jukebox
railed and wailed
from everlasting to everlasting:
Come back, Baby, come back—I need your gravy.
Come back, Baby, come back—I'm weak and wavy.
The talk of the town, I'm Skid Row bound—
and I don't mean maybe!

(O scholars)
this is the ambivalence of classical blues—and the
coins came from the blue-devils' pocket of Dipsy Muse.

Across an alp of chitterlings, pungent as epigrams,
Doctor Obi Nkomo
the alter ego
of the Harlem Gallery
—as a news-waif hallooed, "The Desert Fox is dead!"—
clicked his tongue
—a residual habit from the veld—
and
—stout as a peasant in the Bread-and-Cheese War—
said,
"The lie of the artist is the only lie
for which a mortal or a god should die."

Because nobody was a nobody to him,
when from his thin charcoal lips
irony escaped, it was malice toward none.
The therapy of his slips
by design into primitive *objets d'art*
humanized the patrons of the Harlem Gallery
as much as the masterworks
he salvaged from the Lethe
of the American Way in Black Manhattan.
Mr. Guy Delaporte III cried out before the Regents,
"Mr. Curator, what manner of man
is this?"

Unharassed by the *ignis fatuus* of a lost job,
Doctor Nkomo clicked throatily and, with a chuckle
whispered to me, "It's not this buckle-
head's right or wrong if he does right or wrong."
Like a humming disk came the strophe
of a rebel Bantu song.

Hubris is an evil the Greeks
(Euripides, Sophocles, Aeschylus)
boned and fleshed to wear the mask.
Pride is the lust-
sinewed wench the churchman speaks
of first in the Table of Deadly Sins:
Doctor Nkomo's *All hail to Man*
was a vane on the wing
to winnow the grain
in person, place and thing.

Too many (perhaps) of the Regents' corralled hours
Doctor Nkomo and I
left gored in bull rings of pros and cons:
without a horse-opera god, the Ultra dons
the matador's black of the wherefore and the why,
or hoists the white flag
and lets the red cells in the marrow die.

His *idée fixe* ebbed and flowed across the dinner table:
"Absurd life shakes its ass's ears
in Cendrars'—not Nkomo's—stable.
If,
anchored like hooks of a hag-fish to sea weeds
and patient as a weaver in haute-lisse tapestry,
a Rivera or a Picasso,
with a camel-hair alchemy,
paints in *fresco-buono*
the seven panels of a man's tridimensionality
in variforms and varicolors—
since virtue has no Kelvin scale,
since a mother breeds
no twins alike,
since no man is an escape running wild from
self-sown seeds—
then, no man,
judged by his biosocial identity
in toto
can be,
a Kiefekil or a Tartufe,
an Iscariot or an Iago."

Is philosophy, then, a tittle's snack?
History a peacock's almanac?
He laughed down at me,
a kidney without anchorage,
and said: "You must see through the millstone,
since you're not like Julio Sigafoos and me—
an ex-savage."

His ebony forefinger an assagai blade,
he mused aloud as the box played in Harlem's juke:
"Curator of the Harlem Ghetto, what is a masterpiece?
A virgin or a jade,
the *vis viva* of an ape of God,
to awaken one,
to pleasure one—
a way-of-life's aubade."

Black as cypress lawn,
the crag of a woman crabsidled in.
The breath of a fraxinella in hot weather,
her unlooked-for grin
evaporated; then,
like a well's spew
of mud and oil and raw gas,
she blew
her top.
Dipsy Muse slumped like Uhlan
when his feet failed to prop,
his squeal the squeal
of a peccary ax-poled in its pen.

                              The
                       stem and stern
                  of the Elite Chitterling Shop
                      pitched and ditched
        in the chatter and squawks, in the clatter and guffaws,
                            as a
                    Yarmouth yawl yaws
                when struck by a rogue-elephant sea.
                Scragged beyond the cavernous door,
                clamorous as a parrot against the rain,
                Dipsy Muse's vanity scrabbled in vain
        like an anchor along the neck-gorge of a sea-floor.
                          The jukebox
                       railed and wailed:
        The black widow spider gets rid of her man,
        gets rid of her daddy as fast as she can.
        If you fool around, I know what I'll do—
        like the black widow spider I'll get rid of you.
                A giraffine fellow whose yellow skin
                mocked the netted pattern of a cantaloupe
                    opened his rawhide pocketbook
                      to sniff of dope a whiff,
                with a galley curse and an alley gag;
        then—laughing, choking, brimstoning his spouse,
        he caved in like Ben Franklin's beggarly bag.
                     Doctor Nkomo sighed:
        "The nicks and cuts under a stallion's tail
                    spur him to carry it higher;
                but the incised horsetail of a man
                drains the bones of his I-ness drier."

A black outsider with all his eggs but one
in the White Man's basket, he quaffed his beer,
stretched his beanpole legs;
then
—a rubberneck Robin Hood in a morris dance—
readied a hobby with another color for a ride
beyond the Afrikaner's stance.
"O Romeo," he said, "O Casanova,
prithee, what is chivalrous—what, barbaric?
(Why gnaw one's thoughts to the bone?)
When a caveman painted a rubric
figure of his mate with a gritstone,
Eros conquered Thanatos."

His eyes glistening dots of an ice plant,
he said: "My Western friends
—with deserts to be turned into green pastures—
rent diving bells to get the bends,
curfew morals, incubate tsetse flies,
stage a barroom brawl of means and ends
in a *cul-de-sac*.
(Eagles dying of hunger with cocks in their claws!)
That rebel jukebox! Hear the ghetto's dark guffaws
that defy Manhattan's Bible Belt!
Aeons separate my native veld
and your peaks of philosophy:
I made the trek, Curator,
on Man's vegetable ivory,
in threescore years and ten."

A whale of a man, I thought; *a true,*
but not a typical, mammal.
He absorbs alien ideas as Urdu
Arabic characters.

In a sepulchral corner, I glimpsed
a Scarlet Sister Mary on the make,
her lips dark and juicy like a half-done T-bone steak.

The giraffine fellow eyed us with a dog-ape look
and outed his impatience in a sigh;
a single-acting plunger
cast the die,
"Mister, *who* are you?"
His catarrhal eye
baited by Doctor Nkomo's hair
(the silvery gray patina of a Japanese alloy),
he was but a squeaking Cleopatra boy
when the reply
came like the undershot of a Poncelet water wheel:

"Obi Nkomo, my dear Watson; but that is nil,
a water stair that meanders to no vessel. If you ask
what am I, you dash on rocks the wisdom and the will
of Solon and Solomon.
Am I a bee
drugged on the honey of sophistry?
Am I a fish from a river Jordan,
fated to die as soon as it reaches an Asphalt Sea?"

Not a sound came from
the yellow giraffine fellow—
not a sound
from the bowels
of this Ixion bound
to the everlasting revolving ghetto wheel.

Nearer the ground than Townsend's solitaire,
Doctor Nkomo
raked his hair
. . . his brain . . .
but he did not blink the cliff of ice.
"*What* am I? *What* are you?
Perhaps we
are twin colors in a crystal.
When I was a Zulu
lad, I heard an old-wives' tale
for seven-foot-spear Chakas to be.
In a barnyard near a buffalo trail
a hunter discovered an eagle
eating dung with chickens.
He carried the feathered rex to a mountain top,
although it raised the dickens.
The hunter explained, 'You're not a chicken, Aquila.'
He launched the ungainly bird into space.
A fouled umbrella!
In the wing lock
of habit, it tumbled in disgrace
. . . down . . . down . . . down . . .
a ghostified cock!

"Out of the visaing face
of the sun swooped the falcon baron
clarioning the summons of an aeried race.
Twice
the barnyard eagle answered the Solar City wight;
thrice
he spiraled the simoom-blistered height—
braked and banked and beaked
upward, upward, into transfiguring light.
Old Probabilities, *what* am I?
Mister, *what* are you?
An eagle or a chicken come home to roost?
I wish I knew!"

His character (in the Greek sense)
phrased a nonplus—needed a metaphor's
translation. As an African prince,
kings and chiefs peacocked themselves
behind him;
and he, himself tough-conscienced, had slain
heathenism, the Giant Grim,
without a backward cry.
Scot and plot,
caste and class,
rifted right angles to the curving grain.

The dream of Abraham's bosom bottled long ago,
he walked the Pork Barrel's porphyry
street with the man in the ears;
and the glassy

rivers of talk
—Heraclitean, Fabian, Marxian—
in the lights and shadows of the illuminating gas,
bona fides,
limned a figure and cast
of *Homo Aethiopicus* who knew
all riverine traffickers pass
beyond the Seven Walls of Water—to join
. . . the Last of the Greeks . . .
of the Romans, the Last.

Once in a while
his apology
shaped itself like the symbol
Q
in a skipper's log.
During the falconry
in the chamber of the Regents,
Mr. Delaporte III flew
off at a tangent and off the handle.
Doctor Nkomo's Dandie Dinmount terrier
epithet sprang
across the tables.
My gavel big-talked in slang.
Like a turtle's head,
the session withdrew
into its shell.
The old Africanist bowed cavalierly and said:
"I've called the gentleman a liar
—it's true—
and I am sorry for it."

Wealth of the fettered,
illth of the lettered,
left his realism, like rock dust, unweathered:
one who eyes
the needle of the present to knit the future's garb.
In his own buttoned guise
he seemed to speak to the man Friday in Everyman
boned and lined and veined
for the twelve great fatigues to the Promised Land:

"The golden mean
of the dark wayfarer's way between
black Scylla and white Charybdis, I
have traveled; subdued ifs in the way;
from *vile-canaille* balconies and nigger heavens, seen
day beasts and night beasts of prey
in the disemboweling pits of
Europe and America,
in the death-worming bowels of
Asia and Africa;
and, although a Dumb Ox (like young Aquinas), I
have not forgot
the rainbows and the olive leaves against the orient sky.

"The basso profundo
Gibbon of Putney
—not the lyric tenor, Thomas of Celano—
hymns the *Dies Irae!*"

THETA

In the *château en Espagne* of Vanity,
Bones and Flesh,
Black Keys and White Keys
—Changs and Engs—
argued themselves into apoplexy.

Their hostess,
the Marquise de Matrix,
panged by the pall
of a tribulating moment,
like a Duchess of Malfi at a grand ball,
oiled the waters:

"Something there is in Art that does not love a wall.
Idea and image,
form and content,
blend like pigment with pigment
in a flesh color.
What dread hand can unmix
pink and yellow?
Even a nixie says, 'Nix!'
The weight and fineness of a work of art,
like a sample coin,
must pass *the trial of pyx.*
In spite of an age's smile or frown,
the perennial tooth of this esthetic truth
grows at the root as it wears away at the crown."

Montague's son and Capulet's daughter
the tryst-
ing tree of Art unites
as the wrist
the hand and arm—
unites them as the miracle of the metaphor smites
disparate realms into a form
tighter than a mailed fist.

Ye knights of the Critics' Circus,
why tilt at the fetish
of a sophistry?
Nature and Art,
rejuvenating as the Cybele
to whom we sing *Non Nobis*—
Nature and Art,
dedicated to oneness,
ignore
the outer and the inner
of a person, a place, a thing;
and both alma maters,
eyes unbridled,
explore
the whole of the *rete mirabile*:
the freedom of figurate counterpoint in a
flying fugue or fleeing flea,
the coat of a nucellus,
the testa of a seed,
the integument of a Paltock's flying Indian
can be removed by only the claws of a naked need.

No guinea pig of a spouse
to be cuckolded in a mood indigo,
no gilded in-and-out beau
to crackle a *jeu de mots* about the house—
Art, the woman Pleasure, makes no blind dates,
but keeps the end of the tryst with one;
she is a distant cousin of aeried Happiness
the lovebird seeks against the eye-wrying sun,
in spite of her fame,
dubious as Galen's sight
of a human body dissected,
in spite of the *hap* in her name,
ominous as a red light.

The claw-thrust
of a rutting tigress,
the must
of a rogue elephant—
these con the bull of predictability,
like Happiness,
a capriccio bastard-daughter of Tyche.

KKK, the beatnik guitarist, used to say
to High Yellah Baby
(before he decided to rub
out the light of his eyes
in the alley of Hinnom behind the Haw-Haw Club):
"The *belle dame*—Happiness—the goofy dream of
is a bitch who plays with crooked dice
the game of love."

IOTA

The hour with the red letter stumbles in:
Doctor Nkomo and I counterpoise beside
ebony doors of the Harlem Gallery,
Horthgarian hosts,
closemouthed and open-eyed.
He winks at me, bows to
each ohing, ahing guest
among the gobbler-breasted matrons and their spouses
whose busheled taxes tax strange interludes of rest.

His wits in their Sunday best,
he wears the mask and grins, "Aloha!"
(Please excuse
the beachcomber's ambiguity of this,
which puzzles the Cadillac Philistines.)
Yet none need lose
his good right eye like Agib, who
let curiosity lead him amiss.

From nightingales of the old Old World,
O God, deliver us!
In the Harlem Gallery, pepper birds
clarion in the dusk of dawn
the flats and sharps of pigment-words—
quake the walls of Mr. Rockefeller's Jericho
with the new New Order of things,
as the ambivalence of dark dark laughter rings
in Harlem's immemorial winter.

The East Wing's
rigors and vigors in varicolors,
broods of the ethos and artistic moods,
range from sea level to peak altitudes,
like the cluster of the pinaster.
Ironies and tensions of flesh
going to grass,
paeans and laments of identities
signed in the thought and felt hinterlands of psyches—
now impasted and sprayed and fixed
with waterglass
on dry plaster.
Unlike the teeth of the parrot-fish
fused into a single mass,
polychromatic *heres* and *theres,*
juxtaposed, image the
oddly odd or oddly even
of reality and fable.
Purse pride
of neither gold, nor silver, nor brass,
from porcelain tray and handled sable
fig leaf and barebone in water colors
echo the monastic archetypes
of a haunted master,
or,
facing fate-fating
Now,
subdue the accents, vivify the nuances
of success and disaster.

The West Wing
is no belt of calms:
in the midst of its dramatis personae,
the listening ear can hear,
among the moderns, blue
tomtoms of Benin;
the seeing eye can see fetishes unseen,
via
rue Fromentin and Lenox Avenue.

Painters consecrated like the Brescian Blackamoor
on a holyday
or amused like Somerscales (the eternal naïf)
in his owling way
fetch from streets that have no eyes
and alleys that have no lips
the antique and the newly-made
in our *cis*-Apocalypse.

The sable and camel's-hair
incarnate in oils
an upstage of faces as unsoiled as irisated rain
or repulsive like purulent boils;
a downstage of faces as madder-bleached as dry bones
on an alkali plain
or fissured like agueweeds
in a marsh's toils;
a backstage of faces as empty as a mistigris
or bedeviled like a sea dog's prelithic visage
when the stays lean amiss.

The North Wing's
burnt-in portraits
(colors mixed with wax and resin and verve
liquefied with heat that sings)
enmesh Negroid diversity—
its Kafiristan gaucherie,
its Attic wit and nerve.
This is Harlem's Aganippe
(not America's itching aitchbone)
where characters, flat and round,
project a rhythm, a mood, a scene, a tone.
Sometimes beyond the bourgeois Greek
and yet within the pale,
variegated colors, like those of the agate snail,
blend with the white and yellow
of beaten eggs that mix the juice
from the tender roots of the Smyrna-fig to fellow
light and shadow, line and curve,
grown mellow.

All shapes and sizes and colors of boots
from the ape-cobbler's last
for every actor in the Harlem cast
entertain, absorb, or vex
as the egg trot in the design
goes awry or toes the line
while trafficking,
in the human comedy,
with *Bios* and *Societas* and *X*
as well as the divine.

The South Wing's
orientations of dusky Lion Hearts
(in fresco and secco),
who find
on Toynbee's frontiers
their counterparts,
loom in the varied habiliments of health and blight—
bizarres and homespuns
in a cacophony of colors
as if courage had a copyright.

The idols of the tribe,
in voices as puissant as the rutting calls
of a bull crocodile, bellow:
"We
have heroes! Celebrate *them* upon our walls!"

Heralds' College
(the sceptre's y-fretted retreat;
and, like the Order of the White Eagle,
obsolete)
is dubbed by Doctor Nkomo
afterwit's aftermeat.
He likes to retrek
the vanitied souterrains of history;
puzzle out the kings and queens,
the bishops and knights,
on Prince Eugene's
greenhouse chessboard of heredity.

He chuckles:
"If
a Bourbon should shake his family tree
long enough . . . he
—beyond a Diogenic doubt—
would kneel at the mourners' bench,
dressed in black crepe,
as cannibal and idiot,
rapist and ape,
tumble out."

These Lion Hearts (then) are unsynchronized opposites,
gentlemen and galoots
from Afroamerica;
tone colors of the triple-octaved xylophone
Daddy Blue Note plays on black-letter days;
seven against Thebes
in seven-league Afroamerican boots;
voices of the voiceless
—like the *Iliad,* the *Gilgamesh,* the *Divine Comedy*—
obelized
now and then
by a dusky Origen,
but authentic as a people's autography.

However, this immaturity,
like the stag tick's,
will disappear
like its wings,
when it settles upon a red red deer.

O dry bones of Highgate,
Phidias and Van Gogh and Aristophanes,
Shakespeare and El Greco,
Velasquez and Cervantes,
Orozco and Dante and Pissarro—
all these
(Olympians wombed in the Vale of Tears)
fleshed stout on
the bee bread of self and the beef of history,
like Balzac, the *de*-fetishist, who,
deaf to the phews of irony,
surpasses the Zolas, old and new,
in frescoes of bourgeois reality.

KAPPA

Mr. and Mrs. Guy Delaporte III,
through the shifting maze of Harlem's Vanity Fair,
oh and yawn and ah their way:
mismatched oddlegs:
he,
with a frown like curd;
she,
with a smile like whey.

An Atlantean S
neons
Mr. Delaporte's Success
as President of Bola Boa Enterprises, Inc.,
which left its competitors,
long ago . . . long ago,
dead as the figure of Christ
in a *mortorio*.

His
soul of gold,
like the Ark's mercy seat,
Mr. Guy Delaporte III is the symbol
of Churchianity
at Mount Zion,
the bethel of the Sugar Hill elite—
say the valley people of Mount Sinai
as they wash each other's feet.

When Professor Freez Skerritt's whiskyfied baritone
gropes along the bars of *Sweet Mystery of Life*,
all alone, all alone,
Mr. Delaporte's wonder twills, like surah silk,
about it and about.
Unable to lead his wife
(with her incurves and outcurves of breasts and hips)
captive,
he weeps like Alexander the Fire Burnt Out
because
no brand-new $-world in Harlem gives him pause.

Now,
Hagar's son,
to escape the bone mill of the *ultima ratio*,
needs the agility
of the grand galago.

Before the *bête noire* of John Laugart's
Black Bourgeoisie,
Mr. Guy Delaporte III takes his stand,
a wounded Cape buffalo defying everything and Everyman!
Above and about
Mrs. Delaporte hovers Bishop Euphorbus Harmsworth,
the shield of Sobieski.
Since Doctor Nkomo is one
no harlot of Hush Hush ever gave dead tongue,
among the topsyturvy pros and cons of our patrons,
in a North Wing alcove
he halters me:

"Is it not
the black damp of the undisturbed pit
that chokes the vitals—damns the dream to rot?
The bane of the hinterland,
as well as the outland,
is the mirage of the Status Quo.
No platinum black in the undifferentiated sand.
My village? The *fera* unmanned
in *homo faber*. Alkali water after a rain-
less simoom. Stagnant
blood in a dead-end vein.
Dialectics?
The midwife of reality.
The cream separator of life.
The sieve, Curator, of wheat and chaff.
So, let our eyes,
like Mohammed's,
disappear in the guise
of a crocodile laugh!"

A hurt sea dog, I cut his deck of metaphors:
"On its shakedown cruise,
the *Black Bourgeoisie* runs aground
on the bars of the Harlem Blues."

Doctor Nkomo quicks the quid of an analogy:
"This work of art is the dry compound
fruit of the sand-box tree,
which bursts with a loud report
but scatters its seeds quietly."

We have dined too long, O Harlem, with Duke Humphrey!
In the kitchen,
the chef, I, mixes black and yellow and red
images, leaves You at the table
with brown bread
and the ghost of the thing
unsaid:
Give voice to a bill
of faith at another hour.
My humor is ill.
A night like this, O Watchman,
sends a Derain to Weimar
to lick the Brissac jack boots
of Das Kapital that hawks things-as-they-are.
Then O then, O ruins,
I remember
the alien hobnails
of that cross-nailing Second of September
did not crush like a mollusk's shell,
in café and studio,
the *élan* of Courbet, Cézanne, and Monet,
nor did the self-deadfall of the Maginot
palsy the hand of Chagall,
Matisse,
and Picasso.

LAMBDA

From the mouth of the Harlem Gallery
came a voice like a
ferry horn in a river of fog:

"Hey, man, when you gonna close this dump?
Fetch highbrow stuff for the middlebrows who
don't give a damn and the lowbrows who ain't hip!
Think you're a little high-yellow Jesus?"

No longer was I a boxer with a brain bruised
against its walls by Tyche's fists,
as I welcomed Hideho Heights,
the vagabond bard of Lenox Avenue,
whose satyric legends adhered like beggar's-lice.

"Sorry, Curator, I got here late:
my black ma birthed me in the Whites' bottom drawer,
and the Reds forgot to fish me out!"

His belly laughed and quaked
the Blakean tigers and lambs on the walls.
Haw-Haw's whale of a forefinger mocked
Max Donachie's revolutionary hero, Crispus Attucks,
in the Harlem Gallery and on Boston Commons.
"In the beginning was the Word,"
he challenged, "not the Brush!"
The scorn in the eyes that raked the gallery
was the scorn of an Ozymandias.

The metal smelted from the ore of ideas,
his grin revealed all the gold he had stored away.
"Just came from a jam session
at the Daddy-O Club," he said.
"I'm just one step from heaven
with the blues a-percolating in my head.
You should've heard old Satchmo blow his horn!
The Lord God A'mighty made no mistake
the day that cat was born!"

Like a bridegroom unloosing a virgin knot,
from an inner pocket he coaxed a manuscript.
"Just given Satchmo a one-way ticket
to Immortality," he said. "Pure inspiration!"
His lips folded about the neck of a whiskey bottle
whose label belied its white-heat hooch.
I heard a gurgle, a gurgle—a death rattle.
His eyes as bright as a parachute light,
he began to rhetorize in the grand style
of a Doctor Faustus in the dilapidated Harlem Opera House:

King Oliver of New Orleans
has kicked the bucket, but he left behind
old Satchmo with his red-hot horn
to syncopate the heart and mind.
The honky-tonks in Storyville
have turned to ashes, have turned to dust,
but old Satchmo is still around
like Uncle Sam's IN GOD WE TRUST.

Where, oh, where is Bessie Smith
with her heart as big as the blues of truth?
Where, oh, where is Mister Jelly Roll
with his Cadillac and diamond tooth?
Where, oh, where is Papa Handy
with his blue notes a-dragging from bar to bar?
Where, oh, where is bulletproof Leadbelly
with his tall tales and 12-string guitar?

Old Hip Cats,
when you sang and played the blues
the night Satchmo was born,
did you know hypodermic needles in Rome
couldn't hoodoo him away from his horn?
Wyatt Earp's legend, John Henry's, too,
is a dare and a bet to old Satchmo
when his groovy blues put headlines in the news
from the Gold Coast to cold Moscow.

Old Satchmo's
gravelly voice and tapping foot and crazy notes
set my soul on fire.
If I climbed
the seventy-seven steps of the Seventh
Heaven, Satchmo's high C would carry me higher!
Are you hip to this, Harlem? Are you hip?
On Judgment Day, Gabriel will say
after he blows his horn:
"I'd be the greatest trumpeter in the Universe,
if old Satchmo had never been born!"

MU

Hideho Heights
and I, like the brims of old hats,
slouched at a sepulchered table in the Zulu Club.
Frog Legs Lux and his Indigo Combo
spoke with tongues that sent their devotees
out of this world!

Black and brown and yellow fingers flashed,
like mirrored sunrays of a heliograph,
on clarinet and piano keys, on cornet valves.

Effervescing like acid on limestone,
Hideho said:
"O White Folks, O Black Folks,
the dinosaur imagined its extinction meant
the death of the piss ants."

Cigarette smoke
—opaque veins in Carrara marble—
magicked the habitués into
humoresques and grotesques.
Lurid lights
spraying African figures on the walls
ecstasied maids and waiters,
pickups and stevedores—
with delusions
of Park Avenue grandeur.

Once, twice,
Hideho sneaked a swig.
"On the house," he said, proffering the bottle
as he lorded it under the table.
Glimpsing the harpy eagle at the bar,
I grimaced,
"I'm not the house snake of the Zulu Club."

A willow of a woman,
bronze as knife money,
executed, near our table, the Lenox Avenue Quake.
Hideho winked at me and poked
that which
her tight Park Avenue skirt vociferously advertized.
Peacocking herself, she turned like a ballerina,
her eyes blazing drops of rum on a crêpe suzette.
"Why, you—"
A sanitary decree, I thought. "Don't *you* me!" he fumed.
The lips of a vixen exhibited a picadill flare.
"*What* you smell isn't cooking," she said.
Hideho sniffed.
"Chanel No. 5," he scoffed,
"from Sugar Hill."
I laughed and clapped him on the shoulder.
"A bad metaphor, *poet*."
His jaws closed
like an alligator squeezer.
"She's a willow," I emphasized,
"a willow by a cesspool."
Hideho mused aloud,
"Do I hear The Curator rattle Eliotic bones?"

Out of the Indigo Combo
flowed rich and complex polyrhythms.
Like surfacing bass,
exotic swells and softenings
of the veld vibrato
emerged.

. . .

Was that Snakehips Briskie
gliding out of the aurora australis of the Zulu Club
into the kaleidoscopic circle?

. . .

Etnean gasps!
Vesuvian acclamations!

. . .

Snakehips poised himself—
Giovanni Gabrieli's
single violin against his massed horns.

. . .

The silence of the revelers was the arrested
hemorrhage of an artery
grasped by bull forceps.
I felt Hideho's breath against my ear.
"The penis act in the Garden of Eden," he confided.

. . .

Convulsively, unexampledly,
Snakehips' body and soul
began to twist and untwist like a gyrating rawhide—
began to coil, to writhe
like a prismatic-hued python
in the throes of copulation.

Eyes bright as the light
at Eddystone Rock,
an ebony Penthesilea
grabbed her tiger's-eye yellow-brown
beanpole Sir Testiculus of the evening
and gave him an Amazonian hug.
He wilted in her arms
like a limp morning-glory.
"The Zulu Club is in the groove," chanted Hideho,
"and the cats, the black cats, are *gone!*"

In the *ostinato*
of stamping feet and clapping hands,
the Promethean bard of Lenox Avenue became a
lost loose-leaf
as memory vignetted
Rabelaisian I's of the Boogie-Woogie dynasty
in barrel houses, at rent parties,
on riverboats, at wakes:
The Toothpick, Funky Five, and Tippling Tom!
Ma Rainey, Countess Willie V., and Aunt Harriet!
Speckled Red, Skinny Head Pete, and Stormy Weather!
Listen, Black Boy.
Did the High Priestess at 27 rue de Fleurus
assert, "The Negro suffers from nothingness"?
Hideho confided like a neophyte on The Walk,
"Jazz is the marijuana of the Blacks."
In the *tribulum* of dialectics, I juggled the idea;
then I observed,
"Jazz is the philosophers' egg of the Whites."

Hideho laughed from below the Daniel Boone rawhide belt
he'd redeemed, in a Dallas pawn shop,
with part of the black-market
loot set loose
in a crap game
by a Yangtze ex-coolie who,
in a Latin Quarter dive below Telegraph Hill,
out-Harvarded his Alma Mater.
. . .
Frog Legs Lux and his Indigo Combo
let go
with a wailing pedal point
that slid into
Basin Street Blues
like Ty Cobb stealing second base:
Zulu,
King of the Africans,
arrives on Mardi Gras morning;
the veld drum of Baby Dodds'
great-grandfather
in Congo Square
pancakes the first blue note
in a callithump of the USA.
And now comes the eve of Ash Wednesday.
Comus on parade!
All God's children revel
like a post-Valley Forge
charivari in Boston celebrating the nuptials of
a gay-old-dog minuteman with a lusty maid.
. . .

Just as
the bourgeois adopted
the lyric-winged piano of Liszt in the court at Weimar
for the solitude of his
aeried apartment,
Harlem chose
for its cold-water flat
the hot-blues cornet of King Oliver
in his cart
under the
El pillars of the Loop.

.   .   .

The yanking fishing rod
of Hideho's voice
jerked me out of my bird's-foot violet romanticism.
He mixed Shakespeare's image with his own
and caricatured me:
"Yonder Curator has a lean and hungry look;
he thinks too much.
Such blackamoors are dangerous to
the Great White World!"

.   .   .

With a dissonance
from the Weird Sisters,
the jazz diablerie
boiled down and away
in the vacuum pan
of the Indigo Combo.

NU

Rufino Laughlin
(M. C.)
peacocked to the microphone
as a fixed-on grin lighted his corrugated face
like the island pharos of King Ptolemy.

The M. C. raised his hand,
Rufino Laughlin raised his voice,
in rococo synchronization.
"Ladies and Gents," he demosthenized,
"the Zulu Club has a distinguished guest tonight
who has never let us down.
In a thousand years,
when the Hall of Fame
lies in ruins on genesis-ground,
the poems and the name
of Hideho Heights,
the poet laureate of Lenox Avenue,
will still be kicking around.
Let Harlem give a great big hand,
therefore and *henceforth*,
to a great big poet and a great big man!"

A boiler—a caravan boiler
of applause
exploded.
My thoughts wandered and wondered
. . . *the poet is no Crusoe in the Zulu Club* . . .

His nightly nightmare waterlooed,
the M. C.'s histrionic antics
drooped and crinkled:
leaves of a Bermuda onion
with yellow dwarf.

Colorful as a torch lily,
her hips twin scimitars,
a tipsy Lena
who peddled Edenic joys
from Harlem to the Bronx
plucked the poet's filamentous sleeve and begged:
"If you make me a poem,
Hideho,
I'll make you my one and only daddy-o
till the Statue of Liberty
dates
a kinkyhead."

The poet was no Gallio
who cared for none of these;
so he tossed his palm slap into her buttocks.
Her wiggles were whisky-frisky.
"You're a *female* woman," he said,
grave as the falling accent of a Cantonese scholar; and then
the soul seemed to pass out of the body as he announced,
"Sister, you and I belong to the people."
The tipsy Lena's
giggles were the wiggles
of a coral fish's spinal fin
when it poisons and kills the alien next of kin.

XI

Hideho Heights,
a black Gigas,
ghosted above us
in a fan vaulting of awkward-age lights and shadows.

Sudden silence,
succulent as the leaves of a fat hen, swallowed
up the Zulu Club.

He staged a brown pose that minded me
of an atheistic black baritone
who sang blue spirituals that turned
some white folk white, some pink, and others red.

Hideho's voice was the Laughing Philosopher's
as he said:
"Only kings and fortunetellers,
poets and preachers,
are born to be."

In spite of the mocker's mask,
I saw Hideho
as a charcoal Piute Messiah
at a ghetto
ghost dance.

Does a Yeats or a beast or a Wovoka
see and hear
when our own faculties fail?

Was it *vox populi*
or the Roman procurator
who said to the
Roman who was not a Roman,
"Much learning doth make thee mad"?

In a faraway funereal voice,
Hideho continued:
"The night John Henry was born
no Wise Men came to his cabin, because
they got lost in a raging storm
that tore
the countryside apart
like a mother's womb
when a too-big son is born."

"Great God A'mighty!"
cried Dipsy Muse,
as his arm went halfway round
the calf's-foot
jelly mound
of the Xanthippean spouse
whom the whim
of Tyche
had created in the image
of Fatso Darden.
The Birth of John Henry!
Murmurs ebbed and flowed:
soughing sounds
in the ears of a stethoscope.

. . .

The night John Henry is born an ax
of lightning splits the sky,
and a hammer of thunder pounds the earth,
and the eagles and panthers cry!

. . .

Wafer Waite—
an ex-peon from the Brazos Bottoms,
who was in the M.-K.-T. station
when a dipping funnel
canyoned the Cotton Market Capital—
leaps to his feet and shouts,
"Didn't John Henry's Ma and Pa
get no warning?"

Hideho,
with the tolerance of Diogenes
naked in the market place on a frosty morning,
replies:
"Brother,
the tornado alarm became
tongue-tied."

. . .

John Henry—he says to his Ma and Pa:
"Get a gallon of barleycorn.
I want to start right, like a he-man child,
the night that I am born!"

. . .

The Zulu Club patrons whoop and stomp,
clap thighs and backs and knees:
the poet and the audience one,
each gears itself to please.

Says: "I want some ham hocks, ribs, and jowls,
         a pot of cabbage and greens;
    some hoecakes, jam, and buttermilk,
         a platter of pork and beans!"

John Henry's Ma—she wrings her hands,
    and his Pa—he scratches his head.
John Henry—he curses in giraffe-tall words,
    flops over, and kicks down the bed.

He's burning mad, like a bear on fire—
         so he tears to the riverside.
As he stoops to drink, Old Man River gets scared
         and runs upstream to hide!

Some say he was born in Georgia—O Lord!
         Some say in Alabam.
But its writ on the rock at the Big Bend Tunnel:
    "Lousyana was my home. So scram!"

.   .   .

The Zulu Club Wits
(dusky vestiges of the University Wits)
screech like a fanfare of hunting horns
when Hideho flourishes his hip-pocket bottle.

High as the ace of trumps,
an egghead says, " 'The artist is a strange bird,' Lenin says."
Dipping in every direction like a quaquaversal,
the M. C. guffaws: "Hideho, that swig would make
    a squirrel spit in the eye of a bulldog!"

Bedlam beggars
at a poet's feast in a people's dusk of dawn counterpoint
protest and pride
in honky-tonk rhythms
hot as an ache in a cold hand warmed.
The creative impulse in the Zulu Club
leaps from Hideho's lips to Frog Legs' fingers,
like the electric fire from the clouds
that blued the gap between
Franklin's key and his Leyden jar.
A Creole co-ed from Basin Street by way of
Morningside Heights
—circumspect as a lady in waiting—
brushes my shattered cocktail glass into a tray.
Am I a Basilidian anchoret rapt in secret studies?
O spiritual, work-song, ragtime, blues, jazz—
consorts of
the march, quadrille, polka, and waltz!
Witness to a miracle
—I muse—
the birth of a blues,
the flesh
made André Gide's
musique nègre!

.   .   .

I was born in Bitchville, Lousyana.
A son of Ham, I had to scram!
I was born in Bitchville, Lousyana;
so I ain't worth a T.B. damn!

.   .   .

My boon crony,
Vincent Aveline, sports editor
of the *Harlem Gazette*,
anchors himself at my table.
"What a night!" he groans. "*What* a night!"
. . . I wonder . . .
Was he stewed or not
when he sneaked Hideho's
Skid Row Ballads
from my walk-up apartment?
Then the You advises the I,
Every bookworm is a potential thief.

. . .

Ma taught me to pray. Pa taught me to grin,
It pays, Black Boy; oh, it pays!
So I pray to God and grin at the Whites
in seventy-seven different ways!

I came to Lenox Avenue.
Poor Boy Blue! Poor Boy Blue!
I came to Lenox Avenue,
but I find up here a Bitchville, too!

. . .

Like an explorer
on the deck of the *Albatross*,
ex-professor of philosophy, Joshua Nitze,
sounds the wet unknown;
then, in humor, he refreshes the Zulu Club Wits
with an anecdote on integration,
from the Athens of the Cumberland:

"A black stevedore bulked his butt
in a high-hat restaurant
not far from the bronze equestrian statue
of Andrew Jackson.
The ofay waitress hi-fied,
'What can I do for you, Mister?'
Imagine, if you can, Harlem nitwits,
a black man mistered by a white dame
in the Bible Belt of the pale phallus and the chalk clitoris!
The South quaked.
Gabriel hadn't high-Ced his horn,
nor the Africans invaded from Mars.
It was only the end-man's bones of Jeff Davis
rattling the *Dies Irae*
in the Hollywood Cemetery!
The Negro dock hand said,
'Ma'am, a platter of chitterlings.'
The ofay waitress smiled a blond dolichocephalic smile,
'That's not on the menu, Mister.'
Then the stevedore sneered:
'Night and day, Ma'am,
I've been telling Black Folks
you White Folks ain't ready for integration!'"

The hilarity of the Zulu Club Wits
(unconsecrated like blessed bread)
grows as public as the paeans of Artemis.
The Sea-Wolf of Harlem sneers: "Uncle Tom is dead;
but keep a beady eye on his grandson, Dr. Thomas—
minister without portfolio to the Great White World!"

In two hours
Vincent Aveline will plane South
to fly-fish for sepia baseball stars.
In the skull-shaped mugs
the concocted *Zulu Chief* arrests my eye—
for its legend as an aphrodisiac
out-Marathons Jotham's fable;
but the quixotism that plays
hide and fox in Everyman
incites me to lift my glass.
"Partner, one for the road!"
Aveline becomes enisled for a lost moment.
"Damon," he jives,
your Pithias needs a *Zulu Chief.*"

Later . . . later . . . he
says something startling
as the toast "Drink! Live!"
inscribed on the gold glasses
among the skeletons of the Catacombs:
"Just caught my wife and Guy Delaporte III
between the sheets
of his Louis XIV bed!
A Black Diamond stool pigeon puked it up."
I feel the silence of the *omertà* oozing in.
• • •
Black Diamond,
heir presumptive to the Lenox Policy Racket,
kindles,
with igniting lines from Hideho's *Flophouse Blues,*

the sticks and twigs of greed
on the hearth of his flyaway Jezebel,
whose body, done in the yellow of Minyan pottery,
was exposed and rhapsodized and caricatured
as Miss Bronze America,
to the envy and pride and lust of the
black and tan, black-and-blue, black and white,
in the Harlem Opera House—so Black Diamond says,
"Baby, I play any game that you can name,
for any amount that you can count."

His ego lionized
in the first, second, and third person,
Black Diamond flags down and highballs
Tom, Dick, and Harry—
controls them as
a single stop knob
a set of reed pipes
in an organ.

It was I who taught Black Diamond
his first lesson in the Art of Picasso's Benin,
at Waycross, Georgia—
aeons before Africa uncorked an uppercut:
many a *tour de force* of his
executed in Harlem dives and dead ends
has greened the wide-awake eyes
of such masters as
Giglio and Gentile,
Bufalino and Profaci.

O schoolmasters,
living and half-alive and dead,
the Zulu Club
is not the fittest place to recall,
by fits and starts,
Seneca's young Nero
. . . and . . .
Aristotle's youthful Alexander!

And Black Diamond, now
dwarfing me at my table,
vilifies the Regents of the Harlem Gallery;
swears, on his Grandma's family Bible,
that the sons-of-bitches
had better not fire his beloved teacher,
because his stool pigeons
have dedicated to him
a dossier on *each* and *every one* of the bastards!
And the only reason he doesn't flip the red-hot stuff to
Walter Winchell
(that great truth-serum guy)
is because he has Race Pride,
as a life-member of Afroamerican Freedom, *Incorporated.*
Anyway, he hates to see Race skeletons that whoopee a stink
in top-hat closets dumped in Times Square—
since White Folks are always ready to disinfect the privy
of decent Black Folks like me and him.
Then, too, if an ace boss squeals
in the blackjack game of his free enterprise,
it sets a bad example—*bad* for the little guys!

His Grandma used to dingdong a scripture,
"By their tails ye shall know 'em."
That's the reason he planks down his church dues,
at Mt. Sinai, a year in advance.
You see,
if a fluke flunks in his free enterprise
and the Sweet Chariot swings low, the preacher can't blab
at the biggest funeral in Harlem
and St. Peter can't gab
to the Lord God A'mighty
that Black Diamond's record was in the red—like
a Red editor's among gnawing bellies in Greenwich Village.
. . . Then, too . . .
it's a good example for the little guys.

He jots down
six private telephone numbers
and goads the open sesame deep into my breast pocket.
The gapers are all eyes,
like the tubers of the Jerusalem artichoke.
"Curator," he grins, "you'll never have to turn
on a slab in a morgue and say to Black Diamond,
'Is *that* you, Brutus?' "

Tom, Dick and Harry,
pigmied by the ghetto Robin Hood
(innocuous *now* as a basking shark),
catch the cue, double up like U-bridle irons inverted, and
let loose
geysers of guffaws.

At neighbored tables
the Zulu Club Wits
rant in circles for, against, about
This and *That*.

Shadrach Martial Kilroy
president of Afroamerican Freedom,
his skin soft and moist
like a salamander's,
waxes apocalyptic:
"The White Man is the serpent
in Dolph Peeler's *Ode to the South*."

The Sea-Wolf of Harlem,
Lionel Matheus,
apostatizes:
"To continue the symbolism,
your Afroamerican is the frog I saw
in a newspaper illustration:
the harder the frog tugged outward,
the deeper it became impaled
on the inward-pointing fangs of the snake."

Doctor Nkomo says: "The little python would not let go
the ass of the frog—so the big python swallowed both."
I seem to sense behind the masks of the Zulu Club Wits
thoughts springing clear of
the *terra firma* of the mind—
the mettled forelegs of horses
in a curvet.

Mr. Kilroy's nose,
broad and compressed
as the tail of a salamander,
tilts upward at the ends
in the scrouge of his indignation;
all of a sudden
the promontory of his belly
quakes with cultivated jollity,
like effeminate grains of wet quartz.

"Lionel Matheus," he
pontificates,
"to carry your symbols to a Sublime Porte—
you need to see, you son of a Balaam,
the unerring beak,
the unnerving eye,
the untiring wing,
of Afroamerican Freedom, *Incorporated*—
the Republic's secretary bird."

The gape of Lionel Matheus, a nut-brown Mirabell,
is wider than the eye in the leach of a sail;
then, the image of Agrippa must have buoyed
into his mind, for he says mockingly,
"Almost thou persuadest me to be a nigger-lover."

Mr. Kilroy sighs out his fatigue,
"It is hard for a phobic camel to go
through the eye of a needle of truth."
Metaphors and symbols in Spirituals and Blues
have been the Negro's manna in the Great White World.

Apropos of something or nothing,
Doctor Nkomo interposes:
"Nationalism,
the Sir Galahad of the African republics, has
severed the seventh
tentacle of the octopus of imperialism."

Every hail-fellow-well-met
in propria persona
because of
the white magic of John Barleycorn,
the Zulu Club Wits
become
absent
like the similes in the first book of the *Iliad,*
or
ugly
like the idiom the Nazarene spoke,
or
tight
like ski pants at the ankle.

Hideho Heights,
slumped in the shoal of a stupor,
slobbers and sobs,
"My *people,*
my people—
they know not what they do."

OMICRON

"Life and Art," said Doctor Nkomo, "beget incestuously
(like Osiris and Isis)
the talented of brush and pen.
Artistic instinct draws,
on a rock in the Kalahari Desert,
a crocodile for Bush-born men.
Without Velasquez and Cranach,
what would Picasso be?
Or Léger without Poussin?
Or Amedeo Modigliani without Sandro Botticelli?"

Design trailed design as a scroll saw capered in his mind:
Is *Homo Aethiopicus* doomed,
like the stallion's beard,
to wear the curb of the bridle?
The melon feeds the imago of the ladybird
in the Diadem's diapered plan:
the heritage of Art
—no Triboulet in the tragedy *Le Roi s'amuse*—
nurtures everywhere
the wingless and the winged man.

Unseen,
perhaps,
unheard,
low heels will overtake high heels,
to reach the never-never travelers' rest,
a democracy of zooids united by a stolon
but separated by a test.

An artist makes what he can;
every work of art asserts,
"I am that I am."
So leave the rind to the pedant
and the bone to The Hamfat Man.

O Time, O Customs,
how can an artist make merry
in the tenderloin's maw,
unless he add a head and a wing and a claw
to the salamander of Gerry?

The age,
taut as the neck of a man on a gallows tree,
demands
a Friar Bacon who will cast
a head of brass
to clarion, "Time is,
Time was, Time is past,"
before the graven image topples,
breaks in pieces,
while the necromancer snuggles deep
between the breasts
and in the arms
of the courtesan Sleep.

It is an age that ties
tongues and stones irises;
and no leper cries,
"Unclean! Unclean!"

The idols of the tribe
make the psyche of the artist lean
inward like an afferent blood vessel,
or turn its view
—an adjusting iris diaphragm—
toward the backyard of the Old
or the front yard of the New.

As a skiascope views the changes
of retinal lights and shadows,
the élan-guided eye, in good time, ranges
a land of the leal
that no longer estranges.

In the magnetic field of Art, the creed
of the exploring coil discovers
diatonic nuances of taste
and vintage varieties that need
no philter for lovers.

The net loss of the artist
is
the alms of the rich—
the vice
that consoles the *hoity-toity*
but leaves
the pocketbook of his art
the poorer.

The net profit of the artist
is
the art-fetish delivered
from the black hole of the flesh
by the mercy of the knife.

The pride of the artist
is
the leach of green manure
that slows down
the sleet and snow and ice
of an age's scorn.

The élan of the artist
is
the rain forest sapling
which pushes upward
through bog and snarl
to breathe the light.

The school of the artist
is
the circle of wild horses,
heads centered,
as they present to the wolves
a battery of heels,
in the arctic barrens where
no magic grass of Glaucus
gives immortality.

The grind of the artist
is
the grind of the gravel in the gizzard
of the golden eagle.

The temperament of the artist
is
the buffer bar of a Diesel engine
that receives the impact
of a horizontal of alpine and savanna
freight cars drawn along in the rear.

The sensibility of the artist
is
the fancier of the Brahman and Hamburg and Orington,
the Frizzle and Silky—but
everlastingly he tests to discover
new forms and strange colors,
nor does he balk to wring the neck
of Auld Lang Syne
in any breed.

The esthetic distance of the artist
is
the purple foxglove
that excites
the thermo receptors of the heart
and the light receptors of the brain.

PI

Omega is not *I like.*
In the class chaos under the Order
of *Homo Caucasicus,*
the artist must not barter
the law of measure, the will to refrain,
as the withering chrysanthemum trafficks its water
for rain:
flowers made of hummingbird feathers
the Zoological Gardens in Regent's Park contain.

Even when
his world is ours and ours is his—
a lodestar that leads into its ring
two kingdoms with colors and shapes and textures in high
relief under a single king—
even then
the artist, like a messiah, is egoistic
and the work of art, like the art of God,
is a rhyme in the Mikado's tongue to all save the hedonistic.

Image-breaking?
Perhaps,
to the euclidean; but,
to the perspectivist
—in the curved space of aeons of cultures—
the mixed chalice and wafer bread
may become as dead
as the dead spindles of lathes.

A work of art is a domain
(mediterranean)
of *this* race,
of *that* time,
of *this* place,
of *that* psyche,
with an Al Sirat of its own—
and, beyond its bridge to Paradise, the ritual of
light and shadow,
idiom and tone,
symbol and myth,
pleasures the lover of Art alone
in a bourne where no grapes of wrath are sown.

Without a limitation as to height,
a work of art is a peak in Anthropos
(low as Soufrière or high as Kilimanjaro)
with the temper (sometimes) of a volcano
made by an ape-god of Eros or Thanatos.
O son of profits,
when does the hour come to sight
the anchor? When will the parasitic crater
stifle the bulls of Bashan in the night?

O ye of the Samson Post,
let the remembrance
of things past
season with tolerance
the pigs in blankets.

Is not the stifle shoe
placed on the sound leg
of a stallion to strengthen the weak?
Therefore,
let us beg
in the court of error
no ape of God for a fool,
although
the scriptures of Art
(schools within school)
be
as esoteric, pluralistic, contradictory
as texts of the *Koran,*
the *Book of the Dead,*
the *Bhagavad-Gita,*
the *Vulgate,*
whose disciples
(tempers fermented to a head
like yeasted malt)
babble in the babel of debate
for eternity and a day,
garb heretics in garments
painted with flames and figures of devils
to be led
to the *auto-da-fé.*

Doctor Obi Nkomo said
in his address before the artists
of the Market Place Gallery in Harlem:

"Remember
the Venerable Yankee Poet
on the unfamiliar red carpet of the Capitol
as he visaed the gospel of the Founding Fathers
. . . *Novus Ordo Seclorum* . . .
spieled by every dollar bill.
Remember
Paul Cézanne,
the father of modern Art,
a Toussaint L'Ouverture of Esthetics.
Remember
a genius is not a fence-sitter
with legs wide apart,
a tree crow between
a true crow and a jay.
. . . Remember, yes, remember . . .
Zola, Renoir, Degas, Gauguin, Van Gogh, and Rodin
hailed Cézanne;
but *vox populi* and red-tapedom
remained as silent as spectators in a court
when the crier repeats three times, 'Oyez!' "

Sometimes
a critic switches the dice and gambles on
his second sight,
since the artist's credo is
. . . *now* a riding light . . .
then a whistling buoy in
a Styx' night.

(The Harlem Gallery, too, was grieved by Bunyan's
crabtree cudgel
when Doctor Nkomo threw a stinkpot into
the Market Place Gallery,
among Black Muslims and artists and Good White Friends.
"The Critics' Circus grants an artist
a passport to
the holy of holies," he said, "or a whorehouse;
but never to
Harpers Ferry or Babii Yar or Highgate.")

The critic is an X stopper pausing
between a work of art
and the electromagnet wave causing
the listening ear
to ring and smart.

I visit a work of art: in the garden How
I pluck the pansy; blink the weed;
fish in the dark tarn Auber for the Why;
seek out the What and trace its breed.

The road to Xanadu
is not a jack-o'-lantern of the Hamburg grape.
God is not mocked
(nor is His ape),
for, while our Goliath laves
in aloes and frankincense,
the harlot Now the master paints
aspires to hang in the gallery Hence
with Brueghel's knaves
and Cimabue's saints.

RHO

New Year's Day
Hedda Starks telephoned me
from a Harlem police station.
Her fit of laughing and crying was as convulsive
as the heehaws of a Somaliland she-ass.
So the desk sergeant
waxed human. He juggled the receiver and swore
Hedda was a horned screamer,
as she agonized in her cell at midnight:
"O sweet Jesus,
make the bastard leave me alone!
I'll call The Curator
—the son-of-a-bitch—
and send 'im to Big Mama to get the goddamn rubbish!"

Verbatim was to Sergeant Ghirlandaio
what a glasshouse is to a plant.
"I hope I'm not in Harlem," he said,
"when St. Peter opens the books on Judgment Day."
His chuckle was the impish mockery of an echo
in the bottomless canyon of Hesiod's
—and our—
Brazen Age.

Hedda Starks, alias Black Orchid,
was a striptease has-been
of the brassy-pit-band era—
but listen, Black Boy, to the hoity-toity scholars:
"A vestige is rarely, if ever, present in a plant."

Mister Starks
hailed from Onward, Mississippi—
via Paris, Texas, *via* Broken Bow, Oklahoma.
How he got his *Christian* name is a legend
that tickles the inwards of the Zulu Club Wits.
When he was four years old,
his black mother took him to
the Big House on an *ante-bellum* estate;
and the Lady wanted to know the baby's name
and the proud mother said "Mister."
Since every Negro male in Dixie was
either a *boy* or an *uncle,*
the mistress turned blue and hot
like an arc-welder's torch.
"A pickaninny named *Mister?*" the old doll hissed;
and the maid, slamming the mop bucket down,
screamed: "Miss Leta,
it's *my* baby and I can name it
any damn thing I please!"

The first time Mister Starks, the piano-modernist
of the Harlem Renaissance, lamped
Black Orchid at the Bamboo Kraal,
her barbarian bump and sophisticated grind
(every bump butted by the growl of a horn)
played, with him, the witch,
like the serpentine belly dance
of Congo Leopold's Cleo de Merode, which
captivated Anatole France.

The intelligentsia of Mister's bent
became Hedda's steps on the aerial ladder
of the black and tan bourgeoisie;
but her exhumed
liaison with Mr. Guy Delaporte
(in the *Harlem Emancipator*)
was like the red kimono
that broke Woodrow Wilson's heart.

Did a sibyl say to Aeneas,
"The descent to Avernus is easy"?

Well, Mister Starks needed no Hindu mystic
mulattoed in Atlanta
and
turbaned in Harlem
to tell him—*that*.

And, contrary to what the Cumaean divined,
it was no labor, no task,
for Mister to escape to the upper air:
it was a *beau geste*,
Hardyesque—
fit for the limelight of the Harlem Opera House
in the auld lang syne of Charles Gilpin,
the most .
sinister-smiling
of the Emperor Joneses
inspired by the root of evil.

SIGMA

On a red letter day
pained by the sharp ache of a corn
that protests a tight shoe,
the Angelus Funeral Home received,
by registered mail,
the last will and testament of Mister Starks.

Ma'am Shears, LL. B. and owner,
of long sight, of short breath,
spelled out the letter three times.
Her memory hooked a feather, a wing and a fin:
Mister Starks was to be buried in the tails he'd worn
the night the Harlem Symphony Orchestra
premiered his *Black Orchid Suite;* and
his ebony baton, the gift of a Dahomean witchdoctor,
was to be poised in his hand; and
Hedda Starks was to be exhorted
to turn over to The Curator of the Harlem Gallery
the MS., *Harlem Vignettes,*
which the aforesaid person
(Hedda Starks, alias Black Orchid)
had possessed
with malice aforethought.

Miss Ester Bostic,
the late Dr. Igor Shears' medical secretary,
pieced together the archetype for newsmongers.
Her hobby was making checkerwork
with her fingers or with her lips.

She is now Ma'am Shears' bookkeeper
and *dame de compagnie*
to Trinidad
on the widow's annual forget-me-not pilgrimage
to the twin tombstones that transfigure
the grave of Igor Shears
and the grave-to-be of Ma'am Shears. (But let
us get on with the classic version of the Zulu Club Wits.)
. . . And now . . .
the volatile Miss Bostic
became fixed mercury
as Ma'am Shears,
her arms the flukes of a wounded whale,
swept aside Mr. Abelard Littlejohn—
the springbok impresario of the Angelus Funeral Home.

The pince-nez the third of his six ex-wives had given him,
on St. Valentine's Day,
clattered—broken and unnoticed—upon
the late Dr. Igor Shears' bust
of Frederick Augustus Douglass.
Puffing like Hedley's
Puffing Billy in 1818,
Ma'am Shears grabbed the telephone
and dialed Mister Starks' tenement-room.
"The fool!" she said compulsively. "The fool!"
She'd resurrected his threat to commit suicide
in a scene (in a Sugar Hill juke) that out-Hamleted the
Gloomy Dane.

As he talked with her,
no sign of illness of mind revealed itself
like the twist of a billiard ball.
He was still the highbrow composer,
and his replies came like the answers
at the intervals of a fifth in a fugue.

"Mister, don't try it!" she begged.
"Try it?" he laughed. "I'm a Hannibal—not a Napoleon."
The cryptic words were blisters
along the course of a nerve.
She recalled Reverend Thigpen's subject, *Love of Life,*
two Sundays ago at Mt. Zion.
Sweat trickled down her yellow cheeks.
"It's not like Black Folks to commit suicide."
Her voice sank in a chuckle
as thick as the mother of vinegar.
"Aren't we civilized yet?" he scoffed.
Ma'am Shears groaned, "Civilization and suicide?"
"Soil and plant," he said. "Masaryk speaking—in Vienna."

Mister Starks,
airy as a floating lily pad,
said: "Ma'am Shears,
I want you and Mr. Abelard Littlejohn,
the merry widow-killer of the Angelus Funeral Home,
to meet me
(and the late Dr. Igor Shears)
at Archangel Gabriel's hangout
on Elysian Boulevard.
Au revoir!"

Whiter than Pliny's white
black, Ma'am Shears faced
the end in smoke.

"Angels can do no more,"
Miss Bostic oraculized.

Ma'am Shears
heaved and set the sigh of an old she-walrus
after a futile mating bout.

"This means headlines and $'s for Angelus,"
Miss Bostic finessed
with clicks of her Tru-Grip teeth.

Her spirit
the depressed abdomen of a shrimp,
Ma'am Shears sank upon
her haunches
in her pillowed reclining-chair.

Sergeant Ghirlandaio,
who knew his Conan Doyle from *aardvark* to *zythum*,
discovered a bullet in Mister's heart.
But it was the supt.
who found the .38 hidden in
Crazy Cain's toilet bowl.

. . . New Year's Day . . .
. . . in a Harlem jail . . .
Hedda Starks—alias Black Orchid,
arrested at a marijuana party
and haunted in her cell—
turned over the MS., *Harlem Vignettes,*
to The Curator
and made her peace with God.

O spindle of Clotho,
O scroll of Lachesis,
O scales of Atropos,
the black ox treads the wine press of Harlem!

TAU

The MS., *Harlem Vignettes,*
was done up in a mamba's skin.
On a side along the spine, a snake's head
arrowed a legend inscribed in purple-red ink:
"In the sweat of thy face shalt thou make a work of art."

A snapping turtle on its back,
my memory jumped:
in his youth, Mister Starks had published
a volume of imagistic verse.

. . . Even in this last manuscript . . .
Sanson's images of my own Harlem
burned brightly
like gold and silver paper
at a Chinese funeral.

On the title page
Mister had scribbled:
"I should have followed—perhaps—*Des Imagistes*
down the Macadam Road.
But I'm no Boabdil
at the Last Sigh of the Moor."

So let Tyche pluck, Black Boy, a few oysters
from a planter's bed—a site located in Harlem
strewn with layers of shells, slag, cinders, gravel,
where Art shouts:
"We must shoot General Aupick!
Garrote Guizot's imperative "Enrichissez-vous!"

UPSILON

Mister Starks: A Self-Portrait

My talent was an Uptown whore; my wit a Downtown pimp:
    my boogie-woogie record, *Pot Belly Papa*,
by Alpha & Omega, Inc., sold a million discs.
        (God help *vox populi—vox Dei!*)
        I etch, here and now, a few
of the everybodies and somebodies and nobodies
        in Harlem's *comédie larmoyante*.
John Laugart said: "A work of art is a moment's
antlers of the elaphure in the hunting lodge of time."

        I am no neutral—carbon in fats.
        Like the Fathers of Oratory,
        I am not bound by a vow.
    Sometimes I'm sunk like a ha-ha-wall.
        So what the hell?
    Am I not a Negro, a Harlemite, an artist—
        a trinity that stinks the ermine robes
        of the class-conscious seraphs?
Since a headhunter lets his conscience be his guide,
I'm afraid of the blade that directs water to the bucket.

    I remember the Gaya Bar on Rue Duphot—Jean
Wiener at the piano; Vance Lowry on the saxophone—
        with the Stravinsky of *L'Histoire du Soldat*
        and the Milhaud of *La Création du Monde*
        and the Ravel of *L'Enfant et les Sortilèges*;
    but I did not come home by the weeping cross:
I tried to poise that seesaw between *want* and *have*.

To explain the crossruff,
Harlem used the fig leaf
of Black Orchid,
alias the forbidden wine of Sura 78,
instead of the Rosetta stone.

The Harlem Symphony Orchestra
never, *never* cried:
"Bravo, bravo, Maestro!
Viva! Viva! il grande Mister Starks!"
Yet I deserve no pauper's grave
in a churchyard,
for,
the premiere of the *Black Orchid Suite*—
sunrise on the summit
between
sunset and sunset—
will forever stir my dust and bones
like the strains of *Ecco la marchia*
in the veins of a Mozartian.

Hideho Heights

Plato's bias will not banish,
from his Republic,
the poet laureate of Lenox Avenue—
for he is a man square as the *x* in Dixie,
in just the right place,
at just the right time,
with just the right thing.

I remember his credo versified at
the Market Place Gallery:
"A work of art is a two-way street,
not a dead end,
where an artist and a hipster meet.
The form and content in a picture or a song
should blend like the vowels in a dipthong.
Since this is the means and end in a design,
do I have to moan again,
'Amen'?"

He had the damp-dry eyes of the tragic-comic,
but his humor and pride were feathers
that guised the crissum of a mockingbird.

He said:
"Content is a substance beneath the bark.
Unless a craftsman
is on horseback to lark
a hedge, does he select a piece of wood
(for his artifact)
that is not good?"

To the black bourgeoisie,
Hideho was a crab louse
in the pubic region of Afroamerica.

How did he take it, O Harlem?
Like a fat leaf
about the kidney of a hog.

Dr. Igor Shears

A Jonah crab,
Igor Shears frequented deep water:
a patron of the Arts and a disciple of Walton,
he used to hustle me off to the Florida Keys
after the reneging rigmarole and *rigor caloris* of a season
with the Harlem Symphony Orchestra;
yet, the man inside was an enigma to me—a phrase
(the dove of the distant terebinths)
in the title of a Psalm.

Ma'am Shears

Her character was a cliché in the *Book of Homilies;*
and *what she was* was as legible
as a Spencerian address
in the window of an envelope.

Crazy Cain

In his tradition ran an Eliotic vein of surrender:
a bass rhythm,
florid figurations
—primitive, percussive, often contrary to the bass—
persisted in his style;
so I had to fire him from the Harlem Symphony Orchestra,
in spite of Mrs. Guy Delaporte's vase of tears.
His Negro tradition bitched the night
an Irish field hand raped a Mandingo woman in
an Alabama cottonfield.

The hybrid chattel
with a taint from Blarney
was Cain's great-grandfather:
the noxious tinge
mixed with the blues in his fingers
and the dialect in his veins.

History is a book of seven seals
from no Isle of Patmos;
but a Zulu Club Wit discovered
it was a felony to teach
a black boy his ABC's when
a whale ship was
the Harvard of
a white cabin boy.

Crazy Cain
was as ignorant of his people's past
as Charicleia in *Ethiopica*,
and the only calculus
the descendant of the hybrid chattel had
was in his bladder.
He knew
. . . yet . . .
he knew
that he was the bastard son
of Black Orchid
and
Mr. Guy Delaporte III,
but his knowing fell short of the *Poudres de Succession.*

Doctor Obi Nkomo

His psyche was a half-breed,
a bastard of Barbarus and Cultura;
and the twain shall never meet
on the D-Day dreaded by the Scholar-Gypsy.
Young Nkomo followed the Christ of the African Veld
to the Statue of Liberty,
to Wall Street,
and to Mr. Morgan's Thirteen Galleries of Art
that housed his Byzantine enamels and ivories,
his Renaissance bronzes and marbles,
his French porcelains and paintings
from the fabled Fragonard room.

There the Passion Oratorio of the odyssey stopped
like fermentation checked
by alcohol
in the must of grapes.

Dr. Shears said at a Zulu Club talk-around:
"Obi Nkomo, you are
a St. John who envisions
humanity as a thick mass of bees
with hairs on their legs—
by which they carry the collected pollen
to a collective hive."

In the gale of guffaws Obi
Nkomo's head was erect like the habit of the pagoda tree.

Then he laughed
at himself and laughed at them.
To Dr. Shears, he confided gravely:
"Thou art not the first bridegroom disillusioned by
the darling materialism of the westering star.
She butterflied the bowels of Walt Whitman.
Bedded in the Democratic Vista Inn,
the Good Gray Poet discovered
the materialism of the West was a steatopygous Jezebel
with falsies on her buttocks."

Hideho Heights
downed his *Zulu Chief* in a gulp,
palmed his chin, and said:
"As my ante in the jack pot, I'd say
Obi Nkomo is a St. John who envisions
a brush turkey that makes
a mound of the Old World's decaying vegetables
to generate heat and hatch the eggs of the New."

The aged Africanist looked up surmisingly,
his gaze leveled at Hideho Heights
as straight as the zone axis of a crystal.
"Only an Aristotelian metaphorist,"
he said,
"could conjure up an image like *that!*"

The bouquet was the geometer's horn angle
to me; but the way the Zulu Club Wits
waxed stiller than tissues in paraffin
magicked the nosegay into the cat's pajamas.

The Curator

The Harlem Gallery
. . . the creek that connects the island and the mainland . . .
. . . a *q* in Old Anglo-Saxon . . .
. . . an oasis in the Danakil Desert . . .
. . . and the mascara of dusky middlebrow matrons . . .
became the beccafico that excited the top hats,
the butt that inebriated the Zulu Club Wits,
and the butte that pinked many a butt.

The species itself is strange
in the hand or in the bush,
for wings are found
only on the chosen
and feathers grow only in distinct areas;
a fortiori,
The Curator of this variegated aviary on
Black Manhattan
emerged as a *strange* bird—
a jacobin of horny, reversed epidermal outgrowths.

Sometimes
the Harlem Gallery
was in bad odor; however—
it was not the smell of dead ideas
unembalmed and unburied.

Guy Delaporte solemnized: "I love—God knows I *love*
pictures!"
The Curator groaned: "So does Ike, the painter—except,
of course,
the moderns that give Nikita, the Art critic, a churn of a
bellyache."

The brass-check *Harlem Tattler*
volleyed its barbs of bunkum
at the connoisseur; but

The Curator
stood out
in the
Death's Jest-Book of Harlem like
the Minerva with the Police Gazette Belt
catching a twenty-four-
pound, round
solid missile fired from a cannon
thirty feet away.

Everytime Guy Delaporte III farts—
the phenomenon is headlined in the Negro press;
so, interviewed, he said: "The Curator is a Greenland shark
feeding on the carcass of a whale
in spite of stabs in the head!"

SO—the moods of The Curator
varied from the white stripe over
the goshawk's eye
to the dark patch
back of it.

I remember, oh, I remember how
irony trumped his coat card,
the prodigy
Richard Fairfax.

When the young artist
knuckled under as a gigolo
of Black and Tan Skin-Whiteners, Inc.,
The Curator grew angrier than Cellini, *when,*
behind a hedge,
he saw young Luigi Pulci in the arms
of the whore Pantasilea.

Doctor Nkomo caricatured
The Curator as a dusky
Francis I of France
with an everlasting cartel of defiance;
but among the Harlem middlebrows
there was not even a side-show Richelieu
to check a duel of end men with pasteboard razors!

The Harlem Gallery his *Malakoff,*
I can imagine his saying to
anyone
who advised him to leave,
"J'y suis, j'y reste."

I used to say if I knew the differences between
The Curator and Doctor Nkomo,
I'd know the ebb and flow of tides of color.

Then I made the discovery
in the dawn hours
after the Zulu Club habitués
had floundered into Lenox Avenue.

The janitor—an incognito
ex-chaplain from Alabama Christian College—
performed the ritual of cap and bells
with mop and broom;
the ex-Freedom Rider had explained earlier:
"Gentlemen,
when any Old Ship of State
rams a reef of history,
the passengers
as well as the sailors
are involved."

We chewed this quid a second time,
for Black Boy often adds
the dimension of ethnic irony
to Empson's classic seven.

While The Curator sipped his cream
and Doctor Nkomo swigged his homogenized milk,
I tried to gin the secret of
the mutuality of minds
that moved independently of each other—
like the eyeballs of a chameleon.

"Why cream, O Nestor, instead of milk?"
Doctor Nkomo's guileless question
was a whore at the altar in a virgin's wedding gown.

The Curator's reply
had Taine's smell of the laboratory.

Whether that's good or bad
depends on one's stance,
upstage—or—downstage.

As The Curator spoke, there was no
mule-deer's-tail contrast
of white and black in the way he said it:
"I remain a lactoscopist
fascinated by
the opacity of cream,
the dusk of human nature,
'the light-between' of the modernistic."

Doctor Nkomo's snort
was a Cape buffalo's.
"You brainwashed, whitewashed son
of bastard Afroamerica!"
The Curator grinned
his Solomonic grin,
for the nettle words were stingless like
a mosquito bee.
As a Bach fugue piles up rhythms,
the Africanist heaped his epithets:
"Garbed in the purple of metaphors,
the Nordic's theory of the cream separator
is still a stinking skeleton!"

"Since cream rises to the top," said The Curator,
"blame Omniscience—
not me."
The Curator liked to dangle Socratic bait!

"Perhaps Omniscience deigns to colorbreed."
Lips parted like the bivalves of an oyster,
the ex-chaplain and neo-janitor
put his mop aside and sideslipped toward our table,
his eyes sweethearting a chair.

I needed a shock absorber as
Doctor Nkomo,
with Lionelbarrymorean gestures,
Homerized a spiritual:

"Sit down, servant, please sit down,
sit down, servant, please sit down,
sit down, servant, please sit down,
you done earned your heavenly crown!"

Our crowing laughs and clapping palms
had the scaling motion of
clay pigeons from a trap of the *fin de siècle*.

His D.D. robe
(but not his affidavit of integrity)
in a Harlem pawn shop,
the ex-chaplain continued mockingly:
"Gentlemen,
according to the *Anglo-Saxon Chronicle*,
so potent is one drop of African blood
that, in the zero of a second, it
can turn the whitest Nordic into a Negro.

"Gentlemen,
perhaps there is a symbolism
—a manna for the darker peoples—
in the rich opacity of cream
and the poor whiteness of skim milk."

Among such eggheads,
I was glad that I had on
my thick-lensed glasses,
as the sex image of a Mary of Magdala
with kinky hair and a cream complexion
hula-hulaed across my mind.

(Will mortals ever become mind readers? God forbid!)

The Afroamerican's features of *A Man called White*
paled like the fatty sheath of nerve fibers,
and the African's jet eyes grew
as soft as the fin of a mirror carp.

"Between the ass and the womb of two eras,"
said The Curator, gloomily,
"*taste* the milk of the skimmed
and *sip* the cream of the skimmers."

To the old Africanist,
this eclipse of faith felt and seen in *mens agitat molem*
had the bitterness of dried cones of hops—
without
malt liquors.

"*Mens sibi conscia recti,*"
said Doctor Nkomo
—definitively—
"is not a hollow man who dares not peddle
the homogenized milk of multiculture,
in dead ends and on boulevards,
in green pastures and across valleys of dry bones."

Whatever the effect of this altitude,
it was hidden behind The Curator's mask—
like a tailor bird's nest
behind stitched-together leaves.

Nothing is so desolating
as a deserted night club
with Is seated in the chair of Is Not—
the skull of a way of life that faces the crack of doom
with wine and wit and wiggle.

The Curator and Doctor Nkomo
sat staring into space,
united like the siphons of a Dosinia—
the oddest hipsters on the new horizon of Harlem,
odder
(by odds)
than that
cabala of a funeral parlor
in Cuernavaca,
Mexico
. . . called . . .
"*Quo Vadis.*"

Mrs. Guy Delaporte III

Her temperament
was the mercurial pendulum
of a Riefler's clock—
and her
bent the bias
of a river on a map.
Cultivated in the greenhouse
of an Electra complex,
she was a delicate plant exposed
to the arctic circle of the black Sodom;
so her leaflets closed tight
and her leafstalk drooped in fits of relapsing fever.

John Laugart

Daumier, blind and paralytic, gave up the ghost
in Paris;
Laugart reviled but pot-valiant, a stiletto sucked his veins
dry
in Harlem:
each a bowl from the Potter's wheel
the State buried in a potter's field,
like the one the chief priests bought
in Jerusalem—
for thirty pieces of silver:
his road was a hogback unfit for even
a half-blind black son of Hagar.
The ominous rattle of his bones will never disturb
the tryst of graveyard lovers.

Big Mama

Her conscience was a little clay ball,
baked hard and oiled,
ready for the use of any hand;
and her past was a hidden vanity box in which
she had stashed away many coups of the fleshpots.
When I was a piano-plunker
in her Niflheim speakeasy,
I heard her say once to Dutch Schultz:
"I was born in Rat Alley.
I live on Fox Avenue.
I shall die in Buzzard Street."
I remember the kingbolt guffawed
and slapped her elephantine buttocks
and planted a century note in her bediamonded claw
and said in a funereal voice:
"Big Mama,
you and I were born under the same star."
I remember the faces of his fingermen—
yellowish gray and hard as tala.

One of the Derbies leaned on the upright—winked,
and nodded at the keyboard as I took a swig of bootleg.
Fishing for an apposite figure,
my fingers wandered and wondered
up and down, up and down,
in a corny polka style
reminiscent of Kid Ory's trombone in *Sweet Little Papa*.

"I wanted to be a Caruso," the Derby mused.
(Self-pity is conspicuous consumption of the soul.)
I pitched him a ball with a crazy break. "Sidetracked?"
"Hell, no!" he groused. "Derailed."
His laugh was as hollow as *La fin de Babylon.*
"It happens sometimes in the *best* families, Mister."
His chin was the jut of the *Agamemnon's* prow.
"And any time in the *worst!*" he sharped.

Like all 100-p.c. Negroes,
I knew a white skin was the open
sesame to SUCCESS—
the touchstone of
Freedom, Justice, Equality.
Hadn't a white poet said when they cut off his leg,
"I am the master of my fate . . ."?
So, the class struggle was a myth
manufactured in Moscow by the Red White Russians.
I could see why a 100-p.c. white man said, "Goddamn 'em!"

The guy's getting soft,
I thought.
In the twilight world,
dissonance is white and yellow
directed by a skeleton whose baton is a scythe.

As I explored the theme phrase,
a new rhythm and melody vistaed before me:
the tones feathered into chords
and leafed and interlaced
in fluxing chromatic figures.

Perhaps I'd had too many swigs of bootleg!
Anyway, the cigarette smoke
caricatured not only the Derby but my vision of
the African who had dramatized integration as
the notes of white keys and black keys
blended in the majestic *tempo di marcia* of Man.

The speakeasy was as quiet as
a medicine-subdued pulse;
and Big Mama's face was a
shiny slab of serpentine
marble as Dutch Schultz, a jovial Friar Tuck,
bulged at my elbow.
"If you ever need a job," he said,
"remember my elevator."
But it was the Derby that
became a Socratic gadfly:
"What is it, Mister?"
(Put the notes on the staff, Black Boy!)
My answer was a suspended tone
as I recaptured the African's ethnic metaphors
of the narrow upper keys and the broad lower keys.
I looked up at those faces in man's twilight zone:
staves of mutilated notes on
the music rack of the Great White World's concert grand.
Then I magicked an arpeggio of syncopated colors
(my left hand, like Fats', suggesting a bass fiddle)
and said with a flourish, *"Rhapsody in Black and White."*
It was the feel
for a tangent to a curve with a straightedge—
or the image of Bast in a royal stable.

No ear trumpet was needed:
the theme of
Rhapsody in Black and White
was an answer to
Tin Pan Alley's blues classic—
or, maybe, it was only a buteo
seeking peaks in the breeding season—
a butcherbird
impaling its prey on thorns.
I was—like every other artist—
an incorrigible gambler.
The stakes?
Caesar or God!
(Put the notes on the staff, Black Boy!)
As Caesar seized Alesia,
I grabbed
the bottle of bootleg,
drained it to its vilest dregs,
and stumbled toward the exit guarded by
that Cerebean ex-pug,
Tiger Tyler,
who had fought the Boston Tar Baby
on the apex of the soapy pyramid
when the cauliflowered Master was
Jack Johnson's
Banquo's ghost
of the squared circle—
merry-andrewed.

A man is juice (said Doctor Nkomo) pressed from the
apples of life—juice made hard or sweet or bitter.

Like a biased ball on a level plat of green,
I bowled past the Derby.
Again he stammered, "*What*—is it?"
Big Mama's mind was a rear-vision mirror,
since she said, "You wouldn't understand."
With the hubris of a Hippias,
Dutch Schultz challenged,
"Is my stuff that bad?"
(*Put the notes on the staff, Black Boy!*)

A Magdalene loitered near the subway.
She had the olive complexion of a Brahui
and the smoldering eyes of lighted coals in ashes.
Out of the shadows came a handsome yellow man.
As the cheap melodrama unfolded,
I felt sorry for the unsuspecting woman.
About to pass, I said, "Hello, Officer!"
The surprise of the Vice Squad cop was Macbeth's
when he discovered Macduff
had been ripped alive from his mother's womb.

In the Abraham's bosom of Pisano's café,
I ordered a Dixie Mixie. Later, Pisano whispered,
"I have *The Protocols of the Wise Men of Zion*."
Brows hedged, he leaned between
the beetle and the block.
"Signor," I said, "that corpse stank a thousand years ago."
As if from the upward pressure of a buoy,
the hedge brows lifted.
Then came the sockdolager, "The Antichrist!"
(*Put the notes on the staff, Black Boy!*)

PHI

Harlem Vignettes read,
I felt I should make
(like Hideho)
a second Harlem marriage bed—
take
(like Hideho)
the Daughter of the Wine to Spouse:
sudden sunlight
blinds the mole;
sudden darkness,
the field mouse.

That night in the Zulu Club
the man who had already willed to die
had seen in me
the failure of nerve
Harlem would never see—
the charact in the African
that made
him the better man.

Vanity,
gas
and art
vapor away in Harlem:
I thought the verse of Mister Starks
a smokestack
contrived without book, to prevent
the escape of sparks.

I've walked many a Walk
in Harlem—
seen it crumble away.
I've heard many a Say—
deciphered
its epitaph on its natal day:

the birth-after-the-father-is-buried
Harlem Vignettes
will doubtless fetch
no white laurel of joys,
no black crepe of regrets.

Lice, like men, desert a corpse.
Yet my conscience,
when it has a tittle to do,
feels pricks of *Harlem Vignettes*—like a
horse's foot
in nailing on a shoe.

After the performance of the Angelus Funeral Home,
sophists of the black-and-tan,
anointers of the black-and-blue,
cool, man, cool as bubbles at the spirit level—
entered again the Dollar Cockpit of Custom and the Van;
so, sometimes,
I join the great laughers
. . . Gogol . . .
. . . Dickens . . .
. . . Rabelais . .
in the black world of white Manhattan.

Black Boy,
listen! Let no man lie
in the throat about the Noble Savage
of the Trek of Tears
and the Middle Passage.

Beneath the sun
as he clutched the bars of a barracoon,
beneath the moon
of a blind and deaf-mute Sky,
my forebears heard a Cameroon
chief, in the language of the King James Bible, cry,
"O Absalom, my son, my son!"

Solons of Jim Crow,
sages as far as the beard,
cipher and cipher and cipher—
and ask, "What is a Negro?"
Again,
O bastard son
of occult identity,
we who are we
on the boards of the *Théâtre Vie*
face the prongs of Horton's fork
and the horns of Rimbaud's Ogaden.
I've seen the isms of phile and phobe yeast-
bitten as they brewed their malt and hops
for a Barmecide feast.

His motive burled
like tufted wool,
Shadrach Martial Kilroy
set free the bull
of a fixed idea in the china shop of the Zulu Club:
"O *Homo Caucasicus,*
a specter haunts the Great White World—
the specter of *Homo Aethiopicus,*
the pigmented Banquo's ghost!"

Since he put no Judas in his mouth
to steal away his brains,
Doctor Nkomo said: "As regards the Negro, you
are a people in whose veins
poly-breeds
and
plural strains
mingle and run—
an Albert Rider of many schools,
and *none.*
Since only the unpigmented wear
a cravat
of civil rights,
the vanity
of the Iscariots of
the Republic pancakes
your star of destiny flat
as a depressed appetite; so,
your black dog trapped like an ex-sewage rat,
you go
from the dead end of this to the dead end of that."

The bravado of Mr. Kilroy refused
to let the millstones
grind the grain
of his Race Pride; so he bellylaughed:
"In the five great zones,
the quickie-work *Negro* varies like a Siamese noun
with five different meanings in five different tones."

Doctor Nkomo said:
"Let us not rattle the dry bones of statistics—
like the dead-
alive in an academic waste land.
As man to man,
should you and I grovel in dust and ashes because
of *what* I think of you or *what* you think of me?
God damns that tit for tat!
Even Mr. K would say
every *sookin sin* must find—like Jacob—
his stone, *his* ladder, *his* seed of destiny."

Where are the gray eyes and blond ears?
Ay—Black Boy—there's the rub!
Mr. Kilroy's curiosity
swiveled about the Zulu Club.
No ofays indoors,
he became intimate,
perforce,
like a Puritan in
an illicit intercourse:

"Blackamoors,
this kinky-head, Obi Nkomo, is *rough!*"
Hideho Heights corrected him,
"I say, as the People's Poet, this cat is *tough!*"

The poet, later, gave me a mystifying nod
and began his dubious trek to the bar,
on wobbly legs that reminded me of the
shimmying, shilly-shally
wheels of a car.

He right-angled his shoulders,
shook his senses clear of the devil-may-care
smog of *Zulu Chief;* then his poet's conscience became
an upright like a post in a ladderback chair.

I waited.
"Of course, you've read
Dolph Peeler's *Ode to the South*."
I nodded,
"His symbol of the pig in the boa's coils wasn't bad."
He wiped his mouth.
"Defeatist!"
He pawed his head.
"That bunkum session on the Negro,"
he said,
"has sparked an inspiration."
I thought,
*The old stock mare of poets,
living and dead.*

I was caught up in
the strident hum
of a
whirling Ferris wheel.
"Yo—ho—ho and a bottle of rum!"
he exclaimed.
"The Centennial of the Emancipation Proclamation,
Ye Muses!
As the People's Poet,
I shall Homerize a theme that will rock the Nation!
And every damned Un-American will know it!"

My blab-blab-blab
was a dip to free his sheep
of vermin and scab:
"You poets come too soon or too late,
Hideho Heights,
with too little,
to save the Old Ship of State.
Remember to remember
a tribal anthem
is the yankee-doodle-diddle of a tittle."

To Hideho Heights,
at that moment in the throe
of creation,
I was a half-white egghead with maggots on the brain.
I ate my crow,
for the unconscious of the artist
cannot say to itself *No.*

My clichés at the bar
were bones in the maw of the tomb,
but the idea in Hideho's brain
was an embryo,
head down,
in the
womb!

"What's the big idea?"
I razzed.
Jerked out of his trance,
he put his fists on guard,
jazzed,
feinted,
in the grotesquerie of a boxer's stance.

I waited.
"This is . . . *IT*—
Curator.
Follow the spoor of the symbols—if you have the wit!
Strange but true is the story
of the sea-turtle and the shark—
the instinctive drive of the weak to survive
in the oceanic dark.
Driven,
riven
by hunger
from abyss to shoal,
sometimes the shark swallows
the sea-turtle whole.

"The sly reptilian marine
withdraws,
into the shell
of his undersea craft,
his leathery head and the rapacious claws
that can rip
a rhinoceros' hide
or strip
a crocodile to fare-thee-well;
now,
inside the shark,
the sea-turtle begins the churning seesaws
of his descent into pelagic hell;
then . . . *then,*
with ravenous jaws
that can cut sheet steel scrap,
the sea-turtle gnaws
. . . and gnaws . . . and gnaws . . .
his way in a way that appalls—
his way to freedom,
beyond the vomiting dark,
beyond the stomach walls
of the shark."

I was conscious of the Zulu Club Wits
tied neck and heels by a poetic analogy—
conscious of the poet's posture,
an S-shaped gut on the stool beside me;
but I knew his helm was in line with his keel
as an artist's helm should be.

If fiction is stranger than truth,
I must have been on a bender
when my old T-total crony,
the Jamaican bartender—
who had eased up
to hear Hideho's hot
tale—overhastily downed a double shot
of *Zulu Chief*,
as if it were two per cent in a cider cup.

Above the fluke of a nose,
under a shag of brows,
glowed hard coal embers
that had borne witness to the troubled repose
of crucified Junes and Decembers;
and from the cavern of a mouth
came words quiet and englished and dark:
"God knows, Hideho, you got the low-down
on the black turtle and the white shark
in the Deep South."
Then,
describing a pectoral girdle,
his lower lip curled,
and he blurted—like an orgasm:
"And perhaps in many a South of the Great White World!"
He fumed, he sweated, he paced behind the bar.
"I too hate Peeler's pig in the boa's coils!
I was in the bomb-hell at Dunkirk. I was a British tar.
In Parliament, *white* Churchill quoted one day,
'If we must die, let us not die like hogs . . .'
The words of a poet, my compatriot—*black* Claude McKay."

O Zulu Club Wits,
a tavern is the sunshiniest place
in the black ghetto—
a now paradise
free from
creditors and saviors,
blowflies and lice:
it *is*
a city of refuge,
for those who have fallen from grace,
for those who are tired of the rat-race
(the everlasting—*On your mark! Get set! Go!*)
in the Land of the Gray Flannel Suit
and the Home of the Portfolio!

Never before,
in the tavern of the Zulu Club,
nor in the cabaret downstairs,
had Hideho left the cellar door
of his art ajar, with a Promethean gesture,
so we could get our penny's worth:
"Everybody has a private gallery.
In mine is a whore giving birth
to a pimp's son, Curator, on a filthy quilt.
(In travail a woman shows no sign of guilt.)
I was lucky to get the candid shots
through cracks in the ruins called a flat.
I was a kid
. . . then . . .
with the unbridled intelligence of
Professor Marotelli's cat.

"Maybe, yes, maybe,
an artist's travail is like
a woman's; and her baby is like
a poem, a picture, a symphony—
an issue of the *élan vital* in sweat and blood,
born on a brazen
sea and swaddled
on a raft of life and shaped like a question mark.
If we split hairs, there is no midwife
at one's beck and call
in the Kingdom of Poetry;
and a pregnancy
with its hopes and fears
may encompass many tomorrows,
while the travail may ebb and flow for years.
Then, too,
consider the abortions
of the *howl-howl-with-the-combo* quacks;
the little Eddie Jests and Shortfellows who use no rubbers
when copulating with muses on the wrong side of the tracks;
the new-born sun-god babes snatched
from cradles on the sly;
the bigname poets,
sober or high,
who abandon the little
hybrid bastards of their youth
without
saying,
'Good-by!' "

CHI

Despite his caricatures
of poets and poetasters,
Hideho's joy was Hasidic
among the lives and works of the Masters—
old and new.
He himself was a sort of aged Istanbul
with a young Beyoglu.

He didn't know
I knew
about the split identity
of the People's Poet—
the bifacial nature of his poetry:
the racial ballad in the public domain
and the private poem in the modern vein.

I had overheard the poet say:
"Reverend Eli, in a foxhole
with the banzai in my ears,
one day
I collapsed from battle fatigue.
You know why?
Since I was unable to dig
the immortality of John Doe,
fears
(not Hamlet's . . . not Simon Legree's),
my fears
of oblivion made me realistic:
with no poems of Hideho's in World Lit—
he'd be a statistic!"

Poor Boy Blue,
the Great White World
and the Black Bourgeoisie
have shoved the Negro artist into
the white and not-white dichotomy,
the Afroamerican dilemma in the Arts—
the dialectic of
to be or not to be
a Negro.

From the grandeur that was dusky Rome,
one night I brought Hideho home,
dead drunk,
in a Zulu Club taxicab.
As he lay on the sofa,
ashy-black like a stiff on a slab
in a Harlem morgue,
I chanced to see,
in the modern idiom,
a poem called *E. & O. E.*
(A sort of Pasternakian secrecy, I thought.)
I was again the kid startled by the kettledrum
on the withers of a cavalry horse.
(Cry havoc, Poor Boy Blue.)
That he had been
a bistro habitué,
an expatriate poet of the Black Venus
in the Age of Whoopee—
Clotho had kept hid until then.

For the skeptic
on Lenox Avenue,
for the goof
on Peach-tree Street—
here was the eyesight proof
that the Color Line, as well as the Party Line,
splits an artist's identity
like the vertical which
Omar's *Is* and *Is-not* cannot define.
The face
of no man escapes the common gable roof
of this time, nor the lights and shadows in the design
of that place.

Why should a man,
in an age of anesthesiology,
seek relief
in the bark of the toothache tree?
Yet,
depressed like ondoyant glass,
Hideho Heights,
the *Coeur de Lion* of the Negro mass,
in *E. & O. E.* rationalized:
"Why place an empty pail
before a well
of dry bones?
Why go to Nineveh to tell
the ailing that they ail?
Why lose a golden fleece
to gain a holy grail?"

The Hideho Heights that Afroamerican Freedom, Inc.,
                    glorified
          had recognition marks—plain
     like the white tail of an antelope;
              in the subterrane
         of this poem, however,
     the protagonist aped the dubiety
         of a wet cake of soap.
                    . . .

                    Yet,
         in front of the ramshackle
       theatre that had graduated into
          the Ethiopian Tabernacle,
         like sandstone into gneiss,
     Hideho had left "Bishop" Gladstone Coffin
tongue-tied as a puking slop-bowl gobbler with a con head
that had a Napoleonic forelock, but a naked monkey ass
                    behind.
     Jailed for disturbing the peace, he had said
       later, to the liquored-up Zulu Club Wits:
        "A man's conscience is home-bred.
          To see an artist or a leader do
            Uncle Tom's asinine splits
          is an ask-your-mama shame!"
     The Jamaican bartender had staked off his claim:
     "The drinks are on the house, Poet Defender!"
          A sportsman with ruffed grouse
     on the wing over dogs, the poet had continued:
          "Integrity is an underpin—
            the marble lions that support
            the alabaster fountain in
                the Alhambra."

                    . . .

In the poem, *E. & O. E.,*
The poet's mind kept shuttling between
the sphinx of Yesterday and the enigma of Today,
like the specter of Amphion in Thebes
'twixt fragments of requiems and stones of decay.

Time!
Time?
The poet's *bête noire,* I thought.
We everyday mortals
wrought
on the cis-threshold of the sublime
are concerned with *timing,*
not with *time.*

I remembered the wisdom
of a grand duchess of the burlesque shows,
whose G-string gave repose
to no man's imagination.
"It's all in the timing,"
said Rose La Rose,
Mister Minsky's tigress in heat.
Just as sound,
not spelling,
is the white magic of rhyming
in the poet's feat,
the timing
of a parson's spiel,
of an H-bomb,
of a golfer's swing,
of a curator's budget—
makes the gallery ring!

I
(conscious of my Judas role)
jumped
when Hideho's foot
plumped
against the floor;
but in a second flat
the broken-down flat vibrated again with the snore
of a mine pump's suction hole.

I cudgeled again the eyesight proof:
"I am no ape
of Benares. I have won
no Monthyon
prize. Though I
have cut a G clef and a belletristic S,
naked on
roller skates in Butte Montmartre,
sweated palm to palm
to the down beats of
the tom-tom,
in Sorgue's studio
with the Black Venus,
and, a leaning question mark upon
a blue white metal bar, drunk piccolo
with Salmon, Apollinaire,
MacOrlan, and Picasso—
yet, out of square,
I have not said,
'Hippoclides doesn't care.'"

My unbelief
as I climbed the Peak of Teneriffe
in the poem
. . . grew . . .
indistinct
. . . grew . . .
invisible,
like the veins between the stem and margin of a leaf:

"Beneath
the albatross,
the skull-and-bones,
the Skull and Cross,
the Seven Sins Dialectical,
I do not shake
the Wailing Wall
of Earth—
nor quake
the Gethsemane
of Sea—
nor tear
the Big Top
of Sky
with Lear's prayer,
or Barabas' curse,
or Job's cry!"

PSI

Black Boy,
let me get up from the white man's Table of Fifty Sounds
in the kitchen; let me gather the crumbs and cracklings
of this autobio-fragment,
before the curtain with the skull and bones descends.

Many a *t* in the ms.
I've left without a cross,
many an *i* without a dot.
A dusky Lot
with a third degree and a second wind and a seventh turn
of pitch-and-toss,
my psyche escaped the Sodom of Gylt
and the Big White Boss.

Black Boy,
you stand before your heritage,
naked and agape;
cheated like a mockingbird
pecking at a Zuexian grape,
pressed like an awl to do
duty as a screw-
driver, you
ask the American Dilemma in you:
"If the trying plane
of Demos fail,
what will the trowel
of Uncle Tom avail?"

Black Boy,
in this race, at this time, in this place,
to be a Negro artist is to be
a flower of the gods, whose growth
is dwarfed at an early stage—
a Brazilian owl moth,
a giant among his own in an acreage
dark with the darkman's designs,
where the milieu moves back downward like the sloth.

Black Boy,
true—you
have not
dined and wined
(*ignoti nulla cupido*)
in the El Dorado of aeried Art,
for unreasoned reasons;
and your artists, not so lucky as the Buteo,
find themselves without a
skyscape sanctuary
in the
season of seasons:
in contempt of the contemptible,
refuse the herb of grace, the rue
of Job's comforter;
take no
lie-tea in lieu
of Broken Orange Pekoe.
Doctor Nkomo said: "*What* is he who smacks
his lips when dewrot eats away the golden grain
of self-respect exposed like flax
to the rigors of sun and rain?"

Black Boy,
every culture,
every caste,
every people,
every class,
facing the barbarians
with lips hubris-curled,
believes its death rattle omens
the *Dies Irae* of the world.

Black Boy,
summon Boas and Dephino,
Blumenbach and Koelreuter,
from their posts
around the gravestone of Bilbo,
who, with cancer in his mouth,
orated until he quaked the magnolias of the South,
while the pocketbooks of his weeping black serfs
shriveled in the drouth;
summon the ghosts
of scholars with rams' horns from Jericho
and facies in letters from Jerusalem,
so
we may ask them:
"What is a Negro?"

Black Boy,
what's in a people's name that wries the brain
like the neck of a barley bird?
Can sounding brass create
an ecotype with a word?

Black Boy,
beware of the thin-bladed mercy
stroke, for one drop of Negro blood
(V. *The Black Act of the F. F. V.*)
opens the flood-
gates of the rising tide of color
and jettisons
the D. A. R. in the Heraclitean flux
with Uncle Tom and
Crispus Attucks.
The Black Belt White,
painstaking as a bedbug in
a tenant farmer's truckle bed,
rabbit-punched old Darrow
because
he quoted Darwin's sacred laws
(instead of the Lord God Almighty's)
and gabbled that the Catarrhine ape
(the C from a Canada goose nobody knows)
appears,
after X's of years,
in the vestigial shape
of the Nordic's thin lips, his aquiline nose,
his straight hair,
orangutanish on legs and chest and head.
Doctor Nkomo, a votary of touch-and-go,
who can stand the gaff
of Negrophobes and, like Aramis,
parry a thrust with a laugh,
said:

"In spite of the pig in the python's coils,
in spite of Blake's lamb in the jaws of the tiger,
Nature is kind, even in the raw: she toils
. . . aeons and aeons and aeons . . .
gives the African a fleecy canopy
to protect the seven faculties of the brain
from the burning convex lens of the sun;
she foils
whiteness
(without disdain)
to bless the African
(as Herodotus marvels)
with the birthright of a burnt skin for work or fun;
she roils
the Aryan
(as his eye and ear repose)
to give the African an accommodation nose
that cools the drying-up air;
she entangles the epidermis in broils
that keep the African's body free from lice-infested hair.
As man to man,
the Logos is
Nature is on the square
with the African.
If a black man circles the rim
of the Great White World, he will find
(even if Adamness has made him half blind)
the bitter waters of Marah *and*
the fresh fountains of Elim."

Although his transition
was a far cry
from Shakespeare to Sardou,
the old Africanist's byplay gave
no soothing feverfew
to the Dogs in the Zulu Club;
said he:
"A Hardyesque artistry
of circumstance
divides the Whites and Blacks in life,
like the bodies of the dead
eaten by vultures
in a Tower of Silence.
Let, then, the man with a maggot in his head
lean . . . lean . . . lean
on race or caste or class,
for the wingless worms of blowflies shall grub,
dry and clean,
the stinking skeletons of these,
when the face of the macabre weather-
cock turns to the torrid wind of misanthropy;
and later their bones shall be swept together
(like the Parsees')
in the Sepulchre of Anonymity."
A Zulu Wit cleared away his unsunned
mood with dark laughter;
but I sensed the thoughts of Doctor Nkomo
pacing nervously to and fro
like Asscher's, after
he'd cleaved the giant Cullinan Diamond.

Black Boy,
the vineyard is the fittest place
in which to booze (with Omar) and study
soil and time and integrity—
the telltale triad of grape and race.

Palates that can read the italics
of *salt* and *sugar* know
a grapevine
transplanted from Bordeaux
to Pleasant Valley
cannot give grapes that make a Bordeaux wine.

Like the sons of the lone mother of dead empires,
who boasted their ancestors,
page after page—
wines are peacocky
in their vintage and their age,
disdaining the dark ways of those engaging
in the profits
of chemical aging.
When the bluebirds sing
their perennial anthem
a capriccio, in the Spring,
the sap begins to move up the stem
of the vine, and the wine in the bed of the deep
cask stirs in its winter sleep.
Its bouquet
comes with the years, dry or wet;
so the connoisseurs say:
"The history of the wine
is repeated by the vine."

Black Boy,
beware of wine labels,
for the Republic does not guarantee
what the phrase "Château Bottled" means—
the estate, the proprietor, the quality.
This ignominy will baffle you, Black Boy,
because the white man's law
has raked your butt many a time
with fang and claw.
Beware of the waiter who wraps
a napkin around your Clos Saint Thierry,
if Chance takes you into high-hat places
open to all creeds and races
born to be or not to be.
Beware of the pop
of a champagne cork:
like the flatted fifth and octave jump in Bebop,
it is theatrical
in Vicksburg or New York.
Beware of the champagne cork
that does not swell up like your ma when she had you—*that*
comes out flat,
because the bottle of wine
is dead . . . dead
like Uncle Tom and the Jim Crow Sign.
Beware . . . yet
your dreams in the Great White World
shall be unthrottled
by pigmented and unpigmented lionhearts,
for we know *without no*
every people, by and by, produces its "Château Bottled."

White Boy,
as regards the ethnic origin
of Black Boy and me,
the *What* in Socrates' *"Tò tí?"*
is for the musk-ox habitat of anthropologists;
but there is another question,
dangerous as a moutaba tick,
secreted in the house
of every Anglo-Saxon sophist and hick:

Who is a Negro?
(I am a White in deah ole Norfolk.)
Who is a White?
(I am a Negro in little old New York.)
Since my mongrelization is invisible
and my Negroness a state of mind conjured up
by Stereotypus, I am a chameleon
on *that* side of the Mason-Dixon
that a white man's conscience
is not on.
My skin is as white
as a Roman's toga when he sought an office on the sly;
my hair is as blond
as xanthein;
my eyes are as blue
as the hawk's-eye.
At the Olympian powwow of curators,
when I revealed my Negroness,
my peers became shocked like virgins in a house
where satyrs tattooed on female thighs heralds of success.

White Boy,
counterfeit scholars have used
the newest brush-on Satinlac,
to make our ethnic identity
crystal clear for the lowest IQ
in every mansion and in every shack.
Therefore,
according to the myth that Negrophobes bequeath
to the Lost Gray Cause, since Black Boy is the color
of betel-stained teeth,
he and I
(from ocular proof
that cannot goof)
belong to races
whose dust-of-the-earth progenitors
the Lord God Almighty created
of different bloods,
in antipodal places.
However,
even the F. F. V. pate
is aware that laws defining a Negro
blackjack each other within and without a state.
The Great White World, White Boy, leaves you in a sweat
like a pitcher with three runners on the bases;
and, like Kant, you seldom get
your grammar straight—yet,
you are the wick that absorbs the oil in my lamp,
in all kinds of weather;
and we are teeth in the pitch wheel
that work together.

White Boy,
when I hear the word *Negro* defined,
why does it bring to mind
the chef, the gourmand, the belly-god,
the disease of kings, the culinary art
in alien lands, Black Mammy in a Dixie big house,
and the dietitian's chart?
Now, look at Black Boy scratch his head!
It's a stereotypic gesture of Uncle Tom,
a learned Gentleman of Color said
in his monumental tome,
The *Etiquette of the New Negro,*
which,
the publishers say,
by the way,
should be in every black man's home.

The Negro is a dish in the white man's kitchen—
a potpourri,
an ola-podrida,
a mixie-maxie,
a hotchpotch of lineal ingredients;
with UN guests at his table,
the host finds himself a Hamlet on the spot,
for, in spite of his catholic pose,
the Negro dish is a dish nobody knows:
to some . . . tasty,
like an exotic condiment—
to others . . . unsavory
and inelegant.

White Boy,
the Negro dish is a mix
like . . . and *un*like
pimiento brisque, chop suey,
eggs à la Goldenrod, and eggaroni;
tongue-and-corn casserole, mulligan stew,
baked fillets of halibut, and cheese fondue;
macaroni milanaise, egg-milk shake,
mullagatawny soup, and sour-milk cake.

Just as the Chinese lack
an ideogram for "to be,"
our lexicon has no definition
for an ethnic amalgam like Black Boy and me.

Behold a Gordian knot without
the *beau geste* of an Alexander's sword!
Water, O Modern Mariner, water, everywhere,
unfit for *vitro di trina* glass
or the old-oaken-bucket's gourd!

For dark hymens on the auction block,
the lord of the mansion knew the macabre score:
not a dog moved his tongue,
not a lamb lost a drop of blood to protect a door.
O
Xenos of Xanthos,
what midnight-to-dawn lecheries,
in cabin and big house,
produced these brown hybrids and yellow motleys?

White Boy,
Buchenwald is a melismatic song
whose single syllable is sung to blues notes
to dark wayfarers who listen for the gong
at the crack of doom along
. . . that Lonesome Road . . .
before they travel on.

A Pelagian with the *raison d'être* of a Negro,
I cannot say I have outwitted dread,
for I am conscious of the noiseless tread
of the Yazoo tiger's ball-like pads behind me
in the dark
as I trudge ahead,
up and up . . . that Lonesome Road . . . up and up.

In a Vision in a Dream,
from the frigid seaport of the proud Xanthochroid,
the good ship *Défineznegro*
sailed fine, under an unabridged moon,
to reach the archipelago
Nigeridentité.
In the Strait of Octoroon,
off black Scylla,
after the typhoon Phobos, out of the Stereotypus Sea,
had rived her hull and sail to a T,
the *Défineznegro* sank the rock
and disappeared in the abyss
(*Vanitas vanitatum!*)
of white Charybdis.

OMEGA

White Boy,
Black Boy,
you have played blackjack with Tyche,
you have shot craps with Hap;
yet, things-as-they-are in the ghetto
have sported you for a sap.
Sometimes,
a guy born in a house with the graffito
of doom lucks upon the know-how of a raccoon
that gnaws off its leg to escape from a trap.
Now, the difference between
you and me
is the little matter of
a Harvard Ph. D.
You may have a better brain—
but no Nestor taught you how
to get rid of
its ball and chain.

Those in the upper drawer give a child
the open sesame to the unknown
What and How and Why;
that's *that* which curators, as Pelagians, try
to do
in exhibitions,
when a genius gets through
with a nonpareil of art whose exegesis
exacts patience—the patience of a cow
that sucks lime from a deer
antler dropped at the dawn of the year.

Black Boy,
White Boy,
a lesser dog that diadems an eked-out butt of space
may baffle Palomar's eye;
yet, no Schaeberle thumbs his nose at the discovery
and scowls, "Good-by!"

"At the crossroads, does painting take,"
as Lhote said,
"the direction of the merchant?"
Should the artist stand on his head
in the middle of Main Street,
to get the coppers of the vulgar?
Paint an *ignis fatuus* of *nawiht*,
to win thirty pieces of silver from the elite?

Sometimes a work of art is bitter crystalline alkaloid
to be doled out
at intervals, between the laugh and flout
of an Admirable Doctor; but, if taken too much
at a time, it delivers the cocainizing punch
of a Jack Dempsey nonesuch.

Many mouths empty their waters
into the Godavari of Art—
a river that flows
across the Decan trap of the age
with its lava-scarred plateaux;
and, in the selfheal of the river,
pilgrims lave the bruises of the Rain of woes.

White Boy,
Black Boy,
the meander of a curator leads him by
the house where Illiteracy beds
with Ignorance and all her brats.
Should he
skim the milk of culture for the elite
and give the "lesser breeds"
a popular latex brand?
Should he
(to increase digestibility)
break up
the fat globules and vitamins and casein shreds?
Tonic spasms of wind and wave
assail compass and lamp in the cabined night;
but the binnacle of imagination
steers the work of art aright—
even if the craftsman gives us a dash as he cuts a dash:
Cézanne,
the Zulu of the Brush,
Daumier,
the anatomist of the lawyer's mouth,
Hogarth,
the engraver of harlots for cash.

O Ushas,
I could unweave
a Gobelin arras of irony on graybeard artists
disoriented like Degas when forced to leave
the rue Victor Masse—to make again
a new place for new things and new men.

Black Boy,
White Boy,
out of chaos the dread hand designed
the oval lilac shape
of the rich sweet Tokay;
contrived the helmet-like head of the Cape
buffalo with its diablerie
curved outward, downward, and backward—
then, forward, upward, and inward:
neither man nor beast may hope to escape
when the alarm of the buffalo bird
sets the vicious circle of horns surrealistically flying.

The ape of God
(mind instinct with design)
pricks in the skin of the seafarer's arm
the painted Tyrean form
of the huzzy thrown from a window to the dogs;
blazons the red pallets on the gold
of Aragon's shield;
contrives the triple-rhyming oblong leaf
of the metaphor-maker of Naishapur;
fashions the undulant mold
of the *cyma reversa;*
patterns the mosaics in the baptistries
of San Vitale at Ravenna;
traces the multiple complexities
of shafting in black Purbeckian marble;
fabricates the mordant trill of the grand
pianoforte's warble.

White Boy,
Black Boy,
freedom is the oxygen
of the studio and gallery.
What if a *chef-d'oeuvre* is esoteric?
The cavernous By Room, with its unassignable variety
of ego-dwarfing
stalactites and stalagmites,
makes my veins and arteries vibrate faster
as I study its magnificence and intricacy.
Is it amiss or odd
if the apes of God
take a cue from their Master?

Do not scholars tear their beards—vex
their disciples over the Palestinian and Byzantine
punctuation of the Masoretic texts?

As for the critic,
he is the fid
that bolsters the topmost mast
of Art—an argosy of plunder
from the kingdoms of race and class and caste.
Now and then a State,
when iron fists and hobnails
explode alarms at the citadel's gate,
dons the ill-fitting robes of the Medici
and initiates Project CX,
to propagandize a rubber-stamped pyramid of Art
and to glorify the Cheops at the apex.

Black Boy,
White Boy,
Doctor Nkomo used to dream:
"God's ape
from Giverney gives us new roads
out of the Jardin d'Eau and across the anthroposcape.
If I had the alchemy
of the camel's hair, I'd do, with nuance-by-nuance variety,
as regards
site and trait and light,
a series in a character-history,
like *Cliffs of Etzetat, Coins of Rivière.*
O fruits of the first Harlem harvest,
let the beholder who is neither kith nor kin
recompose the unexpected tones in a dusky Everyman
the painter's brush has disassociated against the milieu—
then boned and fleshed and veined again."

I confess without regret
in this omega of my education:
I no longer have the force of a gilbert,
nor have I ever had the levitation
to sustain a work of art.
I have only pilgrimed
to the cross street
(a godsend in God's acre)
where
curator and creator
meet—
friend yoked to friend at the candle end.

White Boy,
Black Boy,
like the flatted third and seventh notes
in a 12-bar blues,
the identity of the Negro is groovy
in all-God's-children-got shoes.
The moving finger in the Harlem Gallery
paints dramatis personae in the dusk of dawn,
between America's epigraph and epitaph;
yet,
only half an eye has the other half
of the Great White World,
where,
at the crack of doom,
potbellies bellylaugh.

Sometimes the Harlem Gallery
is a harvesting machine without binding
twine; again, a clock that stops
for want of winding:
it is then that the millstones of the Regents
exhaust summer and winter
in grinding
the spirit of The Curator.
But
I envision the Harlem Gallery of my people,
and
(in spite of sounding brass)
I hear the words of Archbishop Trench:
"The present is only intelligible in the light of the past."

Black Boy,
White Boy,
no Haroun-al-Rashid greets the Harlem avant-garde;
in the travailing
dusk of dawn,
a flailing
gibberish may turn one ill-smelling and pale
as characin,
may leave one quailing,
until one discovers it is a
lonely, flailing 666—only
a monkey with a lion's tail.
No Lenox Avenue bar
a-moaning the blues,
no hetaera star
aglitter in the Harlem Opera House,
the day's travel unended and with the night's blended—
I do not expect to hear a Selika's invisible choir
anthem the felicities
of the Beyond's equalizing bar
with its whiffletrees.

Since men of good will are depressed like the rostrum
of the deep-sea Herriotta, since the world's grief
goes unexplained like the why
of the *kind gallows* at Crieff—
send francs (bucks), not *Illuminations,*
to the Afroamerican Djami,
the Harlem Gallery's
faithful Harrari.

White Boy,
Black Boy,
what if this Harlem Exhibition becomes
a *cause célèbre?* The Deluge! I
have no Noah's ark,
no peak of Ararat, to defy
the dusky Regents who,
tasteless as oxygen,
as colorless, too,
can knot the golden purse strings,
while closeted in the Great Amen,
and mix the ingredients of Syncorax' brew!

In the black ghetto
the white heather
and the white almond grow,
but the hyacinth
and asphodel blow
in the white metropolis!
O Cleobulus,
O Thales, Solon, Periander, Bias, Chilo,
O Pittacus,
unriddle the phoenix riddle of this?

Our public may possess in Art
a Mantegna figure's arctic rigidity;
yet—I hazard—yet,
this allegro of the Harlem Gallery
is not a chippy fire,
for here, in focus, are paintings that chronicle
a people's New World odyssey
from chattel to Esquire!

Notes and Commentary to
HARLEM GALLERY

The apparatus that follows should provide a reasonably well prepared and motivated reader a more or less comprehensive guide to what *Harlem Gallery* says and, step by step, what issues it raises. Only incidentally, as a tactic of accomplishing that primary goal, do I pay any particular attention to large patterns in the poem or global concerns of what it may mean. For each canto there is a narrative paraphrase of its action or discussion ("The Argument") and an annotation, as well as I can manage it, of the specific words, phrases, and ideas that require of the reader a knowledge that the poem itself does not provide. The annotations are keyed to line numbers.

I have aspired to make my paraphrases just that—not readings, not appreciations, not interpretations. It is, of course, in the nature of things impossible to keep my understanding of the poem and my affection for it from informing what I conceive it to say, so that I have not thought it worth anyone's while to strain my voice and the reader's credulity by pretending that I was speaking only as a medium for Tolson. Nevertheless, my intention is to be as much transparent, as little intrusive as my responsibilities will allow.

In preparing annotation I have tried to observe the following *don'ts*:

don't spoil jokes

don't belabor the obvious

don't annotate allusions or quotations (crossing the Rubicon, man Friday, open sesame, etc.) that have become familiar idioms in English

don't elaborate upon references (the stingless mosquito bee, for instance, or Galileo's telescope) for which the poem itself supplies the information necessary to make annotation redundant

and the following *dos*:

when appropriate, do try to apply annotation to the unknotting of Tolson's sometimes very knotty figures

do try to let the reader know—again, when appropriate—to what degree the arcane knowledge of an annotation is necessary to the statement a passage makes

to avoid ambiguity, do be explicit about allusions or references I have
   been unable to identify   ,

if one must err in the always tricky business of judging how much in-
   formation is enough, do err on the side of generosity rather than
   stinginess

While observing such strictures as well as I can, I have assumed through-
out that the principle of making a remarkable poem accessible to those who
want to read it precedes all other principles.

Over the years a number of good people have provided me with bits and
pieces of the information necessary to build an approach to Tolson's im-
posing monument. I owe special thanks to Steve Arch, wherever he may be,
and Beth Gargano, both of whom dedicated to this project more time, en-
ergy, and ingenuity than I had any right to ask of them. I should also men-
tion those repositories of knowledge and generosity Brian Balogh, Gordon
Braden, Douglas Day, Mark Elson, Jeffrey Hopkins, Wally Kerrigan, Dan
Larson, Marita McClymonds, Mary McKinley, Ernest Mead, Tom Noble,
Roland Simon, Larry Thomas and Wilburn Williams, even as I shake my
head ruefully over the names I will inevitably have left out. I have, of course,
consulted and profited from the published commentary on *Harlem Gallery*,
as well as Robert Huot's unpublished annotations in his University of Utah
doctoral dissertation of 1971. The published record is not extensive. The
only book-length study devoted to *Harlem Gallery* is Mariann Russell's
Melvin B. Tolson's Harlem Gallery: *A Literary Analysis* (1980). Joy Flasch's
volume on Tolson (1972) in the Twayne American Authors series is in many
ways superseded but still informative. Michael Bérubé's *Marginal
Forces/Cultural Centers* (1992), which considers Tolson in tandem with
Thomas Pynchon, is the most sophisticated literary discussion of Tolson
that has yet appeared. Robert M. Farnsworth established the biographical
record in *Plain Talk and Poetic Prophecy* (1984), which includes as well a
bibliography of Tolson's work and commentary on it to 1984. Farnsworth
also edited and published Tolson's preliminary character sketches in *A
Gallery of Harlem Portraits* (1979), and *Caviar and Cabbage* (1982), the
columns Tolson wrote for the Washington *Tribune* 1937–44.

A Note on the Text

Harlem Gallery was originally published by Twayne Publishers in 1965. The
corrected typescript of Tolson's final draft of the poem is on deposit in the
Melvin B. Tolson Papers at the Library of Congress. There are no substan-
tive discrepancies between the published version and the final draft, and an

examination of the perfectly legible typescript makes it clear that Tolson maintained full control over his text and the way it was to be printed. The text contains a number of minor errors or variations in spelling, several instances of apparently eccentric diction, and what may or may not be a few errors of fact. None of these lacunae, if that is what they are, are major. All of them were apparently introduced by Tolson and withstood his scrutiny. They are identified, tacitly or otherwise, in the annotation but let stand in the text.

Alpha

THE ARGUMENT

In the beginning, in the ambiguous, portentous twilight of W. E. B. DuBois's "dusk of dawn," the Curator is awakened by the challenge of his Gallery. With him awakens the radically interwoven, the fundamental themes of *Harlem Gallery*: social revolution through art and the ironies of racial identity. The first of the Gallery's many symbolic birds sounds reveille: the pepper bird's morning song of African nationalism is complicated by the mocking mock-guffaws of the Australian clockbird, to whose counterpoint is added the raucous, racially apposite, laughlike cries of the goose.

The first picture in the Gallery is also the first assertion of the Curator's persistent, never fully explicated, intuition about the power of art as a weapon in what he conceives to be both a historical and immediate revolution of the world. Francisco Goya's passionate representation of Spanish resistance to Napoleanic imperialism confronts and affronts the old colonial powers, the Great White World, which like Buridan's ass has forfeited its freedom of choice and action, in the same way that John Laugart's *Black Bourgeoisie* will later horrify Guy Delaporte III and the regents of the Harlem Gallery.

Visual arts provide *Harlem Gallery* with a primary technique as well as vital themes. To the eye, this canto becomes, as many cantos or parts of them do, a coherent series of geometric patterns that suggest some deep interplay of verbal and visual images. Tolson was painstakingly inventive of visual puns and analogues, and he prepared his manuscript with great attention to the use of the page as a canvas.

In his image of the Dust Bowl (which is autobiographically suggestive of Tolson as well), and in the image of being ravaged by parasites, the Curator suggests the personal cost of living at the intersection of two racial worlds. In

the reversed roles of the great comic actor Quintus Roscius and the trage-
dian Edmund Kean, he first hints at his own interchangeable racial identi-
ties. To proceed by opposites will become an important method throughout
Harlem Gallery. So will the assumption by necessity of unnatural or unwel-
come responsibilities—as in the image of the Hambletonian, which is not a
horse bred for jumping.

The alternately exhilarated and embittered tone of the canto, further
complicated by the Curator's expression of doubt about the ultimate value
of his undertaking, is deepened by the entrance of the Socratic gadfly with
his mocking "What is it?," the primal question the Curator (and Tolson)
never tires of invoking.

NOTES

1. Afric pepper bird: the term *pepper bird* is used to refer to any of several
species of African hornbills (suborder *Bucerotides*), but the Curator is inter-
ested here more in the imagery of noise and spiciness than in the specifics
of ornithology.

2. people's dusk of dawn: *Dusk of Dawn, an Essay toward an Autobiography
of a Race Concept* (1940) by W. E. B. Du Bois.

5. the Lord of the House of the Flies: Beelzebub (or Baal-zebub), one of the
demonic false gods of the Israelites. See 2 Kings 1:2–3; Matthew 10:25, 11:24.

8. *The Second of May*: One of the two huge canvasses Francisco Goya
(1746–1828) painted in 1814 to commemorate the heroic resistance of the
people of Madrid to Napolean's invasion of May 2–3, 1808.

12. the scimitar of Murat: Joachim Murat (1767–1815) was the French gen-
eral in charge of Napolean's invasion of Spain.

13–14. the Day of Barricades: originally May 12, 1588, when Henry III, king
of France 1574–89, was driven from Paris by a popular uprising. By exten-
sion, any of several such episodes in French history.

14. alarm birds: probably *corythaixoides concolor* (also known as "the go-
away bird"), found in central and southern Africa. Its name derives from its
behavior at the approach of an intruder.

15. Buridan's ass: the French philosopher Jean Buridan (ca. 1300–ca. 1360)
has been credited with the postulation that an ass, placed equally distant
from two equally attractive foods, would lose its ability to make a choice and
starve because of its indecision.

15. not Balaam's: Balaam's ass saw the angel of the lord and kept Balaam
from harm. Numbers 22:21–34.

16. Roscius: Quintus Roscius (d. ca. 62 B.C.E.) was the most famous Roman comic actor of his day.

17. Kean: Edmund Kean (1787–1833), a celebrated Shakespearian tragedian.

18. Sir Henry's flap: the havelock,the piece of cloth attached to the back of a cap to protect the neck from the sun, the invention of which is credited to Sir Henry Havelock (1795–1857).

20. Hambletonian: a strain of American trotting horses, named for the nineteenth-century stallion from which it is descended.

29. Black Boy: the dismissive collective name used in the segregated South, probably reinforced here by allusion to Richard Wright's autobiographical *Black Boy* (1945). Tolson employed it as a generic form of address to his audience in the columns on social issues he wrote for the Washington *Tribune* in 1937–44, just as the Curator does in *Harlem Gallery*.

31–32. the lice and maggots of the apples of Cain on a strawberry tree: the strawberry tree (*Arbutus unedo*), an evergreen found in the warmer regions of the United States, is a real tree bearing mock strawberries. It is also known as the cane apple.

33. the myth of the Afroamerican past: the assumption, baldly stated, that no Africanisms survive among black people in the United States, so that African American culture is simply a badly understood, poorly assimilated derivative of the dominant white culture. This mindset was defined and attacked by the anthropologist Melville Herskovits in his classic study of 1941, *The Myth of the Negro Past*.

41. "*Tò tí?*": the characteristic question ("The What?") attributed to Socrates (d. 399 B.C.E.).

43. clockbird. the kookaburra, or "laughing jackass" (*Dacelo novaequineae*), an Australian kingfisher, begins its strange song at early dawn.

41–48. Although . . . is plain: this final stanza might be visually a stylized *I* or simply a pedestal for the canto. Compare the examples of the conclusion of "Gamma" or lines 153–88 of "XI," but examples are everywhere.

Beta

THE ARGUMENT

The socratic proddings that close "Alpha" touch off in "Beta" a series of characteristically riddling, punning, and allusive variations on the themes of the discovery through art of human nature ("*What* is man?") and the particular artistic identity of the Curator ("what *manner* of man is this?"). That juxtaposition of classical and biblical echoes in the first stanza evokes the lofty standards and sharp judgments that inform the canto throughout.

Once the seeker has gotten beyond simply physical considerations (Biosis, altitudes, "the archimedean pit and pith"), as the Curator advises, he or she should, in inquiring about the human, proceed by contraries. If, for instance, one is inclined to the sharpest realism ("the nth verisimilar") one should consult the mystery and expansiveness of revelation. Those, on the other hand, who like the Homeric lotus eaters are seduced by escapism or risk the loss of a clear sense of distinctions, should seek the discipline of the sharp natural detail, figured in the tiny flowers of the Solomon's seal plant. The object of such dialectical discipline is to enhance one's clarity of mind, thus freeing oneself from the essentially hypocritical reliance on deceit or contrivance in representation. In art as in life one must proceed according to the imperatives of the spirit.

With the invocation of the Babylonian exile in the first lines of the seventh stanza, the Curator turns to ruminations on the ironies of his own racial and professional identity. He is, as always, self-effacing, but he also seems almost perversely prideful about his marginality. Although there is more to him—the core unburnt, the (punningly spelled) spoor undetected—than the world has yet seen, his is a minor role. He feels inadequate to the demands suggested by allusion to the story of Philip and the Ethiopian eunuch, that he interpret great mysteries. No one, he says, can accuse him of carrying either his faults ("emptiness") or talents (like those of the Thracian Bard) to their extremes. His marginality in the contemporary marketplace of art, however, is consoling as well as limiting. As one who is stereotyped, accurately or not, as a failed academic, he forfeits all influence in official art circles, which he in turn cordially despises. As one who lacks pentecostal eloquence and the depth of perception it expresses, he escapes the labeling and susceptibility to faddishness, as well as the power, of the generations of artists who, each in their turn, renew both the common idiom and the possibilities of life.

NOTES

1, 4. O Tempora, . . . O Mores: "Alas for the times . . . Alas for the manners." From Cicero's first speech against Cataline (62 B.C.E.).

5. what *manner* of man is this?: see Matthew 8:27. Mark and Luke also record the disciples' question about Jesus.

6. Guy the ologists in effigy!: Guy Fawkes (1570–1606), who led the Catholic Gunpowder Plot to blow up the British Parliament (1605), was annually burned in effigy on the anniversary (November 5) of his deed. *Ologists*: specialists.

8. archimedean pit and pith: that is, the physical substance. Archimedes of Syracuse (ca. 287–212 B.C.E.), a mathematician, astronomer, and inventer, was most famous for his discovery of the principle of the displacement of water.

9. the Throttler at Gîza: the Great Sphinx at Al Jizah (formerly Gîza). Tolson is apparently alluding to the story of the sphinx's encounter with Oedipus when it had been sent to Thebes to punish the city. It posed its famous riddle to passersby and killed those who answered incorrectly. Oedipus defeated the sphinx by presenting the correct answer, which was "man."

11. Pisgah: the mountain from which Moses looked into the promised land. Deuteronomy 3:27, 34:1.

14. ape of God: the phrase has been used in English at least as early as the mid-sixteenth century to mean the imitator of god, in either a contemptuous or positive sense. It has been used to suggest the peculiar follies, dangers, or glories of the artist at least since the early seventeenth century, and as proximately to Tolson as the novel *The Apes of God* (1930) by Wyndham Lewis (1884–1957). Tolson uses the phrase repeatedly in *Harlem Gallery*, and usually means by it no more than *the artist*.

16. lotus eater: Odyssey 9.82 ff. His sensual indulgence has blinded him to responsibility.

17. green bay tree: Psalms 37:35.

18. Solomon's seal: a plant (*polygonatum multiflorum*) with small drooping white flowers and a rootstock bearing seallike scars.

20. troubled Virgin Pool: Tolson may be referring to the intermittent pool (or Virgin's Fountain) of Gihon, described in Nehemiah 3:15, which formed part of the waters of Siloam, but his usage here is primarily metaphorical rather than allusive.

27–28. a Herod's charger after the Salomean dance: that is, the punishment for prophecy. Matthew 14:3–11; Mark 6:16–28.

30. *non astutia, animo*: Latin, not by cunning, by spirit.

32. tartufish guile: Tartuffe was a hypocritical pretender to piety in the comedy of 1664 by Jean-Baptiste Molière (1622–1673).

36. *The Dialogue of Lees*: almost certainly a nonce-title.

39. in a strange land, strangers: i.e., like Moses in Egypt. Exodus 2:22.

40. the Black Stone's Colonnade: in the Kaaba in the Great Mosque at Mecca, the most sacred shrine of Islam.

41. Amharic eunuch: Amharic is the language of Ethiopia. See Acts 8:27–35 for the story of Philip's spiritual rescue, through interpretation, of the Ethiopan eunuch.

51–52. with eye and tongue: see *Macbeth* 3.2.32.

53–59. like the O . . . descent: the sense of the Curator's figure—that he is a subordinate but necessary strain in a great harmony—is clear. The specific opera or oratorio of St. Bridget to which he seems to refer has eluded identification.

62. *beau geste*: French, a fine, but often empty, gesture.

63. hyacinths: in Greek mythololgy a plant, variously identified but irislike, which sprang from the blood of Hyacinthus, a beautiful youth, loved by Apollo but killed out of jealousy by Zephyrus. Its flowers were marked with an exclamation of grief, AI AI.

65. the Thracian bard: probably Orpheus, to whom this epithet is applied in *Paradise Lost* 7.1.32. His story is also told in Ovid, *Metamorphosis* 11.

76. winter yellowlegs: or greater yellowlegs (*Tringa melanoleuca*), a bird of the sandpiper family that migrates to the southern United States or Central America in the winter. It is a noisy bird and easily hunted.

100. a wheel of prayer: in Himalayan Buddhist countries a prayer wheel is a hand-turned machine that produces continuous artificial prayer.

111. The Lost, The Bright, The Angry, The Beat: In "The Foreground of Negro Poetry" (*Kansas Quarterly* 7 [summer 1975]:30–35), Tolson comments that "since 1920 we have had four periods in both American and Negro literature: the Lost Generation, the Bright Generation, The Angry Generation, and the Beat Generation. Each had its fads and permanencies, its sophistries and realities, its techniques and ideas—all of which are spelled out in our university libraries and little magazines." The Lost Generation, Beat Generation, and Angry Young Men are all familiar names for literary movements. It is not clear what Tolson meant by the Bright Generation.

Gamma

THE ARGUMENT

In "Gamma" as in "Beta" the Babylonian captivity is invoked to represent the condition of the artist with regard to society, Mecca to represent his aspiration and responsibility. Starting from these scriptural metaphors, the Curator elaborates in this dense canto his reflections on the relationship between art and the human ability to comprehend, or even to affect, reality. His initial vision of a dangerous, crowded city, intolerant of heterodoxy, in which art is submerged but attainable, poses an existential problem. The predicament is both recognized and confronted in subsequent evocations of New York and Paris. The canto culminates in a vision of paintings on the grand scale that represent the attainment of art and the transfiguration of the metaphorical city. Here the raw energy and mass of urban life are refined into color and pattern, so that the perverted ("engouled") character of the archetypal wicked city is defeated and Sodom becomes in the "magicked pageant" of art an equivalent of Paradise.

It is the same power of discovering the inherent transcendent in the failed that ennobles Utrillo and his bohemian Paris, or makes of Antonio Bosio's exploration and visual recreation of the Roman catacombs a medium by which the delicate seasoning of human wit (the Attic salt) can survive bloodthirstiness, greed, treachery—the powers of hell itself.

We can encounter reality, the Curator suggests, only through the otherness (altérité) dramatized and thus made tangible in art. We cannot know life from life. Life offers us so much reality that we are overwhelmed by it. The selectivity of art permits us empathy and shared catharsis with the actors who focus our attention on the part of reality they impersonate in a dramatic analogue of life. Consciousness darkens when the stage goes dark.

The stage of Experience is tripartite (line 17) as a reflection of Tolson's understanding of human nature. Humanity is informed, he argued elsewhere, by the three conditions of biology, psychology, and sociology.

In the evocation of his "Afroirishjewish" grandfather the Curator once again suggests his own radically uncategorizable racial makeup. Here he appears to be the heir to the many successive waves of immigration to the United States.

NOTES

1. Shinar: the Hebrew rendering of an Akkadian word meaning Mesopotamia. Later, Shinar became identical in Hebrew usage with Babylonia. See Isaiah 11:11; Daniel 1:2; Zechariah 5:11.

16. Caesar's Gaul: "Gallia est omnis divisa in partes tres." Ceasar, *Gallic Wars* 1.1.

22. Veridic's *Human Comedy*: the monumental body of fiction by Honoré de Balzac (1799–1850), which he in 1841 entitled collectively *La Comédie Humaine*, attempted to reproduce the richness and variety of French life in the nineteenth century.
     veridic (véridique): French, truthful.

25. *altérité*: French, otherness.

32. Utrillo of the Holy Hill: Maurice Utrillo (1883–1955), French impressionist painter, whose favorite themes were the street scenes of Paris. *Holy Hill* is a loose translation of *Montmartre* (mount of martyrs).

33. Montmartre: the Paris neighborhood, famous as a center of artistic and bohemian life.

36. no Atropos said, "No-side": Atropos: in Greek mythology, the Fate who determined the end of life. "No-side" is a rugby term, meaning that time of play has expired.

53. Attic salt: dry, delicate wit.

55. Witches' Sabbath: Walpurgisnacht, on the evening of May 1, initiated the annual increase in demonic activity by the witches.

55. the Catacombs of Bosio: Antonio Bosio (1575–1629), a Roman Catholic priest, sculptor, and antiquarian, reopened and explored the catacombs of Rome near the end of the sixteenth century. He made accurate engravings of the most remarkable paintings and objects he found there. They were published with an explanatory text in *Roma Sotterranea* (1632).

58. from Dō to Dō: i.e., through the full range of the tonal scale, from beginning to new beginning.

61, 62. *The Closerie des Lilas! The Café Voltaire!*: both were famous gathering places for artists, writers, and troublemakers in Paris. The Closerie des Lilas, located on the Boulevard Montparnasse at the edge of the Latin Quarter, was popular through the nineteenth century and well into the twentieth; the Café Voltaire in the Place de l'Odeon operated during the first decades of the twentieth century.

66. like Joseph's coat: the story of Joseph's coat of many colors is told in Genesis 37.

68. Paolo's doomsday *Sodom*: if there is indeed a particular painting in reference here, it is probably *The Flight from Sodom* by Paolo Veronese (born Paolo Caliari, 1528–1599), but Tolson is interested chiefly in establishing a moral and tonal balance for Tintoretto's *Paradise*.

71. engouled: Heraldic: an epithet applied to bends, crosses, saltiers, etc., the extremities of which enter the mouths of animals (*OED*).

73. Tintoretto's *Paradise*: the Venetian artist Jacopo Robusti Tintoretto (1518–1594) painted two canvasses entitled *Paradise*. Tolson is probably referring to the second, begun in 1588 for the ducal palace in Venice. At 30 x 74 feet, it is one of the largest oil paintings in the world.

Delta

THE ARGUMENT

In this complex, sometimes obscure, but centrally important canto, the Curator launches one of his periodic quarrels with the group he calls, generically, "the critics"—against whom, at least in the early cantos, he commonly sides with the artists. Here his discussion of the origins and logic of art is provoked by critics who ask irrelevant questions about the motives—of church, state, money, tradition, psychological need—that fuel creativity. Critics, the Curator asserts, whose true function should be as an invisible, catalytic agent (malic acid) in the process by which art is assimilated, instead call attention to themselves. They also behave like pimps for favorite extraneous ideas. Without their intrusions art-lovers would simply tap the "world-self" for what they needed from it—be it luxury, solace, or reflections of reality.

Art has its own protocol and energy, the Curator insists. In stanza six it moves itself like a Ferris wheel, self-generated and coherent through historical, ideological, and intellectual cycles, while the learned doctors who sought to explain it die and are forgotten. The origins of art, he argues further, are essentially mysterious. Art arises from the suffering, loneliness, and essential humanity of the artist as the trumpet arises from the nature of brass. That is to say, the artist *is* and is not explained by recourse to systems of thought.

As he moves into images of vulnerability and transience (the zinnia yet unhurt by frost, the fatigues rather than the labors of Hercules), the Curator makes the travails of the artist and the miraculous accomplishments wrung from suffering the major focus of the canto. His characteristically misogynic view of the sexual life informs his description of the artist's emotional cycles and volatility. In a moment lust can divert the artist's enthusiasm and flair for life back to the old sexual wars, with their threats of treachery, seduction, and nagging. Socrates' proverbially shrewish wife is a recurring presence in the gallery. The seeress Nix is also one of many Nixies, whose naysaying is reinforced by their mythological hostility to men. These broodings on the perils of the flesh culminate in one definitive image of the artist's fix: to be subject to St. John's agony (beheaded at the climax of a sexual performance) without recourse to the supernatural condition symbolized by St. John's fire. In this predicament, which is largely uncontrollable (something beyond class or taste wills the artist to be earthy or to aspire), the artist can only cultivate courage and discipline.

The final three stanzas of the canto return to the theme of the essential mysteriousness, variety, and ineffability of art. Art works by intuition and desire. For an artist like the Persian mystical poet Hafiz it does not reflect reality (as it may for an audience) but opens windows into it, through which each artist will discover a personal vision. The diogenic cynic asks, metaphorically, about how the absolute value (color) of art can survive time and change. The answer is that particular values, symbolized by primary colors, are appropriate to particular cultures, but all of them are nourished by their contact with the transcendent, just as Elijah was miraculously nourished by ravens.

In the final analysis, art is not subject to analysis. It is known by love, study, and practice. As the canto ends, the Armenian musician-scholar Komitas affords a hint of what a true critic might achieve. His scholarly study of musical notation brings him to the verge of a Keatsian leap into art.

NOTES

9. weeping monkeys: Capuchin monkeys, the mock solemnity of whose name is derived from the resemblance of the hair of their crowns to the cowl of a friar.

10. colorless as malic acid: malic acid is found in various fruit juices and is an intermediate catalyst in the process of fermentation.

10. Hamburg grape: Tolson several times uses this black German grape, especially adapted for hothouse cultivation, as a synecdoche for *wine*.

12. hurrah's nest: confusion, a mess.

16. the black sanders: the Curator is perhaps referring to the prehistoric Sinagua people of the Black Sand desert area near Flagstaff, Arizona, whose culture and its decline were described in a book of 1960, *The Black Sand*, by the American archeologist Harold Colton (1881–1970). Colton speculated that, in addition to utilitarian and ceremonial purposes, one of the functions of Sinagua art may have been simply to pass the time.

19. Gran Galeoto: Spanish, great pimp. In the tragedy *El Gran Galeoto* (1881) by José Echegaray (1832–1916), the great pimp is society, whose slanderous lies about a virtuous woman finally force her to give in to scandalous behavior.

23. balsam apple: either of two small East Indian ornamental vines of the gourd family, with red or orange oblong fruits, which are sometimes used for poultices and linaments.

25. silvered Scarahaeus glass: silvered glass is a form of decorative glassware in which silver nitrate is applied inside double-walled glass to obtain a mirrorlike surface, often etched with designs. Scarahaeus, probably a manufacturer of the glass, has resisted identification.

26. *figuranti*: Italian, in theatrical usage, minor figures, or extras.

40. like Everyman: in the medieval morality play (1485) bearing his name, the allegorical Everyman, facing death, is successively abandoned by the characters representing his friends, his achievements, his physical and intellectual attributes. Only his own good deeds can accompany him into the grave.

51. an evergreen cherry: an evergreen shrub (*prunus caroliniana*) of the southern United States.

54. the twelve fatigues: in Greek mythology the twelve labors performed by Heracles.

55. the Lesbian rule of the seeress Nix: in the sixth century B.C.E. the Greek island of Lesbos was ruled by a group of women devoted to the service of Aphrodite and Artemis. Tolson is, of course, also playing upon the sexual resonance of the adjective.

Nixies, in Germanic mythology, were water sprites, half human and half fish. Although beautiful and at times willing to do favors for human beings, they were for the most part hostile and treacherous.

62. Delilah of Délice: *délice:* French, delight, pleasure. Delilah: the biblical temptress who betrayed Samson; see Judges 16.

64. Xanthippe: the legendarily shrewish wife of Socrates.

65. sonnets from the Portugese: the title of a sequence of affectionate, playful sonnets for her husband by Elizabeth Barrett Browning (1806–1861).

71. the fame flower: a linear-lined herb with light pink flowers (*talinum teretifolium*), found in the eastern United States.

76. St. John's fire: a folk tradition, lighted on the night of St. John the Baptist's day (June 24) to ward off sickness or bad luck.

77. the Vedic god of the snaky noose: Siva (or Shiva), the destroyer, one of the supreme triad of Hindu gods, depicted iconographically with serpents entwined about his blue neck.

79. the noise of block tin: block tin is commercial tin that has been partially refined and cast into blocks for shipping, but still contains small amounts of various impurities. When bent it makes a sharp sound.

85. the Moreton Bay laurel: an Australian tree (*Crytocarya australis*) whose bark contains a poison similar to curare.

92. 'Thou thing of no bowels, thou!': Shakespeare, *Troilus and Cressida* 2.1.49.

104. Hafiz: pen name of the Persian lyrical poet Shans-ud-din Muhammed (1300–1388), the most celebrated of the Sufi mystical poets. Like Omar Khayyám, whom Tolson often invokes, he was a deeply religious writer who nevertheless celebrated both the symbolic and literal joys of wine.

107. Gladstone bag: a light traveling bag, hinged to open into two compartments.

110. a Dog: i.e., a Cynic. The epithet derives from the behavior of Diogenes (ca. 400–ca. 325 B.C.E.).

117–119. Philae . . . Deir-el-Baheri . . . Abydos: each of these ancient holy places was located on the Nile; each has become an important archeological site.

120. by the ravens fed: the prophet Elijah was miraculously fed by ravens at the command of the Lord. See 1 Kings 17:3–6.

122. barrel copper: native copper occurring in small amounts, separated easily from the rock and shipped in barrels to the smelter.

130. Komitas: (or Gomitas) Gevork'ian (or Keworkian or Sogomon) (1869–1935), Armenian composer, performer, ethnomusicologist, and teacher, who based his compositions on his study of Armenian folksong.

131. neums: symbols in the musical notation of the middle ages derived from the Greek system of accents.

132. with a wild surmise: see John Keats, "On First Looking into Chapman's Homer" (1816).

Epsilon

THE ARGUMENT

This sad, bitter final canto of the Curator's sustained introductory manifesto considers the relation of art to political and social power in terms of his now-familiar metaphor of Babylonian captivity. Particularly with its evocations of Psalm 137, the canto is haunted by the central question (left implicit) of that despondent, angry poem, "How shall we sing the Lord's song in a strange land?" Here the artist lives and sings under the reign of the Idols of the Tribe. The phrase is borrowed from Francis Bacon, for whom it signified hindrances to knowledge arising from human nature itself, but the Curator uses it in a more explicitly political sense, referring to groups of relatively powerful people and their hegemony. Their demand that their heroes be celebrated in art is all but irresistible. Until its defiant, individualistic final stanza, the canto is an unrelieved meditation about the power of political economy to determine consciousness.

The examples of Egyptian funerary art and French Enlightment tapestry inspire anew the mocking laughter of the cynics, for their formal designs reveal evidence as persuasive as animal trails or the sounds of life in the womb that all artists, even the Rembrandts and Miltons, must draw upon the local, the ethos of their particular communities, when they seek to represent the general or eternal.

The power and essential ruthlessness of the rulers of those communities ("thy graven images of blood and class") are represented in a series of animal metaphors. The terrible serpent that coordinates the basilisk's stare, the fangs of the venomous reptiles, and the paralyzing coils of the boa constrictor foreshadow the important serpent imagery in the several political allegories of imperialism and Jim Crow that will be woven into the Curator's narratives. The reference to the ferocious Bulls of Bashan, "which oppress the poor, which crush the needy" (Amos 4:1), leads naturally to the explicit resumption of the theme of Babylonian captivity in the sixth and seventh stanzas. By their very ferocity those bulls also represent a moral influence so great that a mere indication of their will has more effect on human attitudes than the subtle arguments of the lame devil himself. We are creatures of the wind, caught in strange weather, as the metaphor shifts, and the quality of our sail of self, with its four dimensions, at the center of which lies our essential self-definition, is regulated by beliefs we assimilate from our political environment.

When they consider the arts, the powerful, of course, favor time-servers. Even awareness does not help the others. Artists who recognize their predicament—who, at the king of Babylon's festive table, see the handwriting on the wall—by their own perceptiveness and honesty discover the most unconquerable of disasters. Unless they are willing to make an equally unsatisfactory choice between God (which would mean a retreat from immediate social involvement) and Caesar, they have recourse only to lamentation or, losing even the creative energy inspired by mourning, the abandoment of art altogether.

The ideological power of social authority thus seems inescapable, but the Curator, overturning his own logic, leaves one way out. He invokes one of the most pervasive motifs of the African American canon by asserting that the determined artist can go underground. Honoring the imperative of art by discovering the true originals and true treasures beneath the surface of things will not make the artist powerful or prosperous, but it can provide him an infusion of hidden courage.

NOTES

1. idols of the tribe: Francis Bacon, *Novum Organum* 52.

1–5. The idols . . . upon our walls!: cf. "Iota," lines 122–26.

6. walking leaf: a fern of the genus *Camptosorus* that reproduces by generating identical new plants from the tips of its fronds, and thus appears to move from place to place.

8. Deir-el-Baheri frieze: one of the colorful, ornate friezes in the temples at Deir el Baheri, on the necropolis of Thebes.

9. Savonnerie tapestry: the Savonnerie factory was established in Paris in the seventeenth century to provide large, intricate, luxurious carpets for royal use or gifts.

12. Siloam: a pool, southwest of Jerusalem, "by the king's garden, and unto the stairs that go down from the city of David" (Nehemiah 3:15). Jesus cured a blind man by bidding him wash in the waters of Siloam (John 9:1–15).

14. laughing Dogs: cf. note, "Delta," line 110.

15, 16. Cavalier, Roundhead: the generic name for the opposing sides, religious and political, in the English Civil War (1642–48).

22. Lord of the House of the Flies: cf. note, "Alpha," line 5.

25. Ishmael: the outcast son of Abraham, opposed by and to all men, but favored by God (Genesis 16:11–12, 20). In nineteenth-century American writ-

ing Ishmael became a common type of the restless, half-wild, spiritually significant American drifter.

33. Pre-Cambrian: the geological period comprising all time prior to 620 million years ago. The period before which the first life appears. Here, a glimpse of reality so bleak and inhuman that it stupefies the imagination.

36. Bulls of Bashan: see Psalms 22:12–13 as well as Amos 4:1.

38. Diable Boiteux: French, lame devil. A comic opera by Jean Françaix (b. 1912), based on the satire by Alain Lesage (1668–1747), *Le Diable Boiteux* (1707), tells the story of a lame devil who betrays the foibles of humanity in return for being liberated from the powers of a magician's vial.

49. A mute swan not at Coole: the mute swan is the common white swan of Europe and western Asia, which makes no loud cries. The uncommon swans of William Butler Yeats's poem "The Wild Swans at Coole" (1916) speak at least metaphorically for the beauty and mystery of nature caught in the imagination.

49. Beaufort's scale: a wind scale in which the force of the wind, from calm to hurricane, is indicated by numbers.

50. Bizan ware: Bizen ware, named for the old Japanese province where it was made, is known for its reddish-brown, bronzelike finish and the elaborate figures of gods, animals, and mythic creatures with which it was at times decorated.

The sense of the dense figure of lines 47–48 may be: the relationship of the Beaufort scale to a non-Yeatsian mute swan on the one hand and the eeriness of Bizan ware on the other is that it is an artificial reduction, stylization, and muting of nature, which creates a strange analogue to the violence and naturalness of the weather. The scale is related to the reef sail of the preceding stanza as another artifact that regulates the metaphorical voyage of the self.

55. by the waters of Babylon: "By the rivers of Babylon, there we sat down, yea, we wept, when we remembered Zion." Psalms 137:1.

58. Belshazzarian tables: the story of Belshazzar's feast and the handwriting on the wall is told in Daniel 5.

63. Chomolungma: or Jo-mo-lang-ma: the etymology of this Tibetan word is not entirely clear, but *elder* (or, *greater*) *elephant* might be close to its meaning. It is the name of the mountain also called Mount Everest.

65. we hang our harps upon the willows: Psalms 137:2.

66. the Ichabod and Sir Toby Belch of the olive leaf:
    1. Ichabod: "And she named the child Ichabod, saying, The glory is departed from Israel: because the ark of God was taken" (1 Samuel 4:21). This

passage provided the controlling allusion for John Greenleaf Whittier's poem of 1850, "Ichabod," about Daniel Webster's support of the Fugitive Slave Law, and among American abolitionists *Ichabod* became a synonym for *traitor*.

2. Sir Toby Belch: Olivia's bibulous uncle in Shakespeare's *Twelfth Night*. Like other alcoholics, he might very well have developed a thiamine (vitamin B1) deficiency that would affect his appetite.

The sense of Tolson's figure here seems to be that Ichabod and Sir Toby are two types of the good person who, because of self-indulgence or political compromise, have made a separate peace (the olive leaf) and thus deprived themselves of moral nourishment.

70. Sicilian Bull: an instrument of torture, made of brass and shaped like a bull, in which people were roasted alive. Its first victim was its designer, Perillus, who was put to death by the tyrant Phylaris (d. 549 B.C.E.). The story is in Pliny the Elder's *Naturalis Historia*.

70. Sicilian Vespers: the wholesale massacre of the French in Sicily, which began near Palermo at the hour of vespers, Easter Monday, March 30, 1282. It initiated a rebellion against French rule.

71. *non obstante*: Latin, notwithstanding, being no hindrance. A legal term in Britain and the United States.

72–78. Art's yen . . . backbone: cf. Melville, *Moby-Dick*, chapters 102, 103, 104 (A Bower in the Arsacides, Measurement of the Whale's Skeleton, The Fossil Whale).

75. fossick gold: gold found by rummaging around in abandoned mines, etc.

Zeta

THE ARGUMENT

The first narrative of *Harlem Gallery* introduces the half-blind but visionary painter John Laugart, to whom the Curator feels inadequate but with whom he finds himself linked as if by fate. The Curator's passing references to the twins Crispin and Crispinian and Castor and Pollux not only suggest that his life and Laugart's are inextricably mingled but establish for them an exalted astrological and religious context. They are interdependent agents of light in the dark Coalsack Nebula that is Harlem.

Laugart's story grows immediately out of the concerns of "Epsilon." His Yiddish proverb reenergizes the Curator's persistent identification of Black and Jew, and as his narrative unfolds he is revealed as the artist-saboteur who has wrestled successfully with, even as he has been wounded by, the tribal angel. His irony has turned the power of the Bulls of Bashan back against them, and he has survived the metaphorical fires of the Sicilian Bull of brass. Other indications of his exceptional nature include the astronomical setting, the catacomb flat, the comparison to St. John the Divine of the Apocalypse, the echoes of Psalms 53, 141, and 142, which deal with the cries of the righteous man in the midst of corruption, and the Pauline allusion of "through a glass darkly," in which "darkly" also echoes venerable racial proverbs.

While such associations make him exemplary of what defiance can achieve, he is also an object lesson of what the achievement costs. His surroundings are sordid; he is himself half-blind, ragged, and alcoholic. By comparing him to characters from Dickens's *Bleak House*, the Curator evokes the bitterness and myopia that arise from the expense of vision and dreams long defeated. His well-being is dependent upon those rulers of the tribe whom he must affront. The Curator's aside in the eighth stanza about the ignorance of the regents and its effect on his budget acknowledges that he was unable to pay Laugart properly for his great painting. In material terms *Black Bourgeoisie* brought its creator a bottle of strong Dutch gin.

Laugart's canvas is based upon the denunciatory traditions of Hebrew prophecy, but takes its title more immediately from E. Franklin Frazier's classic sociological study, which harshly criticized the black middle class for abandoning its own racial community in order to emulate a white community that would never accept it. It is compared in its effect to the work of several painters (Daumier, Gropper, Picasso, Goya) who were noted for their antibourgeois stance and revolutionary practice. The Jeremian cry for relief from judgment (which the Lord will not hear: Jeremiah 11:11) that Laugart will wring from the babbitted souls of the bourgeosie testifies to the sting of both Laugart's painting and Frazier's book.

In light of the centrality of this prophetic function it is noteworthy that Laugart's first explicit statement about art in the canto is formalistic. He balances his rage by cultivating his technique. He has achieved the unhesitating, meticulous draftsmanship of Edgar Degas or the legendary Greek painter Apelles. Out of the conjunction of such opposites—assailant and victim, lord of life and down-and-outer, impassioned oracle and detached craftsman—he becomes a kind of bohemian saint. His observation in the penultimate stanza about crossing the Rubicon establishes one of the norms of *Harlem Gallery*. Among the artists and artistic types in the poem, he and Mister Starks have indeed crossed the Rubicon. Hideho Heights has not. Neither has the Curator, although he sometimes feels guiltily that he should. However, both his nature and his professional role impel the Curator to build rather than to burn bridges. He is a mediator and compromiser (Ulfilas) rather than a challenger. Meanwhile, John Laugart provides a model of artistic integrity, responsibility, and honor to which all else in *Harlem Gallery* is implicitly compared.

NOTES

2. the Bear: the constellation Ursa Major, invoked here simply to expand contexts.

6. to be or not to be: the echoes of Hamlet's dialectical soliloquy are everywhere in *Harlem Gallery*, their significance constantly stretched, extended, reapplied. For Tolson, Hamlet's dilemma has less to do with life or death, action or inaction, than with the innate and unsolvable cussedness of choice itself. The trade-offs involved in any particular decision in *Harlem Gallery* are almost always equally unacceptable. The way out of their confinement is what the poem seeks to discover.

10. parrot-fish: any of numerous marine percoid fish, chiefly tropical, having teeth fused into a parrotlike beak. They are shaped like the bowl of a spoon.

15. Vuelta tobacco: a celebrated tobacco, grown in the Vuelta Abajo district of western Cuba.

29. Through a glass darkly: 1 Corinthians 13:12.

31. among scattered bones in a stony place: Psalms 53:5; 141:6–7.

32. "No man cares for my soul!": Psalms 142:4.

33. isle of Patmos: the setting of the Revelations of St. John the Divine. Revelations 1:9.

37. dusk of a people's dawn: see note, "Alpha," 2.

39. *Black Bourgeoisie*: E. Franklin Frazier's sociological study was published in 1962, so that its insights and controversy were still fresh as Tolson was composing *Harlem Gallery*.

46. Daumier and Gropper and Picasso: the French caricaturist Honoré Daumier (1808–1879), the American Marxist painter William Gropper (1897–1977), and the celebrated Spanish modernist Pablo Picasso (1881–1973) were all leftists and revolutionaries, in trouble with the law, as well as important artists.

47. As a Californian, I thought *Eureka*: perhaps the Curator's reference to the small coastal city in northwest California does link him biographically to the state, but the detail is of no further significance in *Harlem Gallery*. Throughout the poem Tolson locates episodes in the lives of his characters

in real places in the United States, which are used, so far as I can tell, solely for the latent symbolism of their names.

48. Ulfilas: a Gothic bishop (ca. 311–383) who devised the Gothic alphabet and prepared the first translation of the Bible into a Germanic language. He was known for his skill at negotiation and compromise in his missionary work.

53–54. Goya's etching, *She Says Yes to Anyone*: perhaps the etching by Francisco Goya (1746–1828) entitled "They say yes and give their hand to the first comer," the second plate in his series of satires, *Los Caprichos*. The etching shows the sinister wedding of a masked but beautiful young woman to an ugly old gentleman.

55. their babbitted souls: like the soul of George Babbitt, Sinclair Lewis's complacent arch-bourgeois in the novel (1922) bearing his name. Tolson may also be playing on the metalurgical sense of *babbitted*, which would mean lined or reinforced with babbitt metal.

55. a Jeremian cry: Jeremiah 11:11–12; 14:12.

57. beyond the bull of brass: see note, "Epsilon," 68.

71. to gull his face: the Curator's meaning—that he searched for clues in Laugart's face—seems clear enough, but I can find no precedent in English for this usage of *gull*.

72. umbrella bird: a South American bird of the genus *Cephalopterus*, entirely black, with a radiating crest curving forward over the head.

73. haply black: *Othello* 3.3.263.

77–78. the lunar day of Saint Crispin: Crispin and his brother Crispinian, third-century missionaries to Gaul and martyrs, are the patron saints of shoemakers, saddlers, and tanners. Their day is October 25.

81. Castor and Pollux: in Greek mythology, twin brothers, sons of Leda and Zeus, whose astronomical figures form the constellation Gemini.

81. St. Elmo's fire: celestial fireworks; the colorful electrical discharge that is seen around masts, trees, weathervanes, or wingtips during electrical storms.

82. Harlem's Coalsack Way: the Coal Sack is a dark cloud of gas and dust, thirty light years in diameter, in the Southern Cross.

90. a Jacob that wrestles Tribus: the story of Jacob's wrestling is told in Genesis 32:24–32.

93. silver nitrate: a poisonous crystalline irritant salt that has healing properties in external use as an astringent, antiseptic, and germicide.

106. Gomorrhean blues: God's destruction of Sodom and Gomorrah with brimstone and fire is described in Genesis 19:24.

119. seventh facial nerve: the facial nerve is either of the seventh pair of cranial nerves that supply the gustatory function and the muscles of facial expression.

122. terre verte: a grayish green pigment. Tolson is probably also playing on the literal meaning of the French (green earth).

124. a Bleak House grotesque: characters in Charles Dickens's *Bleak House* (1853) become grotesque by expending their lives in the pursuit of futile lawsuits.

126. whispering bell: also, California yellow bells: an annual plant (*Emmenanthe penduliflora*) of the family *Hydrophyllaceae* with pendulous yellow flowers.

128. like a Degas weaver: Edgar Degas (1834–1917), French impressionist painter, was known both for his ability to capture the spontaneity of human motion and for his meticulous draftsmanship.

129. *dégagé*: French, free, easy, unconstrained.

130. Apelles: Pliny, in his *Natural History* tells how Apelles (the most famous painter of his era, ca. 330 B.C.E.) one day called on Protogenes, a fellow painter, and finding him not at home, drew a small fine line through a painting of a table done by Protogenes. Protogenes, in turn, returning home, recognized who had drawn the fine line, and immediately drew a finer one through it. Apelles, returning a second time, drew an even finer straight line through the one drawn by Protogenes, thereby ending the competition. The fine line was his signature.

133. our master Rodin: Auguste Rodin (1840–1917), French sculptor. The French writer Michel Georges-Michel described how Rodin fell into a lyric revery over a dish of tripes, the food of his childhood, in a humble Paris restaurant, and compared the color and texture of the meat to fine cathedral stone.

149. the Acheron: a river of Thesprotia in southern Epirus that in ancient times was reputed to mark the entrance to Hades. Being ferried across Acheron by the boatman Charon marked the passage from life to death.

157. Schiedam gin: a strongly flavored gin, named for the city of its origin in southwestern Netherlands.

Eta

THE ARGUMENT

"Eta" is the only canto in which the action is ostensibly dated. The newsboy's cry of line 18 apparently refers to the death of German General Erwin Rommel in 1944. But that isolated detail is misleading. References to the Angry Young Men and the Beat Generation ("Alpha"), black major league baseball stars ("Xi"), Boris Pasternak ("Chi"), and the Centennial of the Emancipation Proclamation ("Phi"), among many others, suggest that the primary action of *Harlem Gallery* must take place later, within a few years of 1960. In a larger sense, however, time in *Harlem Gallery* has little to do with biographical consistency or historical sequence, and the poem may fairly be said to occupy some enormous present of collective memory and experience, encompassing roughly the years 1930–60.

The canto introduces another exemplary central character, Dr. Obi Nkomo, the Curator's professional associate and, as it were, alternate self. He shares many characteristics and attitudes with the Curator but also represents, in contrast to the Curator's radical racial mixture, the proverbial wisdom, emotional resource, and relatively uncomplicated moral vision of an unmediated ancestral past. He is a Bantu—of the linguistic group characterized by its artistic and intellectual legacy—and a Zulu, of the Bantu tribe famous for courage and martial exploits. There are several allusions to his warrior's heritage (lines 22, 90, 209–11, 271).

With its noise, raciness, and low-life sexual comedy, the physical setting of "Eta," like the name of Aunt Grindle's establishment itself, brings together opposed cultural values and indicates the range of class and cultural contexts in which Nkomo and the Curator feel comfortable. The raucous sexual energy of the place, expressed in the jukebox blues, the prostitute of line 174, and the contretemps between Dipsy Muse and his wife, defies, as Nkomo observes, the Christian moralism of the West (162–63). At Aunt Grindle's the idiom of the blues is allied with Nkomo's "rebel Bantu song."

Nkomo is introduced in answers to three questions about him: Guy Delaporte III's, the yellow-skin doper's, and his own. He begins as an objectified alter ego, defined and described by the Curator, and concludes with his own account of his experience and its meaning.

The characterization of Nkomo following Guy Delaporte III's echo of the disciples' question about Jesus, "What manner of man is this?," is essentially artistic in nature. Nkomo's quotation of Picasso's aphorism about the "lie of the artist" indicates that he shares the Curator's priorities concerning art. So does his alternately ironic and angry contention with the philistinish judgments of the regents. Articulating his *"idée fixe"* about art and life, he all but repeats the Curator's argument from "Gamma" about the selectivity of art as a way of knowing reality and understanding character. Nature is so complex, Nkomo says, the various aspects of human tridimensionality so interwoven, that no individual taken in his or her entirety can be known as fully as characters (Iago, etc.) from books are known. The Curator's playful, perhaps too exclusively Western challenge to this theory, asking whether philosophy and history are thus merely empty shows, provokes him to hint that the Curator may be burdened with too much complexity and inspires a new series of provocative questions.

Nkomo's ruminations about the complexity of life and the clarity of art also lead him to conclude that the pure villainy represented by a Judas Iscariot or Iago is not to be found in nature. That affirmation extends the implications of his *"All hail to Man,"* which is contrasted to classical and Christian reifications of the idea of evil. He is characteristically respectful and generous with regard to others ("nobody was a nobody to him") and progressivist in outlook.

The comic interlude of Dipsy Muse and the misogynic doper leads Nkomo to reflect, first, on the bad tricks the penis ("incised horsetail") can play on a man, then on the comparative value of the erotic in African (or generally "primitive") and Christian Western cultures. The primitive used his acknowledgment of Eros to confront death, but the Westerner stifles, deforms, or is indifferent to the life force. He is like an eagle so out of touch with its own nature that it cannot nourish itself on its natural prey (there is also clearly a bawdy pun on "cocks" in Nkomo's exemplary metaphor). Nkomo, however, has in his own life and experience resolved this and other oppositions between the primitive and civilized worldviews. He is, again like the Curator, but in other applications, a bridger and unifier.

The second question, the giraffine doper's unwitting echo of the great Socratic challenge, provokes Nkomo to riddles about the relationship of identity to environment, with their obvious racial applications. His retelling of the African folktale about the eagle who thought he was a chicken is both historically and personally suggestive, but it only returns him to the Socratic question.

His "I wish I knew" acknowledges the tacit third question of the canto, and it invites a response from the Curator, who finds Nkomo's character too complex to be expressed directly. He undertakes a metaphorical history of a man who has by assimilation and rejection added to his preeminent African identity the powers of Christianity, and by experience and attention the powerful Western ideas of change, particularly socialistic ones. The result is a true cosmopolitan, like the world citizens of the classic past.

He has a temper, Nkomo, and is not above winning an argument by resorting to a venerable double entendre, but he is clear-eyed and sees beyond roles to the essential humanity and the great objectives. His own understanding of his unfinished pilgrimage is that his powers of balance and memory have brought him through a number of valleys of the shadow to an appreciation of the nature of history. He is a rationalist and a realist. He concludes his lyrical reverie with the prediction that Apocalypse or Armageddon, whether political or moral, will be a function of history rather than of revelation.

NOTES

4. dinoceras: not a dinosaur, more like a mammoth: a large prehistoric elephantlike mammal with a small brain.

7–10. *Come back, Baby . . . don't mean maybe*: this funky quasi-blues verse appears to be Tolson's own.

18. Desert Fox: the epithet was applied to General Erwin Rommel (1891–1944) because of his success in armored combat against British forces in the North African desert early in World War II.

22. the Bread-and-Cheese War: a peasant uprising in North Holland in the late fifteenth century.

33. Lethe: the river in Hades whose waters caused forgetfulness in those who drank of them.

34. Black Manhattan: i.e., Harlem; the allusion is to James Weldon Johnson's (1871–1938) historical study, *Black Manhattan* (1930).

36–37. what manner of man is this?: see note, "Beta," 5.

57. horse-opera god: i.e., *deus ex machina*; a horse opera is a western movie.

57. Ultra: an extreme or radical conservative. The word was used chiefly in reference to ultraroyalists in French politics of the early nineteenth century. The colors of lines 58–60 reflect European political symbolism of the revolutionary era: black for anarchy, white for reaction, red for leftist revolution.

62–63. Absurd life shakes its ass's ears in Cendrars'—not Nkomo's—stable: Tolson elsewhere attributed the sentiment to *Eloge de la vie dangereuse* (1938), by Blaise Cendrars (1887–1961), French traveler and man of letters.

65. hag-fish: primitive marine fishes of the order *Cyclostomata*, or jawless fishes. Parasites and scavengers, they lurk in muddy bottoms waiting for prey, and have rows of horny teeth that enable them to fasten themselves to other fish and eat their way into the fish's body.

66. haute-lisse: French, high-warp.

67. Rivera: Diego Rivera (1886–1957), Mexican painter, known for his socialism and his monumental public frescoes.

69. *fresco-buono*: the art of painting on a freshly spread moist lime plaster with pigments suspended in a water vehicle.

72. Kelvin scale: a scale for measurement based on absolute zero.

75. an escape running wild: in botany, an *escape* is a commonly cultivated plant that has run wild or has sprung up from self-sown seeds of a cultivated individual.

81–82. Kiefekil . . . Iago: obviously a list of familiar literary villains, but Kiefekil remains an unfamiliar name.

87. the millstone: in Matthew 18:6 and elsewhere in the gospels, the millstone symbolizes the oppressive burden of the unredeemed worldly life.

88. Julio Sigafoos: Tolson's note (in his papers at the Library of Congress) on this character reads: "a feral 12-year-old boy found in the woods near Cleveland (?). He had been raised by wild dogs. He went on all fours and had the habits of the canine. He was captured, schooled, and became a specialist in astrophysics. He was killed, I'm told, chasing a car!"

90. an assagai blade: an assagai (or assegai) is a slender hardwood spear, tipped with iron, used in southern Africa.

94. *vis viva*: Latin, living force; the force of a moving body calculated as the product of its mass and the square of its velocity.

98. cypress lawn: a silk or cotton gauze fabric, originally made in Cyprus, often used for mourning garments. Tolson evokes it simply for the peculiar shading of its black color.

100. fraxinella: a perennial herb (*Dictamnus albus*) whose flowers, in hot weather, emit a flammable vapor.

107. Uhlan: a uhlan is a mounted soldier of Tartar origins, whose service, individually or in units, in various European armies, has been long and distinguished. Tolson's use of Uhlan as if it were a personal name is not clear, but may owe something to the comic ballad *Breitmann as an Uhlan* (1871) by the American dialect humorist Charles Godfrey Leland (1824–1903).

117. *Yarmouth yawl*: of the several towns in the eastern maritime United States and Canada named after the English port, Yarmouth in southeastern

Maine is probably best known for the building of traditional sailing craft. A yawl is a light vessel, with a large mainmast forward and a much smaller mast far aft.

125–128. *The black widow . . . get rid of you*: Memphis Minnie (Minnie Douglas 1897–1973) recorded "Black Widow Spider" in 1939. Tolson's lines do not appear to be traditional blues, but may be based on her version of the song.

135. Ben Franklin's beggarly bag: "An empty bag cannot stand upright." *Poor Richard's Almanac* 1740.

145. morris dance: a traditional English dance, performed by men at pageants, processions, and spring festivals, in which the dancers often assume oversized costumes representing folk heroes.

154. ice plant: an Old World herb (*Mesembryananthemum crystallinum*) that gets its name from the glistening vesicles that cover its leaves.

168. vegetable ivory: the hard white opaque endosperm of the ivory nut, which can be substituted for ivory, especially in the manufacture of buttons. Nkomo seems to be using it as a generic term for the artifacts of civilization and as an invitation to the Curator's pun.

171–172. *as Urdu Arabic characters*: Urdu is a grammatically and phonetically Indic language, but it is written in a modified form of the Arabic alphabet.

174. Scarlet Sister Mary: a fallen woman, after the novel (1928) of sexual freedom and Christian penitence by Julia Peterkin (1880–1961). The novel, which won a Pulitzer Prize and was dramatized in 1930, dealt with Gullah life in South Carolina.

184. a squeaking Cleopatra boy: *Antony and Cleopatra* 5.2.219–21: "I shall see / Some squeaking Cleopatra boy my greatness / I' the posture of a whore." Cleopatra is speaking and she is using *boy* as a verb.

186. like the undershot of a Poncelet water wheel: i.e., very quickly. A poncelet waterwheel is an undershot waterwheel used on rivers with a high volume of water but short falls.

193–194. a fish from a river Jordan . . . Asphalt Sea: the Romans and Greeks called the Dead Sea the *Sea of Asphalt*, as did the Jewish historian Flavius Josephus. The Jordan's strong current carries many fish to the Dead Sea, where they die in the highly saline water.

199. Ixion: the Greek Cain, whose earthly offense was in murdering kin and who subsequently offended Zeus by his attentions to Hera. Zeus cast him into Erebus where he was bound upon a revolving wheel of fire.

211. Chakas: Chaka (1773–1828), the greatest of Zulu heroes. From 1818 to 1828 he was the primary ruler and military genius of the Zulus, whom he led on a conquest of what is now Natal.

217. Aquila: Latin, eagle.

243. the Giant Grim: in part 2 of John Bunyan's *Pilgrim's Progress* the Giant Grim, a slayer of pilgrims, tries to stop Mrs. Christian's journey to the Celestial City, but is instead slain by Mr. Great Heart.

245. Scot and plot: Tolson is probably playing on *scot and lot*, a now archaic usage meaning: obligations of all kinds taken as a whole.

248. dream of Abraham's bosom bottled: that is, Nkomo has given up on Christianity. For Abrahan's bosom, see Luke 16:22.

253. Heraclitean, Fabian, Marxian: Nkomo would have been talking and listening to talk about change—change as the constant principle of reality as the Greek philosopher Heraclitus (6th–5th century B.C.E.) defined it; or slow, orderly change in the forms of society, as the Fabian socialists of late nineteenth- and early twentieth-century England wished to develop it; or change as violent revolution in the Marxist sense.

259. Seven Walls of Water: the seven seas.

264–265. the symbol *Q*: "q. (in a ship's log) = squalls" (*OED*).

271. Dandie Dinmount terrier: the dandie dinmont terrier is a small, short-legged, rough-coated Scots breed, developed to hunt small animals. It is known for its intelligence, affectionate good nature, and utter fearlessness.

279–281. I've called . . . sorry for it: the model for Nkomo's verbal mischief is the Anglo-Irish playwright and legislator Richard Brinsley Sheridan (1751–1816), who upon being asked to apologize for insulting a fellow member of Parliament replied: "Mr. Speaker, I said the honorable member was a liar it is true and I am sorry for it. The honorable member may place the punctuation where he pleases."

293. black Scylla and white Charybdis: see *Odyssey* 12 for the classical parable about the narrow line of discipline and sanity humanity must maintain if it is to find a way between the equally difficult and forbidding horrors of the inhuman life.

295. *vile-canaille*: French, vile rabble.

295. nigger heavens: the balconies to which patrons of color were restricted in segregated theaters.

301. a Dumb Ox (like young Aquinas): Albertus Magnus, his tutor, said of the young Thomas Aquinas (1224–1274), Italian theologian and philosopher,

"The dumb ox will one day fill the world with his lowing." The nickname derived in part from Thomas's great bulk and taciturnity.

305–307. Gibbon . . . *Dies Irae!*: Edward Gibbon (1737–1794), the English historian of the monumental *Rise and Fall of the Roman Empire* (1776–88), was born at Putney, Surrey. Thomas of Celano (ca. 1200–1255), Italian Franciscan friar, is the reputed composer of the *Dies Irae* (Latin, *Days of Wrath*), or Mass for the Dead.

Theta

THE ARGUMENT

This brief interlude in the developing narratives of *Harlem Gallery* extends Dr. Nkomo's sense, in "Eta," of being a trekker between two worlds. It is a meditation on the dialectical relationships between nature and art, their essential congruence of sustenance and vision, their differing consistencies and satisfactions. It also clarifies and refines the pervasive metaphor by which art is defined in relation to the sexual life.

The canto opens in a discord of elements, biological and cultural, that should be as complementary and mutually interdependent as Siamese twins. In calming their fury the hospitable Marquise de Matrix significantly qualifies the famous first line of Robert Frost's "Mending Wall." Her emendation emphasizes that hers is an artistic resolution, a cultivated synthesis of form and content, thought and feeling, black and white, male and female. Art creates bonds as strong and "natural" as biology's; it makes marriages that defy both the restrictions of the local or circumstantial and the quixotic rationalizing of critics. It can be known and tested only according to its own authenticity and durability. In its essential integrity and impenetrable unity it is like nature itself. Both nature and art are insusceptible to analysis and false oppositions; both are primal sources of nourishment.

However, the acknowledgment of "naked need" at the end of the fifth stanza announces a new dialectical opposition, which builds upon the inherent difficulties and tragic consequences in the marriages of the Duchess of Malfi and Romeo and Juliet, so that the disparities between art as a reality of the synthesizing imagination and happiness (or unhappiness) as a reality of natural life are explored. Although art must be wooed like a lover, one's alliance with it resembles marriage rather than concupiscence. It differs from concupiscent happiness, to which it is related, by its qualities of virtue, control, culture, and fidelity. Happiness is defined rather as a whim of nature, in terms of treachery, shallowness, lust, and chance.

The final stanza both dramatizes the cost of pursuing a purely natural happiness and brings "Theta" full cycle. The canto opened in a jangle of elements, all daydream and illusion, in need of art, unqualified by the realism of the natural. It ends in a naturalistic nihilism and violence (whether murder or suicide), in need of restraint and decorum, unalleviated by the resourcefulness of the imagination. KKK's name and behavior realize the latent violence in the metaphorical black and white keys of the opening stanza. The fanciful, inconsequential setting of castles in Spain is displaced by the terrible fires of the Valley of the sons of Hinnom, where the heathen gods live on and unclean things are brought to be destroyed.

NOTES

1. *château en Espagne*: French, castle in Spain.

4. Changs and Engs: Chang and Eng (1811–1874) were the original Siamese twins, so called because of their place of birth. They were exhibited in the United States and abroad, became American citizens, and in 1843 married two sisters.

10. Duchess of Malfi: from the tragedy of that name (ca. 1614) by John Webster (ca. 1580–ca. 1625), in which the duchess marries out of her class and is eventually murdered because of her action.

12. Something there is in art that does not love a wall: cf. Robert Frost, "Mending Wall" (1914): "Something there is that does not love a wall."

17. What dread hand: the fearsome creative power of William Blake's "The Tyger" (1794).

19. a nixie says, "Nix!": see note, "Delta," 55.

22. *the trial of pyx*: the process, in Great Britain, whereby sample coins are tested for weight and fineness.

26. Montague's son and Capulet's daughter: i.e., Romeo and Juliet.

34. Ye knights of the Critics' Circus: cf. "Delta," 9.

38. Cybele: in Greek mythology, the Great Mother, primarily a goddess of wild nature and fertility.

39. *Non Nobis*: Latin, not to us. In Psalm 115 which these words begin, the sense is: not to us [but to Thee] the praise or glory.

45. alma maters: Latin, beloved mothers.

48. *rete mirabile*: Latin, wonderful net, a small but dense network of blood vessels formed by the breaking up of a larger vessel into branches that usually reunite into one trunk.

51. nucellus: a mass of thin-walled cells that composes the central and chief part of the body of an ovule and that contains the embryo sac and is surrounded by one or more integuments.

53–54. the integument . . . a naked need: Robert Paltock (1697–1767), English lawyer and author, was best known for his novel *The Life and Adventures of Peter Wilkins, a Cornish Man* (1751). Marooned like Robinson Crusoe, Wilkins meets Indian-like creatures who are capable of flying but are encased by their wings when not flying. Wilkins discovers when he tries to make love to one of the creatures that the wings' membrane (integument) is extremely tough and resistant.

56. mood indigo: according to Duke Ellington and Barney Bigard, "You ain't had blues until you've had this mood indigo." This famous song, recorded in October 1930 under the title "Dreamy Blues," was Ellington's first popular hit.

58. *jeu de mots*: French, witty words.

64–65. dubious as Galen's sight of a human body dissected: Galen (ca. 130–ca. 200) the Greek physician and scientist, developed experimental anatomy and systematized the medical knowledge of his time. So far as is known, his dissections were confined to animals. The sense of Tolson's figure is not entirely clear but may be that Art, like Galen, is resistant to too much unmediated reality.

74. *a capriccio*: Italian, whimsical.

74. Tyche: in Greek mythology, fortune or chance.

79. the alley of Hinnom: the valley of the sons of Hinnom is west of Jerusalem. It is one of the sinister places of the Hebrew scriptures, in ill repute because of the connection of Tophet, a high place in the valley, with Molech worship. See especially 2 Kings 23:10, 2 Chronicles 28:3 and 33:6, Jeremiah 32:35.

80. *belle dame*: French, beautiful lady. Almost certainly Tolson has in mind the fearsome seductress of John Keats's "La Belle Dame Sans Merci."

Iota

THE ARGUMENT

The collections of the Harlem Gallery are both guarded and made accessible by the Curator and Dr. Nkomo, who greet the fashionable opening-day crowd generously but with considerable irony. With his characteristic wit and urbanity, Nkomo wears, in Paul Laurence Dunbar's phrase, "the mask" that hides both racial and social anger. His mockingly ambiguous "aloha" only faintly echoes the "dark laughter" of the racial wisdom the gallery expresses. Here the conventional nightingales of Europe are displaced by the African pepper bird, which again announces the revolutionary art and the revolution invoked in "Alpha."

The exhibition is housed in four wings. Paintings are organized, not by the usual historical or generic categories, but according to technique and the spiritual resource of modern black people each room makes available to a common humanity. The Curator and Nkomo thus stand at the intersection of the converging lines of force of the African American tradition (cf. "the four dimensions of A-is-A", "Epsilon," 47), to which they are guides.

The East Wing holds stereochromatic murals ("waterglass on dry plaster"), both historical and visionary, depicting the sweep and rhythm of a prophetic and ethical tradition. Echoes of Isaiah define its tone and grandeur. In these appropriately large documentary paintings, the collective successes and defeats of a people, impressed in the sensibilities of individual artists, are by the artist's craft fixed in plaster. They represent a tradition wrung more from experience than revelation, a moral resource and discipline that can instruct one's response to the challenge of the eternal "*Now.*"

The West Wing exhibits paintings based upon, or containing, elements of "primitive" art or primitivism of vision, which the Curator several times invokes in the course of *Harlem Gallery*. Artists who recover the freshness of perception and straightforward artistic vocabulary of traditional peoples give character to the otherwise featureless streets and alleys of our modern world. At the same time, they earn the capacity to envision fundamental innocence, nobility, and suffering—as if the human drama were "prelithic," almost purely natural, uncomplicated by concerns of time and civilization.

The North Wing houses portraits in encaustic, the medium appropriate to the intense compassion of the racial vision expressed there. This part of the exhibit celebrates the rich variety of character and psychic resource of "Negroid diversity," from the sort of country-boy innocence suggested by "Kafiristan gaucherie" (although "Kafir" also carries a bitter ambiguity), to the height of cultivation ("Attic wit and nerve"). This human plentitude, rather than American social problems, is the wellspring of inspiration ("Aganippe") for African America. It summons the full capacities of painterly technique and imagination.

The South Wing displays portraits of immediate African American ancestors in fresco and secco, the modes perhaps reflecting the oppositions and contradictions in this part of the collection. The "dusky Lion Hearts," gentlemen and galoots, who were involuntary pioneers on the moral and cultural frontiers of white America are now treated as Idols of the Tribe and thus associated with the cultural tyranny of the bulls of Bashan. Their portraits are hyperbolic and amateurishly done. Even though the reverence paid these elders inspires mirth in Nkomo, who understands the ironies of genealogy, the Curator, perhaps because of his Americanness, views them with mixed emotions. He notes the courage and authenticity of these voiceless forerunners and feels that the pretentiousness, lack of discrimination, and tastelessness by which they are painted are simply signs of cultural immaturity.

Even though the native "Lion Hearts" have for the moment been preempted by the fashionable and powerful, they represent the true racial vernacular. The canto ends with the Curator's invocation of artists who, cultivating the complementary studies of self and history, have achieved, through the particularities of the vernacular, a triumphant human statement.

NOTES

4. Hrothgarian hosts: in *Beowulf* Hrothgar is king of the Danes, who presides over the great mead hall Heorot.

11. he wears the mask:
> We wear the mask that grins and lies,
> It hides our cheeks and shades our eyes,—
> This debt we pay to human guile;
> With torn and bleeding hearts we smile,
> And mouth with myriad subtleties.
> —Paul Laurence Dunbar, "We Wear the Mask" (1895)

11. "Aloha!": the Hawaiian word is used to express either greeting or farewell.

16. Agib: the third calendar (a member of a begging order of dervishes) in the *Arabian Nights*. He lost one of his eyes because of overcuriosity.

23. Mr. Rockefeller's Jericho: in 1933 the Rockefellers commissioned the Mexican artist Diego Rivera to paint six inspirational murals near the main entrance of the RCA building in Rockefeller Center in New York City. The socialistic murals Rivera produced became the subject of intense public controversy and the Rockefellers had them secretly brought down (like the walls of Jericho: Joshua 6) during the night. The poet Archibald MacLeish "replaced" the murals with six "panels" of his own in "Frescoes for Mr. Rockefeller's City" (1933).

24. the new New Order of things: "Novus Ordo Secolorum" (a new order of the ages) appears on the Great Seal of the United States, as well as on the one-dollar bill. The phrase was also used in the 1930s and 1940s to describe the realignment of nations under Germany and Japan. It has been used since.

25. dark dark laughter: in the novel *Dark Laughter* (1925) by Sherwood Anderson (1876–1941), the protagonist, John Stockton, abandons his comfortable middle-class life to become a drifter and common laborer. The story of his travels is accompanied by a chorus of "dark laughter" and song by the unrepressed black people who are contrasted with the spiritual sterility of machine civilization.

31. pinaster: or, cluster pine (*pinus pinaster*), a pyramidal pine of the Mediterranean region.

32–33. Ironies . . . grass: see Isaiah 40:4–8.

37–38. waterglass on dry plaster: the method of painting stereochromatic murals. Waterglass is a water-soluble substance consisting of sodium silicate of various compositions, used industrially and otherwise chiefly as an adhesive.

39. teeth of the parrot-fish: see note, "Zeta," 10.

61. tomtoms of Benin: Benin was the center of a black African kingdom that flourished from the fourteenth through the seventeenth centuries. Benin ironwork, carved ivory, and bronze portrait busts rank with the finest African art. The area is identified with the appearance of African artifacts in Europe early in the twentieth century, which, particularly through Picasso, greatly influenced the development of modernism.

64. rue Fromentin and Lenox Avenue: familiar streets, central to writers and artists, in Paris and Harlem respectively.

65. consecrated like the Brescian Blackamoor: perhaps Moretto da Brescia, or Il Moretto (Alessandro Bonvicino, 1498–1554), Italian painter, master of the Brescian school, who was active and much admired as a painter of altarpieces and other religious works. His assumed name (*il moretto: the brunette*) means only that he was dark complexioned, but it is related etymologically to the word for *moor*.

67. Somerscales (the eternal naïf): there appears to be no very persuasive candidate for the subject of this reference. Robert Huot suggests the self-trained Victorian British painter of maritime subjects, Thomas Jacques Somerscales (1842–1927), but while his is the only name that anyone has turned up, he does not make even an awkward fit for Tolson's allusion.

77. madder-bleached: madder bleach is a method of bleaching cotton goods in order to obtain a pure white ground for printing.

79. agueweeds: or boneset, is a name given to several American herbs, genus *Eupatorium*, having white flowers and leaves that appear to be pierced by the stem, once used as a household remedy.

81. mistigris: a card game, or, in it, a blank card or joker that can be used as a wild card.

89. Kafiristan: a Kafir is a member of a group of southern African Bantu-speaking peoples of Ngoni stock. *Kafir* is also used disparagingly by South African whites to describe black South Africans.

91. Aganippe: in Greek mythology, a nymph, and her spring on Mt. Helicon, a source of inspiration sacred to the Muses.

97. agate snail: of the African family *Achatinadae*, which includes the largest land molluscs. Its shell is iridescent and multicolored, like the chalcedony stone for which it is named.

99–100. the juice from the tender roots of the Smyrna-fig: the milky juice of the fig tree was recommended by Cennino Cennini in the fifteenth century as an additive to egg tempura.

107. the egg trot in the design: in colloquial British usage, an *egg trot* was a gentle amble, like the pace of an egg-wife riding to market with her wares.

117. on Toynbee's frontiers: Arnold Joseph Toynbee (1889–1975) British historian, who postulated in his highly influential *A Study of History* (1934–54) that all civilizations at some point reach natural barriers to their growth — that is, frontiers, like the Great Plains in the history of the United States.

123–127. The idols . . . our walls!": cf. "Epsilon," 1–5.

128. Heralds' College: or, College of Arms, a British corporation, dependent upon the crown, whose chief responsibility is the designing, grant, and registration of armorial bearings.

130. the Order of the White Eagle: historically, there are several noble societies or awards bearing this name, but Tolson uses it here without historical reference, as a synecdoche for white obsessions about racial purity.

138–139. Prince Eugene's greenhouse chessboard of heredity: Eugene, Prince of Savoy (François Eugene de Savoie Carignan, 1663–1736), general in the service of the Holy Roman Emperor, was one of the great soldiers of modern history, especially famous for his victories against the Turks. He spent the whole of his adult life fighting battles in Europe, often in wars of succession, sometimes against his own relatives.

142. a Bourbon: the French family, champions of legitimism, which ruled in France and other European countries from 1589 until well into the twentieth century.

145. mourners' bench: in evangelical Christianity, a seat near the pulpit during revivals, reserved for those particularly concerned about their spiritual condition.

155–156. seven against Thebes in seven-league Afroamerican boots: these references to Greek tragic myth and fairy tale mean no more than that the Lion Hearts have been apotheosized.

159. obelized: marked as doubtful or spurious.

161. Origen: (ca. 185–ca. 254), Christian theologian and scholar, one of the Greek Fathers of the Church, famous for his teaching and his zeal for truth.

164. stag tick's: not a tick but a fly (*Lipoptera cervi*) of the family Hippoboscidae, parasitic upon the red deer. It has wings upon maintaining its maturity, but sheds them soon after settling upon its host.

168. dry bones of Highgate: Tolson several times, in *Harlem Gallery* and elsewhere, uses *Highgate* to mean some proverbial place of suffering. He appears to have derived this synecdoche from *Sublime Porte*, as a generic name for the regime of the Ottoman Turks. See note, "Xi," 340.

The valley of the dry bones is described in Ezekiel 37:1–11.

176: bee bread: a bitter yellowish brown pollen stored up in honeycomb cells and used mixed with honey by bees for food.

177–180. like Balzac . . . bourgeois reality: Balzac's (see note, "Gamma," 22) celebration of the whole life of his time and place is contrasted to the dispassionate naturalistic and scientific analyses of Emile Zola (1840–1902).

Kappa

THE ARGUMENT

A dangerous moment occurs during the course of the first day's exhibition when Guy Delaporte III, the poem's chief representative of the cultural power of capitalism, comes face to face with John Laugart's denunciatory *Black Bourgeoisie.* The antagonism of forces is deepened and made more precarious by the circumstances of Delaporte's position with the Board of Regents of the Gallery, the sentimental, if hypocritical, Christianity by which he justifies himself, and the tactics of conquest and destruction he has developed in his career as a businessman. He is also having trouble controlling his voluptuous wife and may thus be in psychic need of a situation in which he can assert himself. For the moment, his confrontation with Laugart's painting results in a standoff, but the explosiveness of the coincidence that brought together the various factors of position and character is acknowledged by the Curator's reference in "Lambda" to the concussive assaults of chance.

Upon encountering *Black Bourgeoisie,* Delaporte intuitively, spontaneously accepts its authenticity and power. While his wife is shielded from its heathen influence by a euphoniously but ironically named churchman, Delaporte feels that he has been isolated and set at bay, like Ishmael, and is compared to the African Cape Buffalo, which is notorious for its ferocity when wounded.

Standing aside, observing the episode, Dr. Nkomo and the Curator react differently to the danger it poses. Nkomo sees in it the initiation of a purposeful, creative dialectical process. The status quo, he says in a series of figures, is a sort of death, so that we should view the assault on Delaporte's complacency with a restrained and wary amusement. The Curator, however, sees the tense moment as an example of the irresistible power of the Idols of the Tribe that he had analyzed pessimistically in "Epsilon." To Nkomo's analogy of the sand-box tree, which suggests that they ignore the misleading emotional violence of the moment and let art go about its quiet work, he replies that he is out of patience, tired of doing without. As he calls Isaiah's watchman to witness, his spirits have sunk so low that he can feel the despair that drove the important Fauve painter André Derain when he acknowledged what Marx called "the iron law of Necessity" by, in effect, selling out to the power of an oppressive German state.

However, as he did in "Epsilon," the Curator suddenly reverses his mood at the end. Here, he seems to respond to Nkomo's faith in the processes of history by invoking historical memory, thus resolving their disagreement. His heroic example of European modernists who spiritually defied the German conquests of France in 1870 and 1940 defeats the implicit argument of a Derain and the implications of his own dark broodings.

NOTES

2. Vanity Fair: the novel of 1847–48 by William Makepeace Thackeray (1811–1863) describes the ultimately futile and meaningless lives of socially ambitious people. Thackeray drew his title from John Bunyan's *Pilgrim's Progress* (1678), in which the fair in the town Vanity, where all sorts of worldly delights are for sale, is set up by Beelzebub, Appolyon, and Legion. Bunyan took *his* symbolism from the lament of the preacher: "Vanity of vanities, saith the Preacher, vanity of vanities; all *is* vanity" (Ecclesiastes 1:2).

4. oddlegs: an oddleg is a caliper with the points of its legs bent in the same direction.

9. Atlantean S: that is, held (for display) aloft, as Atlas holds up the world.

12. Bola Boa Enterprises: Mr. Delaporte's company name coordinates the names of two constrictors: the great snake of the South American jungle and the bola, a weapon that consists of two or more stone or iron balls attached to the end of a cord, used for hurling at and entangling an animal.

16. *mortorio*: Italian, funeral, or, mass for the dead.

19. the Ark's mercy seat: the mercy seat is a golden plate resting on the Ark of the Covenant. See Exodus 25:17.

23. Sugar Hill: the wealthy neighborhood overlooking Harlem, named from the slang term for money.

27. *Sweet Mystery of Life*: this song, lyrics by Rida Johnson, music by Victor Herbert, from Herbert's musical comedy *Naughty Marietta* (1910), remained popular for decades.

29. surah silk: a soft, light lustrous fabric, usually made of silk or rayon in twill weave.

30. about it and about: cf. Edward FitzGerald's *Rubáiyát of Omar Khayyám* (4th ed., 1879), quatrain 27:

> Myself when young did eagerly frequent
> Doctor and Saint, and heard great argument
> About it and about: but evermore
> Came out by the same door where in I went.

38. Hagar's son: Ishmael (Genesis 16:11–12, 20)

39. *ultima ratio*: Latin, final reckoning; last resort.

41. galago: also known as "bush baby," a small, nocturnal African primate of the *Loris* family. It is extremely quick and agile.

47. Euphorbus Harmsworth: in the *Iliad* Euphorbus wounded Patroculus and was later killed by Menelaus. The Greek philosopher and mathematician Pythagoras (6th century B.C.E.) claimed to have been Euphorbus in a previous life. Tolson seems however to be using the name chiefly for the fun of its sound and the word play of *Euphorbus* (etymologically "good-bearer") against *Harmsworth*.

48. the shield of Sobieski: John III Sobieski (1624–1696), king of Poland 1674–96, a plotter and schemer who became the champion of Christian Europe against the Turks, raising the siege of Vienna and defeating Kara Mustapha's Turkish army.

60. platinum black: a soft, fine dull black powder of metallic platinum, obtained from solutions of its salts, used as a catalytic agent.

61. *fera*: Latin, wild beast.

62. *homo faber*: Latin, man the maker.

70. like Mohammed's: the prophet Mohammed, it is said, never laughed a full laugh so that the inside of his mouth could be seen; he only smiled. The crocodile laugh that would be achieved by imitating Mohammed would (by analogy to "crocodile tears") be a restrained or deceptive laugh.

79. sand-box tree: a tree (*Hura crepitans*) found in tropical America that bears a furrowed roundish fruit about the size of an orange. When ripe, the fruit bursts explosively and scatters the seeds.

82. We have dined . . . with Duke Humphrey: a Britishism, to dine with Duke Humphrey is to go dinnerless.

92. *A night like this, O Watchman*: see Isaiah 21:11.

93. *Derain*: André Derain (1880–1954), one of the most prolific of the French Fauvist painters, who made a significant contribution to modern painting and enjoyed a marked success before World War I. During the 1920s his critics became increasingly harsh and he grew embittered and lonely. He continued, however, to exhibit in Germany as late as 1935.

93. *Weimar*: the German Weimar Republic, established after World War I, became increasingly oppressive under Nazi influence and eventually gave rise to the Third Reich.

94. *Brissac jack boots*: the Brissacs were a noble French family, especially influential during the fifteenth to eighteenth centuries. Politically astute, they

managed always to stay proximate to the centers of power, and they provided several generations of Marshalls of France. Jackboots, by their association with the Nazi uniform, have become symbolic of brutal force.

95. *Das Kapital*: the first volume of Karl Marx's treatise in historical materialism was published in 1867.

100. that cross-nailing Second of September: on September 2, 1870, in the Franco-Prussian War, Napoleon III and his army of 100,000 men were defeated and captured by the German army at Sedan. The Germans laid seige to Paris and within six months the war was over. Many French artists and writers, including Courbet and Monet, fled the country.

102. Courbet: Gustave Courbet (1819–1877), French realist painter and a radical socialist, who was associated with the brief emergence of the Paris Commune during the Franco-Prussian War.

102. Cézanne: Paul Cézanne (1839–1906), one of the French postimpressionist masters and the spiritual father of cubism.

102. Monet: Claude Monet (1840–1926), major French impressionist painter.

103. self-deadfall of the Maginot: the Maginot Line, named for French Minister of War André Maginot, the elaborate string of defensive fortifications built by the French after World War I from Switzerland to the borders of Belgium and Luxembourg, was based upon traditional concepts of warfare and proved ineffective against the German invasion of France in the spring of 1940.

104. Chagall: Marc Chagall (1887–1985), Russian-born French cubist and surrealist painter, like many important European artists and intellectuals, remained active in the United States during the Second World War.

105. Matisse: Henri Matisse (1869–1954), major postimpressionist and Fauvist painter, remained and worked in Paris during the war.

106. Picasso: Pablo Picasso (1881–1973), whose Marxist sympathies exposed him to danger in both his native Spain and France, spent most of the war in Paris.

Lambda

THE ARGUMENT

The Curator and Dr. Nkomo's painful reflections are interrupted by the raucous entrance into the Gallery of Hideho Heights. His arrival, too late for the social occasion of the opening, introduces perhaps the most complex and influential character of the poem, who incarnates the various types, styles, strengths, and problems of the modern African American writer. He is the character who offers the most serious challenge to the Curator's vision of the primacy of European high art, and he is also perhaps the character his author loves best. It is noteworthy that although Hideho's noisiness, string of social and racial insults, and barroom style, as well as the declassé poem he performs, are all clearly intended to disrupt and offend, the Curator welcomes him with relief and affection.

"Lambda" has the restorative power of an interlude, in which Hideho is a brash refreshment from the stuffiness and menace of Guy Delaporte III and his crowd, but even here the poet expresses some of the contradictions that will be developed as his narrative continues. In his populist style (but not in his personality) he resembles such folk-oriented public poets of the Harlem Renaissance as Langston Hughes or Sterling Brown, but he also betrays an Olympian distance both in his stance before the Gallery and the rhetoric, "in the grand style of a Doctor Faustus," of his poem. His mode is celebratory, yet there are whispers of mortality in it, and he injects at least a hint of mortal vulnerability into his jazz-portrait of Louis Armstrong.

The poem he has written while still flushed from the experience of an Armstrong performance imitates the spontaneity, improvisation, and lack of polish of club jazz. However, it also incorporates, almost as a separable entity in a different genre, a formal lament for the lost masters of a great musical tradition, and it is highly stylized. Despite its energy and enthusiasm it falls flat—or at least apparently so—before the unsympathetic auditors in the Gallery. Hideho's public style, like the art of the jazzman or the preacher, demands the give and take of an engaged audience that he will enjoy in his later performance at the Zulu Club. Now, his poem signals an end to the reception, a dispersal of the crowd, and an abrupt shift of setting.

NOTES

9. Tyche: see note, "Theta," 74.

10. Hideho Heights: the poet's name derives from the musical signature ("hidee hidee hidee hi; hidee hidee hidee ho") of jazzman Cab Calloway (b. 1907) and (according to Joy Flasch) the name of one of Tolson's favorite students at Langston University.

12. beggar's-lice: prickly or adhesive fruits or seeds that stick to clothing.

20. Max Donachie: apparently a fictitious painter and apparently a bad one.

20. Crispus Attucks: (1723–1770) was involved in the colonial action that precipitated the Boston Massacre. He was at least in part of African ancestry and the first American to die in the Revolution. He is one of the Lion Hearts of the South Wing of the Gallery.

22. the Word: see John 1:1: "In the beginning was the Word, and the Word was with God, and the Word was God."

25. Ozymandias: Percy Bysshe Shelley's poem of 1818 describes a ruined statue and inscription that are emblems of the vanity of human aspiration. Of the statue remains chiefly "a shattered visage . . . whose frown, and wrinkled lip, and sneer of cold command" betray the wisdom and mockery of the sculptor.

31. Satchmo: the name by which Louis Armstrong (1900–1971), jazz coronetist and virtuouso, was commonly known. Although Armstrong's musical importance is primarily as one of the revolutionary figures in early jazz, by the late 1950s he had become a much-loved American institution, whose records were popular hits and who performed in concerts all over the world, *from the Gold Coast to cold Moscow.*

41. parachute light: an intense white light, supported by a parachute, for the illumination from the air of military objectives.

42–43. the grand style of a Doctor Faustus: that is, elevated and demonstrative in a way appropriate to Christopher Marlowe's tragedy (ca. 1588) of the man of great mind and talent who sold his soul to the devil.

43. the dilapidated Harlem Opera House: the Harlem Opera House was opened in 1889 by Oscar Hammerstein.

44. *King Oliver*: Joseph "King" Oliver (1885–1938), jazz coronetist and bandleader, whose band gave the young Louis Armstrong his first important public exposure.

48. *Storyville*: a 38-block area in New Orleans that from 1897 to 1917 was the most famous red-light district in the United States and the incubator of classic jazz.

52. *Bessie Smith*: (1898?–1937), American blues singer.

54. *Mister Jelly Roll*: Ferdinand Joseph La Menthe "Jelly Roll" Morton (1885–1941), jazz pianist, composer, and bandleader, and one of the masters of the New Orleans school.

56. *Papa Handy*: W[illiam] C[hristopher] Handy (1873–1958), blues composer and bandleader, author of "St. Louis Blues."

58. *Leadbelly*: Huddie Ledbetter (1888–1949), blues singer and guitarist, who spent much of his life between 1918 and 1934 in prison. He became a central figure in the recording and dissemination of traditional blues.

63. *hypodermic needles in Rome*: on June 23, 1959, while touring Italy, Armstrong suffered a severe heart attack and received considerable attention from the international press while he recovered at St. Peter's Hospital in Rome. He surprised everyone by appearing unannounced at a concert on July 4.

65. *Wyatt Earp's legend, John Henry's, too*: the outlaw/lawman Wyatt Earp (1848–1929), like the legendary black folk hero John Henry, whom Hideho will celebrate later, relied upon his own strength and skill to confront a hostile world.

73–74. *the Seventh Heaven*: in Islamic tradition there are seven heavens, the seventh formed of divine light beyond the power of words to suggest.

Mu

THE ARGUMENT

At the Zulu Club, where the Curator, as much as Hideho Heights, feels as comfortable as an old hat, the art in question turns to jazz, which is tacitly contrasted in its earthiness, improvisation, and lack of inhibition to the more finished and distant artifacts of "Iota" and "Kappa." The jazz artist puts the act of creation, rather than the result, on display. The audience differs too. There is none of the passivity, the whispered comment, the ohing and yawning and ahing, of the exclusive crowd at the opening. The patrons of the Zulu Club participate in the act of creativity in all of its excitement and messiness; their job is not to observe but to get down.

The Zulu Club is not exclusive; it is frequented by professional people, entrepeneurs, race leaders, the criminal fringe, and working people, "ecstasied maids and waiters, pickups and stevedores," as well as artists and curators. Art, for them, is not the property or expression of power of a class. Jazz does, however, have a peculiar racial flavor, and the racial distinction the Curator prepares thoughtfully in response to Hideho is important. Jazz is not exclusive of anyone, but for white people it represents an opportunity (philosopher's egg) for new remedies or discoveries, while for black people it is the very furnishing of the soul, as intimately a part of the domestic life as the music of Franz Liszt was for the Weimar bourgeoisie. The implications of such intimacy are not entirely comforting.

The action of "Mu" is a simultaneous, mutually stimulating musical and sexual drive to climax. The pentecostal music excites, inhibitions relax, the musicians and the dancers egg each other on until everyone gives in and recreates in the Zulu Club the culminative, celebratory debaucherie of Mardi Gras. To this erotic and cultural arousal the curator and the poet respond with a characteristic difference. Hideho is all engagement; he is effervescent, his senses heightened, released from proprieties. For him, jazz is the intoxicant (marijuana) that can open the way to great mysteries. His rejection of what he considers a dinosauric self-centeredness and his immersion of himself in the community created by the music will lead to an important collapse at the end of "Xi."

The Curator's response, even to this music he loves, is characteristically muted and suspicious. His ambiguous acknowledgment of both the glory and danger of giving oneself over to the logic of jazz recalls his meditations on art and happiness, marriage and concupiscence in "Theta." He locates the dancers in their "lurid lights" of smoke and shadow, recognizes the seductiveness of the willow woman and the latent violence in the reptilian copulatory dances of Snakehips Briskie and the generic Penthesilea, with her flaccid Sir Testiculus. His familiar misogyny reasserts itself. Throughout this and the other cantos set in the Zulu Club he is haunted by the percussiveness of the sexual life and the scoldings of the generic Xanthippe. The climax of the erotic revelry leads him not to participate, but to lose himself in the solipsistic intellectual reflections from which Hideho mockingly recalls him. He concludes the canto in a dissonance, troubled by a whiff of Shakespearian evil. But it has been great fun.

NOTES

5. spoke with tongues: see Acts 2:1–18.

16. Carrara marble: a white statuary marble named for the town in Italy where it is mined.

29–31. harpy eagle . . . house snake: a harpy eagle is a large, voracious South and Central American eagle with remarkably strong beak and claws. A house snake is a harmless African predator of rodents. The sense of the stanza appears to be that Hideho is beating the price of drinks at the Zulu Club by sneaking swallows from his own bottle; when he offers an illicit drink to the Curator, the Curator refuses, either because he doesn't want to cheat the club or because he fears discovery by the bartender. The animal imagery is used for its literary and mythic rather than its zoological reference.

33. knife money: ancient Chinese bronze money, having the shape of a knife.

41. sanitary decree: the Curator's meaning seems to be that the woman, not knowing who is being familiar with her, is protecting her reputation by feigning outrage. Apparently she and Hideho are already acquainted.

42. a picadill flare: probably Tolson's variant of *pickadil*, meaning that her smile was stiff, artificial.

50. alligator squeezer: or, crocodile squeezer, a lever device with powerful jaws, used for metal shingling.

54. Eliotic bones: doubtless an allusion to the T. S. Eliot of *The Waste Land*, although the Curator's talk of willows and cesspools has no immediate referent in Eliot's work. Probably Hideho is mocking the Curator's Eliotic association of sexual expression with filth.

61. Snakehips Briskie: in a note in the Library of Congress papers Tolson says of him, "an imaginary character, although I remember the prototype in the old Harlem Opera House." Mariann Russell (Melvin B. Tolson's *Harlem Gallery, A Literary Analysis*, 1980), associates him with Earl "Snakehips" Tucker, a popular Harlem dancer of the 1930s.

62. aurora australis: the southern lights.

67. Giovanni Gabrieli: (ca. 1555–1612), Italian composer, known for the ingenious choral and instrumental arrangements with which he exploited the acoustics of St. Mark's in Venice.

80–81. the light at Eddystone Rock: the Eddystone Rocks and their lighthouse are located near the western end of the English Channel, southwest of Plymouth.

82. Penthesilea: in Greek mythology, an Amazon queen who led a troop of Amazons against the Greeks during the Trojan War. She was killed by Achilles, who then fell in love with her corpse.

83. tiger's-eye: a yellow-brown ornamental chatoyant stone, used here to refine the evocation of color.

90. *ostinato*: (music) relating to any frequently repeated motif or passage.

98–100. The Toothpick . . . Stormy Weather: these individuals and groups are all, Tolson said, "real *ancients* of the Jazz World," although their identities are not always readily recoverable now. The legendary Gertrude "Ma" Rainey (1886–1939), the earliest professional blues singer, is the best known name in the list. Speckled Red (Rufus Perryman 1892–1973), blues singer and pianist, made many records during the 1930s and 1940s. The influence of the Funky Five was acknowledged by the archaic blues singer of the 1940s, Montana Arthur Taylor. The others are better known to memory than to the public record.

102. High Priestess at 27 rue de Fleurus: Gertrude Stein (1874–1946) conducted her famous salon at this address in Paris for many years. She attributed the notorious remark of line 103 to herself in *The Autobiography of Alice B. Toklas* (1933).

104. a neophyte on The Walk: the main public event of initiations in the mysteries of Eleusis was the great autumn procession of initiates, escorting sacred objects, from Athens to Eleusis. The procession became ecstatic in mood and was characterized by dancing and rhythmic shouting.

106. *tribulum*: Latin, threshing machine or threshing-floor.

108. philosophers' egg: 1. the first matter of the philosopher's stone; 2. a medicine made of saffron and the yolk of an egg, once considered a cure for plague or poison.

121. *Basin Street Blues*: the song of 1938 by Spencer Williams about the street in New Orleans was introduced by Louis Armstrong and has become part of the classic dixieland repetoire.

122. Ty Cobb: Tyrus Raymond Cobb (1886–1961), the Georgia Peach, hitter and base-stealer extraordinaire, among the most memorable figures of baseball's early years.

123–124, 132. Zulu, King of the Africans . . . Comus on parade!: The final day of Mardi Gras in New Orleans begins with the arrival of King Zulu, whose parade and float burlesque the gaudy shows of the white Krewes, their parades and kings. The last parade of the day features Comus, the oldest of the Carnival Kings, chosen by the Mistick Krewe of Comus, a white organization.

126. Baby Dodds': Warren "Baby" Dodds (1898–1959), a jazz drummer who worked with Louis Armstrong and King Oliver.

130. callithump: a noisy, boisterous parade.

133. All God's Children: a line from the old spiritual was adapted by Eugene O'Neil for the title of his play about interracial marriage, *All God's Chillun Got Wings*. The play caused considerable controversy, much of it ugly, when it was produced in 1924.

135. charivari: a confusion of noises, derived from the French term for a mock serenade with pots, pans, kettles, etc., used to deride an unpopular person or marriage.

139. Liszt: Franz Liszt (1811–1886), Hungarian composer and pianist, spent his life after 1848 in Weimar, where he directed the opera and concerts, composed and taught.

144–147. King Oliver . . . of the Loop: Oliver was particularly identified with the development of jazz in Chicago. See note, "Lambda," 45.

150. bird's-foot violet: a common violet (*viola pedata*) of the eastern United States. It bears large pale blue or purple flowers that resemble pansies.

153. a lean and hungry look: *The Tragedy of Julius Ceasar*, 1.2.194–95.

158. the Weird Sisters: the sinister, prophetic witches of *Macbeth*.

161. vacuum pan: a tank with a vacuum pump and condenser for rapid evaporation and condensation by boiling at a low temperature.

Nu

THE ARGUMENT

As the music falls silent, "Nu" provides an interlude in which Hideho Heights is detached from the community of jazz he had so happily celebrated and is prepared to become, in "Xi," the agent through whom communal art is expressed. This brief canto does little to advance the action, but it intensifies an increasingly insistent sense of artistic and psychic danger.

While the mood of the Zulu Club continues to be festive, the details of Hideho's recruitment for his performance are disturbing. Both the master of ceremonies who announces Hideho to the crowd and the drunken street-walker who urges him on are represented figuratively in terms of self-interest, hyperbole, hypocrisy, and sickness unto death.

The Curator resumes his familiar role of observer as Hideho's ego and libido are manipulated and aroused. Hideho wills himself so fully to the crowd, the Curator thinks, that he seems to be vacating his own body. Now he is prepared to perform as a truly public poet, the voice and impersonation of the people.

NOTES

5. the island pharos of King Ptolemy: Pharos is an island in the bay of Alexandria, Egypt, which because of the fame of the lighthouse King Ptolemy II built there (ca. 280 B.C.E.) became a generic term for lighthouse. Ptolemy's lighthouse was unusally bright and visible and was counted among the Seven Wonders of the World.

9. demosthenized: a neologism derived from the name *Demosthenes* (ca. 383–322 B.C.E.), the most celebrated of the Greek orators.

22. caravan boiler: the term appears not to be lexical, but its evocation of noise and sequence is clear enough.

31. yellow dwarf: a virus disease of the onion, characterized by yellowing, crinkling, and drooping of the leaves, and stunting of the bulbs.

32. torch lily: a showy tropical plant (*kniphofia uvaria*) with scarlet flowers. Also called the torch flower or the red-hot-poker.

44. Gallio: Junius Annaeus Gallio (d. ca. 65) was a Roman administrator and the brother of Seneca. Acts 18:12–17 recounts how he, as deputy of Achaia, refused to adjudicate religious disputes between Jews and Pauline Christians because he "cared for none of these things."

Xi

THE ARGUMENT

Hideho begins his performance under dramatically arranged lighting, in a flurry of metaphors and allusions that associate him with giantism, prophecy, and the incarnation of spirit. For those in the club with him, including the Curator, he is transfigured because, it seems, he has overcome the personal self and become invested with the powers of collective identity and the inspired native voices (preacher, shaman) who express it. The artistry he assumes is at once sophisticated and traditional. *The Birth of John Henry* is, as an artifact, not much like the aristotelean object, detached from both its maker and the circumstances of its creation, toward which most Western art has aspired. It is more like a tribal ghost, or ancestor dance, during which the communities of the living and dead are given voice and reach communication with each other through the agency of the artist. Hideho thus accepts both extraordinary power and extraordinary danger.

The Birth of John Henry is based closely on traditional material, particularly folksong, about the mythic black railroad man who died at the triumphant conclusion of his worker's duel with a steam drill. For regulars at the Zulu Club it is a familiar item in Hideho's repertoire. Because it is already known and admired, inviting participation rather than interpretation, it does not rely on either time for development or any degree of close attention from its audience. Both Dipsy Muse and Wafer Waite respond to it at once, as if they were in church. The structure of call and response, which is at the heart of much African American preaching, oratory, and music, carries the narrative along and defines an increasingly intimate relationship, "the poet and the audience one." However, this is a secular art, and the echoes of the sacred and the prophetic are to some degree overwhelmed by the boisterous response of Rufino Laughlin and the Zulu Club wits to Hideho's exhibitionistic drinking. The raffishness of the performer is as inspirational and much admired as is the substance of the performance.

The first and most intense effect of Hideho's reenactment of the legend of John Henry is a kind of ecstasy of mutual interaction among poet, musicians, and audience that takes on overtones of bacchanalia or even holy communion and releases a bolt of creative electricity. The Curator, reassuming his familiar role of observer, records the power of the moment by his uncharacteristic absorption in it. The cocktail glass he has apparently broken in his excitement and his fantasies about monastic secrets alike express the heady sense of form and freedom conjoined, the miracle of incarnation, that is stirred by Hideho and his community's triumphant celebration of life redeemed by art.

Stimulated by its inherent logic and by the responses it provokes from its audience, Hideho's poem evolves. His own reference to the traditional birthplace of John Henry prompts Hideho to evocations of the recent past of the people gathered in the club—histories of migrations north and hard times. With their self-deprecating humor and underlying bitterness, his broodings are taken up and elaborated in the personal preoccupations about race and conflict expressed by Vincent Avelino, Lionel Matheus, Joshua Nitze, and Black Diamond. At least psychically, Hideho's voice is now submerged in theirs as they deliver their tales of sexual betrayal, criminality, and racial frustration. The Curator, observing them, is witness to other versions of the blues. For a moment Black Diamond, once the Curator's student, inspired by the power of Hideho's lines, assumes Hideho's physical stature and, rhetorically, his capacity to affront the regents. With his New York inflection, godfatherly style, and eagerness to impress his old teacher, he is a strangely charming character, but he is also clearly a lost soul who has put the Curator's gifts of knowledge and truth to uses the Curator now finds embarrassing. His distortions of the Curator parallel the Zulu Club patrons' diversions of the creativity Hideho has given them, so that he becomes representative of the sinister implications of charisma, memory, and storytelling.

As the race-men, Shadrach Martial Kilroy and Lionel Matheus, the salamander and the lone wolf respectively, engage with Dr. Nkomo in a competition of racial metaphor and allegory, the sources of Zulu Club inspiration have passed from the verses of Hideho Heights to the potent Zulu Club drinks. Hideho has been exhausted. His generous, communalist creativity has been appropriated, reduced, and expended carelessly by an audience that could feel but not understand it. He has become, this people's poet, a familiar sort of sacrifice. His collapse and outcry define both the majesty and inadequacy of his vision of art.

NOTES

2. Gigas: this word derives from the Greek for *giant* and is used as an adjective in English. It refers to any plant with a multiple chromosome structure that gives it a thicker stem, taller growth, thicker and darker leaves, and larger flowers and seeds than a corresponding plant with a normative chromosome structure.

9. atheistic black baritone: Paul Robeson (1898–1976), singer and actor. His association with communist causes and his winning of the International Stalin Peace Prize (1952), as well as his outspokenness on matters of race, made him a controversial, often unwelcome, figure in the United States.

12. the Laughing Philosopher's: the Greek philosopher Democritus of Abdera (ca. 460–ca. 370 B.C.E.), who is most famous for his seminal theory of atoms, was called the "laughing philosopher," probably because of his ethical ideal of cheerfulness.

19–22. Piute Messiah . . . Wovoka: Wovoka (ca. 1858–1932) aka Jack Wilson, was of the Paiute nation of the southwestern United States and the prophet of a messianic religion sometimes called the Ghost Dance Religion. Among many native peoples the ghost dance is a circle dance for communication with the spirits of the dead. Wovoka claimed that on January 1, 1889, he had revealed to him in a vision that if the ghost dance were faithfully performed a time would come when the earth would die and be reborn, and all white people would die, leaving all Indians, living and dead, to reunite in a world free of disease, death, and misery. Wovoka's teaching was widely accepted among Plains Indians, but not always to their advantage, since it encouraged a certain recklessness in their conflicts with whites.

22. Yeats: William Butler Yeats (1865–1939), the Irish poet, was a visionary who experimented with communication with the spirit-world and invoked the power of Celtic legend and myth as a basis for the renewal of Irish culture and an impetus to political action.

25. *vox populi*: Latin, the people's voice.

26–29. Roman procurator . . . make thee mad: in Acts 26:24 the Roman procurator of Judea, [Marcus Porcius] Festus (ca. 60), having been told by Paul about the meaning of Christ's sacrifice, death, and resurrection, "said with a loud voice, Paul, thou art beside thyself; much learning doth make thee mad." Paul was being tried before the Romans because, in order to avoid the judgment of the Jewish court, he had claimed the legal privileges to which he was entitled as a Roman citizen.

48. Fatso Darden: probably a nonce-name.

58. Brazos Bottoms: the Brazos River arises in western Texas and flows southeasterly to the Gulf of Mexico at Freeport. The *bottoms* are south of Waco, in the Blacklands, the richest agricultural land in the state.

59. M.-K.-T.: the Missouri-Kansas-Texas Railroad.

61. the Cotton Market Capital: the Dallas Cotton Exchange opened in 1907. For many years Dallas was the world's largest inland cotton market.

66. the tolerance of Diogenes: that is, impatiently. The cynic whose skeptical wisdom has been frequently invoked in *Harlem Gallery* was not known for his tolerance.

97. the University Wits: a group of Elizabethan playwrights and pamphleteers, known at the time as much for their raucous fellowship and youthful self-indulgence as for their intellectual achievements. The group included Robert Greene, Thomas Nashe, John Lyly, and Thomas Lodge.

101. "'The artist is a strange bird,' Lenin says": the idiom is not Lenin's, but the sentiment might be a reasonable paraphrase of the ideas Lenin expressed in remarks about the avant-garde or in his papers on Leo Tolstoy. In any case, the comment is intended to say more about the egghead who delivered it than about Leninist theories of art.

102. quaquaversal: a structure that dips from its center to all points of the compass.

114. Leyden jar: the earliest form of electrical condenser, invented in Leyden in the eighteenth century. Tolson is referring, of course, to Benjamin Franklin's kite-flying experiment of 1746.

116. Morningside Heights: a middle-class community near Columbia University, overlooking Harlem.

119. Basilidian anchoret: a hermit who has renounced the world and accepted the discipline established by St. Basil the Great (ca. 329–ca. 379), Christian apologian, reformer, and bishop, one of the greatest of the Greek Fathers of the Church.

127–128: *André Gide's musique nègre!*: the French writer André Gide (1869–1951) was also an accomplished pianist, with a great interest in African and African American art and music. In the diaries he kept during his travels of 1924–25 in central Africa, *Voyage au Congo* (1927) and *Le Retour du Chad* (1928), Gide repeatedly described African dance and music. He was particularly detailed and enthusiastic about the twelve-time, improvisational, polyphonic communal singing, which could not be accurately transcribed in conventional European notation. See especially the chapters "Sur le Logone" and "Retour en Arriére" in *Le Retour du Chad*.

130. *a son of Ham*: see Genesis 9:21–25.

132. *a T.B. damn*: Tolson is probably adapting the slang "total blank," meaning, *complete failure.*

154. the *Albatross*: there have been several vessels of this name used for oceanographic research. Tolson may have had in mind the Swedish schooner that sounded the ocean floor in 1947–48 or the American research ship used in a study of the Bering Sea 1893–1906.

159. the Athens of the Cumberland: Nashville, an intellectual and cultural center that boasts a full-scale replica of the Parthenon.

162–163. the bronze . . . of Andrew Jackson: the statue, a replica of the statues of Jackson in Washington and New Orleans, is on Capitol Hill in Nashville.

173. *Dies Irae*: see note, "Eta," 307.

185. the paeans of Artemis: in Greek mythology Artemis was a daughter of Zeus and sister of Apollo, identified with wild nature, hunting, and the moon. Paeans were exultant public hymns of tribute, addressed chiefly to Apollo.

186. The Sea-Wolf: a reference to Jack London's naturalistic novel of 1904, the protagonist of which, Wolf Larsen, is an utterly ruthless, selfish, primitivistic reduction of humanity to its purely natural impulses.

195. Jotham's fable: is about the justice of succession, hatred between brothers, and destruction by fire. See Judges 9:1–21.

197. hide and fox: the Curator's revision of *hide and seek. Fox* is a verb.

201–202. Damon . . . Pithias: in the semilegendary story of the fourth century B.C.E. Pythagorean philosophers, Pythias (more correctly, Phintias) was condemned for political crimes against Dionysus of Syracuse. While Pythias arranged his affairs in preparation for death, Damon assumed his place, expressing willingness to die if Pythias did not return for execution. Pythias returned at the last moment, and Dionysus was so moved by the strength of the friendship that he issued a pardon.

212. *omertà*: the code of silence among criminals, especially associated with the Mafia.

214. Policy Racket: i.e., the numbers, a popular, illegal, highly profitable daily lottery.

219. Minyan pottery: a fine, gray or yellow wheel-made pottery of exceedingly smooth and graceful surface, dating to ca. 1900 B.C.E., named for the prehistoric tribe that inhabited the area of its discovery in Greece.

236. the Art of Picasso's Benin: Picasso's introduction to the power and stylization of African art in 1906–7 was an important element of his development toward cubism and modern abstraction.

237. at Waycross, Georgia: see note, "Zeta," 47. In his Washington *Tribune* columns, Tolson often used Waycross as a synecdoche for small-town, white America.

243–244. Giglio . . . Profaci: Giglio and Gentile (Gentile da Fabriano, ca. 1370–1427, the first master of the Umbrian School), might be the names of painters, but more likely they are masters of another kind. Gentile is probably Daniel "Danny Brooks" Gentile, at least once allegedly a murderer, who held the policy racket concession in Greenwich Village during the mid-1940s. Like Joseph Profaci (1896–1962) and Russell Bufalino (1903–) he was for years a prominent figure in the New York Mafia. The Giglio family was famous among Italian mafiosi; it is not clear to what degree its influence may have extended to the United States.

250–252. Seneca's young Nero . . . Alexander!: the Roman philosopher Lucius Annaeus Seneca (ca. 4 B.C.E.–65) was appointed tutor and later adviser to the young emperor Nero; Aristotle (384–322 B.C.E.) was famously the teacher of Alexander the Great. Like Black Diamond, those students found other applications for their education than their instructors had intended.

263. Walter Winchell: (1897–1972), radio commentator and newspaper columnist, who is usually credited with the invention of the gossip column. Between 1930 and 1950 he was one of the most influential and feared people in the United States.

292. the tubers of the Jerusalem artichoke: the Jerusalem artichoke is a perennial American sunflower (*Helianthus tuberosus*). Its tubers are potato-like.

298. basking shark: one of the largest species (*Cetorhinus maximus*) of shark. It gets its name by lying at the surface and basking in the sun. It feeds on plankton and other minute life.

299. U-bridle irons: strong, flat iron bars so bent as to support, as in a stirrup, one end of a floor timber.

306. Shadrach Martial Kilroy: this interesting name is compounded of Shadrach, who, with Meshach and Abed-nego, was cast into the fiery furnace by Nebuchadnezzar, but by the power of the Lord emerged triumphant (Daniel 2–3); Martial (ca. 40–ca. 104), the great Roman epigrammatic and satiric poet; and Kilroy, who, during the Second World War, was here. Go ahead and make something of it.

312. Dolph Peeler's *Ode to the South*: the poet and the poem are Tolson's inventions.

340. a Sublime Porte: French, High Gate; the Ottoman Turkish court and government, named for the palace gate at which, originally, justice was administered according to the stern Islamic code.

341. son of a Balaam: in Numbers 22–24 Balaam, a prophet, was recruited by Balak, king of the Moabites, to curse the Israelites and drive them from the land. By the intercession of the Lord and angels of the Lord he was brought to a recognition of the truth, so that instead of cursing, he blessed Israel.

346. secretary bird: a large, long-legged raptorial bird of southern Africa (*Sagittarius serpentarius*), named for the resemblance of its crest to a bunch of quill pens stuck behind the ear. It eats snakes.

347. Mirabell: in William Congreve's play *The Way of the World* (1700) Mirabell is the witty, attractive, but dissembling lover who, by keeping his wits and his powers of manipulation, winds up with both the money and the lady.

349–351. Agrippa . . . a nigger-lover: Matheus has in mind Herod Agrippa II, the last of the Herodian dynasty that ruled Palestine for the Romans (37 B.C.E.–70). Paul's exposition, during his legal defense, of Christian doctrine, which had Festus believing him mad, leaves Agrippa almost persuaded to be a Christian (Acts 26:28).

364. *in propria persona*: Latin, in one's own person or character.

370. the similes in the first book of the *Iliad*: the absence of the characteristic Homeric extended, or epic, similes in book 1 of the *Iliad* has been suffi-

ciently noteworthy to have provoked commentary since late antiquity. See, for example, Alexander Pope's final note to book 1 in his translation of the *Iliad* (1715).

372–373. ugly . . . Nazarene spoke: the dialect spoken by Jesus would have been Galilean Aramaic, which, as Matthew 26:73 indicates, was distinctively different from the other dialects encountered in and around Jerusalem. Tolson may be using *ugly* in its chiefly American sense of *confrontational* or *offensive*.

381–383. My *people* . . . what they do: cf. Luke 23:34.

Omicron

THE ARGUMENT

Perhaps as a response to the radical error in vision that was exposed by Hideho's symbolic collapse, Dr. Nkomo's aphorisms invoke first principles and launch a discussion of the relationship between art and its kindred, life. After the Curator comments about the play of Nkomo's mind in the first line of the second stanza, his voice and Nkomo's are, for once, not distinguished but intertwined.

The relationship of art to life — specifically, the life lived in human communities — is incestuous because it is both concupiscent and dialectical. It arises from a kind of copulation of closely related aspects of the human and proceeds incrementally by mutual stimulations. The artist changes life by reimagining it, reordering it, as the crocodile drawn on the rock reorders and transforms the desert. This new life then inspires a new generation of artists, who compose in their turn new visions of it. Thus we arrive, through the painters of the Renaissance and the images of life that they received, renewed, and transmitted in their personal styles, at a Picasso, a Leger, a Modigliani.

The "there" that lies at the end of this dialectic is curiously utopian. There, *Homo Aethiopicus* will be unbridled, the have-nots (low heels) will overtake the haves (high heels), and the law will not estrange — there, in that democracy where life is simultaneously individualistic and communal because artists could imagine the new kind of organic community (stolon) that makes it so. Even though the narrative voice is wistfully aware that such aspirations are unrealistic, an indulgence in our hunger for never-never land, these stanzas make one of the most affirmative statements in *Harlem*

Gallery. At this moment the artist is fully engaged and fully in flight, the creator, master, and celebrant of a redeemed reality. Much of the Curator's persistent reference to the aping or imitation of god is culminated here.

Confronted by the Idols of the Tribe and the impulsions of the spirit of the age, both of them unclean, both to be resisted, the artist "makes merry" by trusting to and expressing the integrity of his or her own nature. The age and the powerful who rule the age are subverted when the artist with a few deft additions turns the cynical perversion of the salamander, the gerrymander, into a dragon, more morally accurate and more interesting as an artifact than the political grotesque. Or the artist turns away from the immediate, toward the past or future, or inward, where is to be found the true dwelling place of light and the precise flavor of things. What the common good requires is an artistry that, unlike Friar Bacon's, is not wasted.

The canto culminates in a series of metaphors for artistic attributes that emphasize integrity and durability in a context of natural process and renewal. Like nature itself, the artist is fertile; the artist is vital; the artist has physicianlike powers to warm the heart and enlighten the mind. Art, fully conceived and fully rendered, is a natural force, with all the creative and transformational implications of other natural forces.

NOTES

2. Osiris and Isis: in Egyptian mythology, the children of the earth god Geb and the sky goddess Nut. They were both brother and sister and husband and wife. Isis was the goddess of nature and fertility; Osiris was the god of agriculture and civilization.

5, 6. Bush-born men: a nomadic tribe of the Kalahari Desert in southern Africa, the Bushmen, or San, are in many ways primitive, but have a remarkably complex language and are famous for their drawings, which are often found on rocks or in caves.

7–10. Diego Rodríguez de Silva y Velázquez (Spanish, 1599–1660), Lucas Cranach (German, 1472–1553), Nicolas Poussin (French, 1594–1665), and Sandro Botticelli (Italian, ca. 1444–1510) are exemplary painters of the Renaissance whose stylizations became part of the artistic idiom of Pablo Picasso (Spanish, 1881–1973), Fernand Léger (French, 1881–1955), and Amedeo Modigliani (Italian, 1884–1920).

15. ladybird: a common regional name for the familiar ladybug beetles (family *coccinellidae*).

16. diapered: here used in its sense of patterned, in a design growing out of the repetition of small geometric figures.

18. Triboulet in the tragedy *Le Roi s'amuse*: in Victor Hugo's drama of 1832, Triboulet, the hunchback jester, kills his own daughter, who has been seduced by the king, thinking he is killing the king.

24. low heels . . . high heels: in Jonathan Swift's *Travels into Several Remote Nations of the World . . . by Lemuel Gulliver* (1726) the politics of Lilliput are dominated by the dispute between low heels and high heels, a satiric allegory of the contemporaneous British contention between low church and high church factions, with their implications of social class.

26. democracy of zooids united by a stolon: a stolon is an extension of the body wall from which buds are developed, giving rise to new zooids, and thus forming a compound animal in which the zooids usually remain united by the stolon. A zooid is a more or less independent animal produced by other than direct sexual methods, especially a single animal of such compound organisms as coral.

30. I am that I am: Exodus 3:14.

32. The Hamfat Man: *Hamfatter,* a dismissive term for an actor of poor quality, was probably used with regard to minstrel companies. It may be derived from "an old-style Negro song called 'The Ham-fat Man'" *(Dictionary of Americanisms on Historical Principles,* ed. Mitford M. Mathews, 1951).

37. the salamander of Gerry: in 1812 Elbridge Gerry (1744–1814), the governor of Massachusetts, used his influence to have an election district in the northeastern part of the state recast for party purposes. The resulting irregularly shaped entity resembled the outline of a salamander, and the punning coinage that named it passed almost immediately into American political usage.

41–50. a Friar Bacon . . . courtesan Sleep: the learning and achievement of Roger Bacon (ca. 1214–ca. 1294), English scholastic philosopher, scientist, and Franciscan monk, made him the subject of many legends. The story of the brazen head was circulated in pamphlets and other forms but is most familiar from Robert Greene's play of 1594, *The Honorable Historie of Friar Bacon and Friar Bungay.* With the help of Bungay, Bacon casts a head of brass and summons the devil to learn how to make it speak. The head would speak within a month, he was told, but if he didn't hear it, all his labor would be lost. The head speaks and is broken as Bacon sleeps and his servant fails to awaken him.

52. stones irises: the meaning of this strange image is not clear. Tolson might 1. be using *stones* in the sense of "removing the stones/seeds from" (although irises, which grow from bulbs, don't fit well with that sense), or 2. in the sense of walling up, or throwing stones at, the irises of the eye.

57. afferent blood vessel: one that returns blood to a central organ.

59. iris diaphragm: a diaphragm that can be adjusted to change the aperture and hence the focal plane of a camera or microscope.

62. skiascope: measures the refractive state of the eye by the process Tolson describes.

65. land of the leal: *leal* is by derivation related to *legal* and other words having to do with the law. In Scots usage *leal* has come to mean loyal or true. Poetically, the land o' the leal is the happy place where the living and blessed departed are reunited.

68. exploring coil: also flip coil, a coil of wire used to measure magnetic fields by suddenly flipping the coil and measuring the resulting change in current.

104. magic grass of Glaucus: there are many versions of this Greek myth of the fabled fisherman of Boeotia who saw that a dead fish that was laid on a certain grass was restored to life. He ate some of the grass and, leaping into the sea, was transformed into a sea-god.

114. alpine and savanna freight cars: the topographical images are invoked for the sake of an allegory of art, but in railroading terms they appear to signify nothing more than raised or flatbed cars.

118–119. the Brahman and Hamburg and Or[p]ington, the Frizzle and Silky: all are ornamental domestic fowls.

127. purple foxglove: a biennial foxglove (*Digitalis purpurea*) of Western Europe. Its dried leaves are the source of the cardiac stimulant, digitalis.

Pi

THE ARGUMENT

The Curator resumes the elaborate rumination of "Omicron" about the social powers and responsibilities of the artist. For the first time in *Harlem Gallery* he extends the implications of his descriptions of art to the practice of criticism, which he identifies with art by its capacity to illuminate moral boundaries and original causes and so share in the communal work of inventing the good place of the imagination—in "Omicron" the land of the leal; here, the happy bourne, or Xanadu. The artist and the critic are not equal in their capacities, but both must struggle to discover a narrow path of conduct and interest between the extremes of the merely personal ("Omega is not I *like*") and the merely regimented (the discipline of the bulls of Bashan).

Solipsism and reflexive response to stimuli are dismissed immediately. In a world of social randomness the artist must not barter away norms of personal and artistic discipline. Willy-nilly, he or she is responsible for the task of imagining new institutions of reality that will mate such opposites as art and nature, the internal and the external, the individual and the communal. Even when the opposition is not obvious, as in a fully realistic reimagining of the immediate world, the successful completion of the task is miraculous.

The nature of social responsibility is not so easily defined as the fact of it. Art is a function of the integrity of a particular personality (*that* psyche), but it is also the expression of the integrity of a place, a people, and a time. It may be iconoclastic, particularly if icons are conceived in flat (Euclidean) and therefore brittle ways, but it is not arbitrarily so. The art of perspective, in which depth and relative size are represented, provokes a sense of reality that leaves even the most fixed, the most sacred of symbols to the natural transformations of time. Just as art is not proscribed in the way that religious symbols or texts are proscribed, it is not intolerant in the way that they are intolerant. Rather it is, as in "Omicron," like a natural force, majestic but volcanic, with the same unstable potential for destructive or cleansing eruptions.

Caught as a condition of being human in the chaotic orders of society and nature, the artist must discover principles of strength and stability (Samson post or stifle shoe), by which even a limited artist may resist conformity and contribute somewhat to the common enterprise. In the figures of Robert Frost and Paul Cézanne, Dr. Nkomo offers alternate models of the artist's social engagement. The poet and the state arrive at an accommodation through differing but congruent interpretations of a shared ideal, while Cézanne acquires a phalanx of revolutionary supporters and by defeating inertia routs the status quo.

Such shifting, even apparently contradictory, artistic tactics often oblige the critic, who is by nature derivative of them, to fall back on luck or instinct. The imagery of gambling, however, defines both the radical limitation and the imperative of the critic's social responsibility. Although perhaps inadequate to the transcendent social and historical issues suggested by such notorious places of carnage as Babi Yar, the critic can enhance the personal experience, sacred or profane, of both artist and audience. Strategically placed between the work and the reception of the work, looking on the one hand to the mystery of origins, on the other to the sting of recognition, the critic's contribution, like the X stopper's, is to clarify. It is not the majestic vocation of the artist, but it earns something of the artist's wages. In

Xanadu the landscapes and the citizenry alike are always new and always glorious.

NOTES

9. Regent's Park: a large park on royal property in London. It contains the British national Zoological Gardens, and did contain for many years the gardens of the Royal Botanic Society.

18. a rhyme in the Mikado's tongue: i.e., exquisite and rare. Rhyme is not used as a structural or temporal principle in classical Japanese poetry, so that a successful rhyme in the very delicate and suggestive context of the spare Japanese poem would have an extraordinary effect.

28. mediterranean: Tolson is using the word in its etymological sense of *amid the earth, earthbound.*

33. Al Sirat: in Muslim eschatology the bridge over the chasm of hell over which the righteous will pass to Paradise, while the unrighteous fall into the flames. It has been described as finer than a hair, sharper than a sword, and beset on each side with briars and thorns.

39. grapes of wrath: see Revelations 14:18–20.

42. Soufrière: there are two volcanoes of this name in the West Indies, one on St. Vincent, one on Guadeloupe. Neither attains a height of 5,000 feet.

42. Kilimanjaro: an extinct volcano, the highest mountain in Africa, rising to two points of 19,340 and 17,565 feet.

46–47. sight the anchor: to pull up an anchor sufficiently to determine whether it is foul or clear.

47. parasitic crater: in physical geography, a subordinate volcanic cone, developed on the side of the principal cone.

48. bulls of Bashan: see note, "Epsilon," 36.

49. Samson Post: any of various posts used in architectural or industrial applications where great strength is requisite. Derived from Samson, judge of Israel, and the support pillars he pulled down to crush the Philistines (Judges 16:25–31).

50–51. the remembrance of things past: alludes to 1. Shakespeare, Sonnet 30; 2. Marcel Proust's thirteen-volume novel, *A La Recherche du Temps Perdu* (1912–22).

53. pigs in blankets: Tolson's final intentions for this line are not clear. Different issues of the first edition of *Harlem Gallery* read alternately "pigs in blankets" and "pigs in baskets." Indications of priority are inconclusive. We have

let stand "pigs in blankets" because it is the reading in the last available manuscript, even though Tolson might subsequently have changed it to avoid associations with a popular fast food.

However the line is to be reconstituted, Tolson may be alluding in it to versions of the children's story of the three little pigs in which the pigs attempt to hide in baskets or under blankets when the wolf is at the door. The sense of the figure developed in the stanza appears to be: those (of the Samson post or the parasitic crater) who have the power to bring things crashing down should temper their wrath with humanity so that the merely weak or foolish may be spared when the wicked are destroyed. That is, get the bulls; spare (or strengthen) the pigs.

54. stifle shoe: the convex surface of the stifle shoe is placed on the sound leg of a stifled (suffering from a dislocated or diseased stifle bone) horse, causing it to throw its weight on the leg with the weak joint, thereby strengthening it.

78. *auto-da-fé*: Spanish, act of faith. During the Inquisition, the public execution of heretics.

83–86. the Venerable Yankee Poet . . . *Seclorum*: Robert Frost (1874–1963) was invited by John F. Kennedy to participate in Kennedy's inauguration as president in 1961. For the occasion Frost composed a poem in couplets, called "Dedication," in which he explored the implications of the motto *Novus Ordo Seclorum* (Latin, a new order of the ages), which is on the Great Seal of the United States, as well as the obverse of the dollar bill. On the bright, windy day of the inaugural the eighty-six-year-old poet found himself unable to read from the typescript of his poem, and instead recited "The Gift Outright" from memory.

89. Paul Cézanne: see note, "Kappa," 103.

91. Toussaint L'Ouverture: Pierre Dominique Toussaint L'Ouverture (1743–1803), the leader and hero of the revolution of Haitian slaves and free blacks against French and British rule in Hispaniola (1791–1798). As founder and ruler of the first independent black nation in the Western Hemisphere, he became an important symbolic figure in African American history.

95. tree crow: any of various Asian birds, intermediate between crows and jays, such as the genera *Cryspsirhina* or *Dendrocitta*.

107. riding light: the light shown at night by a vessel at anchor.

108. whistling buoy: a buoy that makes a whistling noise because of the action of the waves, usually used to mark a shoal or a channel entrance.

109. Styx': another infernal river (cf. "Zeta," 150) over which the souls of the dead were ferried by Charon.

110–111. Bunyan's crabtree cudgel: in part 1 (1678) of John Bunyan's *Pilgrim's Progress* the giant Despair imprisons Christian and Hopeful in Doubting Castle and beats them with a "grievous Crab-tree Cudgel."

114. Black Muslims: members of the Nation of Islam, the militant, separatist black American Islamic sect made into a national force among urban black people by Elijah Muhammed (1897–1975). In the late 1950s and early 1960s its most articulate spokesman in Harlem would have been Malcolm X (1925–1965). It is not easy to imagine an occasion in which Black Muslims would have sat down with a lot of Good White Friends to listen to Dr. Nkomo lecture on the nature of criticism.

119. Harpers Ferry: part of Virginia in October 1859 when abolitionist John Brown (1800–1859) conducted his raid on the federal arsenal there.

119. Babii Yar: or, Babi Yar: the site near Kiev of a Nazi massacre of approximately 33,000 Jews in June 1941 during the German invasion of Russia.

119. Highgate: see note, "Iota," 168.

120. X stopper: in radio, a resistor or capacitor designed to damp out specious or parasitic oscillations.

127. the dark tarn Auber: the French composer Daniel François Auber (1782–1871) remains popular for his "Le Lac des Fées" (Lake of the Fairies, or Enchanted Lake). His dark tarn was situated in "the ghoul-haunted woodland of Weir," at least in Edgar Allan Poe's "Ulalume" (1847), to which Tolson is alluding here.

129. The road to Xanadu: the title of one of the most influential studies (1927) of Samuel Taylor Coleridge, by John Livingston Lowes (1867–1945). It is an exhaustive recreation of the poet's imagination and creative activity.

130. Hamburg grape: see note, "Delta," 10.

131. God is not mocked: Galatians 6:7.

133. Goliath: the champion of the Philistines, slain by David (1 Samuel 17).

137. Brueghel's knaves: Pieter Brueghel the Younger (Flemish, ca. 1564–1637) is known as "Hell" Brueghel because of his paintings of devils, hags, and robbers.

138. Cimabue's saints: Cimabue, originally Cenni di Peppi (ca. 1240–ca. 1302), Florentine painter, and one of the fathers of the Italian Renaissance, famous particularly for his frescoes in the church of St. Francis at Assisi.

· Rho

THE ARGUMENT

From his extended revery about the golden world of art, the Curator turns again to a cautionary tale about the realities of an artist's pilgrimage through the brazen world. "Rho" is the first of four cantos dedicated to the life, mysterious death, and literary remains of the musician Mister Starks, the last major exemplar of the tragicomedy of art to be introduced in *Harlem Gallery*.

The peculiar trials of Starks's life are revealed by the sordid situation in which his widow finds herself at the opening of the canto. His peculiar powers both to inspire and disturb are revealed by her frenzied conviction that he is haunting her. Like all of the important fictive artists of *Harlem Gallery*, Starks is a little bit larger than life, a figure out of romance rather than documentary realism. By the circumstances of his naming, which is the stuff of racial legend, he is a symbol of defiance; by the symbolic waystations of his upbringing, he is a type of the modernist. His inherent quality is suggested by his metaphorical association with Aeneas, who was both fated and privileged to descend to Avernus. Although Starks proves unequal to that heroic responsibility, the Curator acknowledges his stature with his wistful, affectionate celebration of his friend's "escape to the upper air."

His flaw was not so much cowardice or selfishness as it was the unwisdom of love, or, more particularly, the sexual life, with its lusts and its treacheries, which is, persistently, one of the common enemies in *Harlem Gallery*. In "Rho" the alternately xanthippean and salomean character of the Black Orchid, Hedda Starks, is clearly developed as the force that impels Starks to his dramaturgical suicide. In subsequent cantos the account of both the motives and agency of his death will be complicated considerably.

NOTES

8. horned screamer: a bird (*Anhima cornuta*) of northern South America, with a long slender hornlike process on the forehead. It has a loud trumpetlike call.

20–22. Hesiod's . . . *Brazen Age*: the brazen age was the terrible, violent precursor to our own time when people had fallen away from the purer life of the golden and silver ages, in the poet Hesiod's (8th century B.C.E.) *Works and Days*.

29–30. Onward . . . Oklahoma: see note, "Zeta," 47.

54. Congo Leopold's: Leopold II; original name Louis Philippe Marie Victor (1835–1909), king of Belgium (1865–1909) and sovereign of the Congo Free Republic (1885–1908), who became notorious for abuses of people in the Congo region.

54. Cleo de Merode: (1873–1966), French dancer and a much-celebrated beauty of her day, mistress of Leopold II.

55. Anatole France: pseudonym of Jacques Anatole François Thibault (1844–1924) French novelist, critic, poet, and playwright, a preeminent social critic and satirist as well as a master stylist. Nobel laureate 1921.

62–63. the red kimono that broke Woodrow Wilson's heart: the reference is almost certainly to Wilson's prolonged relationship with Mary Peck, which disturbed both of his marriages and at one point frightened him badly with prospects of scandal. The particulars of the garment have proved elusive. However, the incident in question is probably the confrontation of Mary Peck by Wilson's first wife. Mrs. Peck answered the door in her wrapper, and Mrs. Wilson pointedly described the scene in great detail to her husband.

64–65. a sibyl . . . Avernus is easy: in Virgil, *Aeneid* 6.126, the Cumaean sibyl tells Aeneas, who wishes to visit the Underworld to see his father and receive a vision of the future of his race, "Facilis descensus Averno," and goes on to say that it is the way back that is difficult. Avernus was the Italian lake that in the ancient world was regarded as the entrance to hell.

75. Hardyesque: perhaps an allusion to Thomas Hardy (1840–1928), English novelist and poet, whose essentially decent characters, time's laughingstocks, are defeated in their struggles against their physical and social environments, their own impulses, and the malevolence of chance. Or Tolson's term might refer to Oliver Hardy (1892–1957), the fat man of the team of comic actors, Laurel and Hardy, whose bumbling responses to worldly dangers enabled them to escape a myriad movie disasters. The various connotations of *beau geste* and the hint of the operatic in line 76 suggest that a hard-and-fast distinction between the two possiblities might be reductive.

76. Harlem Opera House: see note, "Lambda," 44.

77–80. Charles Gilpin . . . Emperor Joneses: Gilpin (1878–1930) was the most famous black American singer and actor of his day. He was particularly admired for his title role (1920–24) in Eugene O'Neill's *The Emperor Jones*, an expressionistic psychological drama about a black Pullman porter who becomes the ruler of a West Indian island, enriches himself at the expense of his subjects, and, when the inevitable rebellion occurs, undergoes a melodramatic psychic retrogression through phases of racial history from the civilized to the savage state.

Sigma

THE ARGUMENT

The Curator manages to have this canto both ways. His heart is with Mister Starks, but he tells Starks's sad story with an amused detachment, probably because he is recounting the undoubtedly racy version of it he learned from the Zulu Club Wits. His account of Starks's suicide, a matter of death imitating art, continues with a description of the effect of Starks's will upon Ma'am Shears. Farsighted, short-winded, she is a familiar type of the domestic tyrant, affectionately described, whose name, in the dominantly comic tone of the canto, carries some symbolic weight. It might be said to translate "Atropos," with whose invocation the canto is concluded, just as Miss Bostic with her checkerwork might be said, if we don't take all this too solemnly, to imitate Clotho, and Hedda Starks Lachesis.

As both a lawyer and mortician, Ma'am Shears is well qualified to appreciate Starks's testament, but she responds to it according to neither of her professions. The scenario she creates is rather like a routine out of Laurel and Hardy, an all but vaudevillian genre piece about the follies of the vestigial vestal ladies and the unmanned vestigial man, all of them on death's payroll, complete with false teeth, pince-nez, and the generic bust of Frederick Douglass, upon which the spectacles have incongruously fallen.

The telephone conversation in which Ma'am Shears attempts to dissuade Starks allows us our one opportunity to hear his terse, urbane voice — he has fewer lines to speak than any other major character in *Harlem Gallery* — and reveals both his effervescence of mind and his bitterness. The comic characters and action in "Sigma" enhance by juxtaposition the bite of his dry wit and the moral pressure of his disillusionment. His triumph is that in the face of death he can make so witty and graceful a response to the wreckage of his life. He has contrived a situation in which he exits on his own terms and with all the best lines.

Just as the canto is about to end on this bittersweet note it is complicated by the introduction of another genre piece, this one out of detective fiction, hinting that Crazy Cain may have taken over the matter of Starks's death. However, the mystery story does not reach closure; the only scraps of evidence are the putative fact of the .38 hidden in the toilet bowl (which seems an unlikely place to hide anything) and the implications of Crazy's name.

Later there will be some indications of a possible motive, but they are at best inconclusive. We are left without sufficient evidence to decide unambiguously whether Starks killed himself or was killed, and, in keeping with so much of the treatment of this elusive character, we are probably meant by our author to acknowledge that frustration of our desire for clarity. Why draw fine lines of motive or agent when the black ox so easily obliterates them?

In other words, it is all fate, all destiny, even if there is something mockheroic about it.

NOTES

29. *dame de compagnie*: French, lady's companion.

38. became fixed mercury: i.e., froze up.

42. springbok: a swift, graceful South African gazelle.

48–49. Hedley's *Puffing Billy*: William Hedley (1779–1843), English colliery official and inventor, invented the first commercially practical steam locomotive using smooth wheels on smooth rails. Called *Puffing Billy*, it began operation in 1813.

63. "I'm a Hannibal—not a Napoleon": Hannibal (247–182 B.C.E.), the Carthaginian general and sworn enemy of Rome, after defeat and exile committed suicide to avoid capture by the Romans. Napoleon Bonaparte (1769–1821) surrendered to the British after Waterloo. During the few years of exile before he died, probably of stomach cancer, his wife broke contact with him and secretly married again.

71. mother of vinegar: a slimy membrane that develops on the surface of alcoholic liquids. It is an agent of fermentation and is added to wine or cider as a starter to produce vinegar.

74. Masaryk . . . in Vienna: Thomas Masaryk (1850–1937) Czech political leader and philosopher, first president and chief founder of Czechoslovakia, received his doctorate from the University of Vienna in 1876. He published his first important work, *Der Selbstmund als sociale Massenerscheinung der modernen Civilisation* (Suicide as a mass phenomenon of modern civilization), while he was teaching there.

85–86. Pliny's white black: in 7.51 of his encyclopedic *Naturalis Historia* Pliny (Gaius Plinius Secundus) the Elder (23/24–79), Roman historian and naturalist, considers the grandchild of an adulterous union between a Roman woman and an African man to be white, not Ethiopian, because the color of her skin would not distinguish her from most Romans.

102. Conan Doyle: Arthur Conan Doyle (1859–1930), English physician and author of popular romances, is famous for his series of Sherlock Holmes detective stories.

115–117. Clotho . . . Atropos: in the division of labor among the classical Fates, Clotho spins out the thread of life, Lachesis shapes it, Atropos cuts it.

118. the black ox: a traditional symbol of bad luck or dark fate.

Tau

THE ARGUMENT

This brief canto locates Mister Starks, who would become fully an artist only in his music, among the honorable company of poets. The sorcerer's trappings with which he has decorated his manuscript, and his allusive acknowledgment of the common source and burden of creativity, identify him, at least in his own mind, as a kind of spoiled priest of modernism.

The Curator's memory and senses are stirred. He acknowledges once again the miracle of art by which the past provides fuel for the imagination, so that time and mortality are defeated.

The achievement of Starks's *Harlem Vignettes* is real, even though he did not pursue the possibilities of his idiom to either the logical or the heroic conclusions reached by some larger modernist poets. It harvests a few small maturations of the life of art, defiant and spirited, whose germ Starks had planted in the historical debris of Harlem.

NOTES

2. mamba's skin: the mamba is any of a kind of large, extremely venomous, cobralike tropical or southern African snake (genus *Dendroaspis*).

5. In the sweat of thy face . . . : cf. Genesis 3:19.

11. Sanson's images: i.e., original mappings. Nicholas Sanson (1600–1667), French geographer and cartographer, made maps of all the known regions of the world.

17. *Des Imagistes*: the title of Ezra Pound's anthology of 1914 is used here to indicate the group of poets—besides Pound, Hilda Doolittle, John Gould Fletcher, Amy Lowell, Richard Aldington, and D. H. Lawrence—who adopted imagism, the idea that the image is the essence of the poem, as their standard for the purification and modernization of poetry. As a philosophy of art, imagism was limiting, and soon abandoned in its pure form,

while its emphasis on the energy and priority of the image continued to have important results, particularly in the high modernist work of Pound.

19–20. Boabdil . . . the Moor: Boabdil is a Spanish corruption of abu-Abdullah, who as Mohammed XI, was the last Moorish king of Granada (1482–1492). The place where he formally surrendered to Ferdinand and Isabella and from which he tearfully looked back for the last time at the Alhambra was traditionally known as "the last sigh of the Moor."

25. General Aupick: Jacques Aupick (1789–1857), general, ambassador, and senator of France, was the stepfather of Charles Baudelaire. He forced Baudelaire to attend military school, was shocked by his immoral behavior, and disregarded his literary talents. Baudelaire hated him.

26. Guizot's imperative Enrichissez-vous: François Guizot (1784–1874), French historian and statesman, became premier of France in 1847. He was overthrown in the February Revolution of 1848. "Enrichissez-vous" is from his address of March 1, 1843, in which he counseled workers to enrich themselves by hard work and thrift instead of trying to reform electoral laws.

Upsilon

THE ARGUMENT

Mister Starks's Harlem Vignettes, which Hedda Starks apparently believed could be used for blackmail, is assigned a remarkable spatial and moral priority in Harlem Gallery. As a fiction-within-a-fiction, it opens a new window onto the relationships between art and life with which the Curator, Dr. Nkomo, and Hideho Heights have been wrestling throughout the poem. The insights Starks offers, however, are not necessarily to be taken as correctives to those offered previously. His perceptions are not entirely reliable and, as a voice from the grave, he is accountable to no one but himself.

His self-portraits at both the beginning and the ending of the canto are full of guilty introspection, compromise, frustration, and a sort of heroic wistfulness. Although in possession of the peculiar freedom of the outcast and inspired by his generational expatriation among the awakening geniuses of European modern music, he has (in his own harsh metaphor) prostituted his talent in order to satisfy his desire for Black Orchid. Yet he insists that he should not be judged strictly according to his failures, because what he truly is and has truly achieved are defined by the composition of

Black Orchid Suite. That single full realization of the imperatives of high art, he thinks, will live.

The same insistence on the transformative power of the uncompromised work of art—this one in potential—sustains his sense of integrity in a remembered episode of what should be some thirty to forty years earlier (although, as always in *Harlem Gallery*, the sequence of historical time has been collapsed), when he was the piano player in Big Mama's speakeasy. The *Rhapsody in Black and White*, which would coordinate the powers of African, African American, and European music, is the great work of which, in his own way, each of the artists of *Harlem Gallery* dreams, but it seems naive even to dream about it in this world of crude power, harsh bootleg liquor, and cheap flesh, in which the exemplary fame belongs to a punch-drunk boxer. To some degree Starks redeems that world and rescues himself from his own frailties by accepting a gambler's chance and walking away from Big Mama and Dutch Schultz, by his perfectly spontaneous and self-less gesture of warning the streetwalker about her peril, and by refusing to participate, even verbally, in the sort of conspiratorial bigotry that has made him an outcast. These are small episodes in a sad comedy, but they become normative.

In his next portrait, Starks celebrates Hideho Heights as an artist who because of his racial and bohemian rigor has achieved a greater stature than his own, but in his first stanza he establishes a strangely equivocal context for praise. What does it mean, after all, to be a poet whom Plato would not banish when the poets Plato would banish were those who refused to be censored, insisted on giving voice to slaves, and reported the misbehavior of the gods? What does it mean to be the solid center of *Dixie*? What does it mean to have a portrait begin with images of classical order and the agora, but conclude with images of the excremental and parasitic? Starks does not develop such hints; instead he takes at face value Hideho's version of himself as public poet. He does not know, as we and the Curator will know, that Hideho is bifacial.

In the sketches of Dr. Igor and Ma'am Shears, Starks turns to characters who will figure in the mystery surrounding his death. They are appropriately enigmatic, even as they are studies in unshaded contrast. Dr. Shears is a creature of deep waters and distant roosts, whom Starks has not sounded but whose profundity he invokes. Yet it is not clear whether or not the mystery inside the man is anything more than emptiness. Neither is it clear *which* cliché is represented by Ma'am Shears, who appears to be nothing more than an accumulation of social conventions. *What she was*, however, refers to a character fully known to Starks, but only fleetingly to us from the hints we might glean from "Sigma."

Of all the enigmatic players who enter the poem through the whodunit of Starks's death, the musician Crazy Cain is perhaps the most enigmatic, a particularly explosive version of the stock figure of the tragic mulatto, who seems fated to repeat the history of his quasi race, without ever gaining the power to understand either it or himself. In his desperate attempts to find keys to Cain's character, Starks is thrown back on historical analogies and some curiously racist theories of genetic determinism. But perhaps the solution lies in the name, and Crazy Cain can best be understood as simply another episode of the mystery of iniquity, Eliotic in his surrender to his own spiritual impotence, thrown up by the whims and vagaries of history.

The portraits of Dr. Obi Nkomo and the Curator, which follow, are the most ambitious in *Harlem Vignettes* and both of these characters are invested with a size and moral heroism that Starks, for all his admiration, never assigns to Hideho Heights or John Laugart. Nkomo is represented as a transracial, transcultural John the Baptist, not yet sure what savior he is to announce, while the Curator is an embattled spirit of integrity and defiance, who doggedly persists in arousing the enmity of the philistines on whom he must depend. Most of the Curator's portrait is dedicated to a description of his engagement in a verbal contest with Nkomo, after hours at the Zulu Club, about the social and artistic moral to be wrung from the metaphor of milk, in which cream is associated with elitism and high art, skim milk with the cultural and physical poverty necessary to support the elite, and the division between them, elusively, with race and class. It is, of course, a restatement of one of the dominant themes and most intractable problems to be addressed in the poem, and it is complicated further by the presence of an aggressive minister and civil rights activist who pushes hard on a strictly racial allegory that the Curator and Nkomo cannot reject, but neither could they fully affirm. In the genuinely friendly and witty exchange between the two friends, the Curator finally comes down on the side of compromise, suggesting reluctantly that because we are caught in the interregnum between cultural systems we must take what nourishment we can from each of the mutually exclusive, morally unequal sources that are offered by the categories of the status quo. The socialistic Nkomo, however, sees such pragmatism as moral surrender, and apparently wins the game by asserting that righteousness will not compromise the ideal of racial and cultural homogenization. He is reversing here the position he had implicitly assumed earlier (see "Kappa," line 67). Whoever wins or loses, the two friends conclude their game in the empty Harlem night almost as new kinds of people, in a séance of comradeship.

After the olympian gamesmanship of the Curator and Nkomo, the brief sketches of Mrs. Guy Delaporte III and John Laugart seem almost perfunctory, even though Mrs. Delaporte inspires Starks to some surprisingly sentimental and exculpatory Freudian analysis, which hints at yet another story yet untold. Laugart, on the other hand, is treated with a terse, almost formulaic stoicism that by its very restraint suggests the depth of Starks's feeling. He is the uncompromising moralist who is rewarded with crucifixion, but not resurrection. After life's fitful fever, he sleeps well.

Big Mama represents one last fully consistent, psychologically appropriate defense against the conditions of Harlem life, a selfish, hard-bitten nihilism that allies her morally with the gangster Dutch Schultz. Her portrait quickly dissipates into the story of Starks's emerging *Rhapsody in Black and White*, so that her sordid criminal milieu makes Starks's quiet courage and decency the more persuasive by contrast. We leave Starks as he is stirred once again by the voice of the creative imperative that saw him through as much of his world as he could abide.

NOTES

Mister Starks: A Self-Portrait: It is all but impossible not to notice the similarities of circumstance that relate Starks's *Harlem Vignettes* to the collection of verse biographies, influenced by Edgar Lee Masters's *Spoon River Anthology*, that Tolson left unpublished at his death and has since been edited by Robert Farnsworth and published as *A Gallery of Harlem Portraits*. The biographical coincidence is remarkable, and Starks is one of Tolson's alter egos, but in fact the style and concerns of *Harlem Vignettes* do not much resemble those of Tolson's abandoned manuscripts, certainly not in the direct way that Hideho Heights's closet masterpiece *E. & O. E.* resembles Melvin Tolson's "E. & O. E."

4. *vox populi—vox Dei*: Latin, the people's voice, god's voice.

7. *comédie larmoyante*: French, tearful comedy: a kind of sentimental, edifying comic drama, in which pathos is derived from realistic depictions of the tribulations of everyday life. Its development is attributed to the French playwright Pierre Claude Nivelle de La Chaussée (1692–1754).

9. elaphure: a large grayish deer (*Elaphurus davidianus*) with long slender antlers, probably of Chinese origin but now found only in domesticated herds.

10. neutral—carbon in fats: *neutral*, chemically neither acid nor alkaline. As the figure develops, Starks may be referring to the molecular structure of

fats, in which four to twenty-four carbon atoms are arranged in a chain. Unlike the Fathers of Oratory, the carbon atoms are "bound" on four sides.

11. the Fathers of Oratory: the Oratory of St. Philip Neri (1515–1595), also known as the Congregation of the Oratory, is an Italian order of priests living in community without vows, for the purposes of prayer and preaching.

13. ha-ha-wall: a sunk fence, a ditch with a retaining wall, used to divide properties without defacing the landscape.

18–19. Since a headhunter . . . to the bucket: the key to this strenuous figure may be Mister Starks's use of *headhunter* in one of its metaphorical slang senses, meaning *a portrait artist in search of subjects.*

20. the Gaya Bar on Rue Duphot: a night club of the 1920s frequented by Parisian artists and musicians.

20. Jean Weiner: (1896–1982), French pianist who performed several of Stravinsky's works in the late 1920s and founded the Weiner concerts of contemporary music. In the early 1920s he earned his living by playing in night clubs, including the Gaya Bar.

21. Vance Lowry: black banjoist and saxophonist, who was Weiner's partner in night club appearances.

22–24. Stravinsky . . . *Sortilèges*: the composers Igor Stravinsky (Russian, 1882–1971), Darius Milhaud (French, 1892–1974), and Maurice Ravel (French, 1875–1937), could all have been seen and heard by Mister Starks, perhaps in the Gaya Bar, since all of them spent time in Paris during the 1920s. Milhaud did visit the Gaya Bar and says in his autobiography that he first heard jazz there. The compositions mentioned here—*L'Histoire du Soldat* (1918), *La Création du Monde* (1923), and *L'Enfant et les Sortilèges* (1925) were influenced by ragtime and jazz. All three composers knew and occasionally worked with Jean Weiner.

25. weeping cross: in medieval times, a cross erected by the highway for the devotions of penitents.

27. the crossruff: that is, the crossruff "between *want* and *have*." A crossruff is a tactic of cardplaying whereby partners alternately trump different suits and lead to each other for that purpose.

30. the forbidden wine of Sura 78: sura is 1. palm wine; 2. one of the numbered sections of the Koran. Wine is forbidden in several suras, but it is not mentioned, nor is anything specifically forbidden, in Sura 78, which is a wrathful general warning to those who resist truth.

31. Rosetta stone: a slab of black basalt, bearing inscriptions in Greek, Egyptian hieroglyphics, and demotic, discovered in 1799, which allowed hieroglyphics to be deciphered for the first time.

44. *Ecco la marchia*: the march "Ecco la marcia" (Italian, here's the march) opens the finale of act 3 of Wolfgang Amadeus Mozart's opera of 1786, *Le Nozze di Figaro* (The Marriage of Figaro).

46–47. Plato's . . . Republic: in book 3 of the *Republic*, Socrates leads his interlocutors to agree that poets are rare givers of pleasure who nevertheless imitate slaves and other common people, report on the scandalous doings of the gods, and sometimes linger on unhappy or frightening subjects. They are thus dangerous to the hierarchical social order of the ideal state and must be sent away.

65. crissum: the anatomical structure and the feathers covering the cloacal opening of a bird. The word is derived from the New Latin *crissare* (said of a woman), to wriggle the backside while having sexual intercourse.

69. to lark: in horsemanship, to ride across country or over obstacles.

79. Jonah crab: a large crab of the eastern coast of the United States, usually found in deep water.

81. Walton: Isaac Walton (1593–1683), author of *The Compleat Angler; or, the Contemplative Man's Recreation* (1653).

83. *rigor caloris*: this phrase appears not to be good Latin (it would mean the stiffness or stern discipline of heat). Probably it is Starks's coinage, an antonym of *rigor mortis*, to mean the discipline of heated activity.

85–87. a phrase . . .title of a Psalm: the Psalms are untitled. Starks is probably referring to the enigmatic inscriptions appearing above many of them, which may once have been instructions for liturgical use but are now incomprehensible.

Terebinths are small European trees yielding Chian turpentine. Their doves may mean no more than something elusive but may also remind us of the wings of the dove of Psalms 55:6 or 68:13.

88. *Book of Homilies*: in the Church of England, two books of homilies (1547, 1563) were appointed to be read in churches.

90. a Spencerian address: spencerian was a form of slanted cursive script introduced by P. R. Spencer (1800–1864), widely used as an instructional model in the mid-nineteenth-century United States.

92. an Eliotic vein of surrender: a sense of spiritual lassitude and incapacity to overcome the fallen state of sinfulness characterized the poetry of T. S. Eliot through the publication of "The Hollow Men" (1925).

108–109. a book of seven seals . . . Patmos: in Revelations (ca. 95) John receives his vision on the Isle of Patmos. God is envisioned (5:1) holding a book sealed with seven seals, which can be opened only by the Lamb. As each seal is unsealed, John sees seven different terrific visions of the fallen world.

113–115. a whale ship . . . cabin boy: Herman Melville, *Moby-Dick* (1851), chapter 24, "The Advocate": "a whale-ship was my Yale College and my Harvard."

118. Charicleia in *Ethiopica*: Charicleia is the heroine of a prose romance by Heliodorus (4th century B.C.E.). Because of the proximity of a portrait of a white Ethiopian princess at her conception, she is born white, even though both her parents are black. Her mother, fearing that her father will not believe the child is his, gives Charicleia away, and she grows up ignorant of her royal and racial past.

129. *Poudres de Succession*: Tolson told a correspondent that the *poudres de succession* were "real," but the phrase (literally, *powders of succession*) offends the French. It is either a very bad pun or, more likely, an error in transcription of the legal term *pouvoir* (or *droit*) *de succession* (power of succession), which is obviously what is troubling Crazy Cain.

133. the D-Day dreaded by the Scholar-Gypsy: the narrator of Matthew Arnold's poem "The Scholar Gypsy" (1853) reimagines an old legend of a poor scholar who left Oxford to wander with the gypsies and learn their secrets. The narrator dreads the thought that the "glad perennial youth," who has discovered hope and freedom, might some day be brought back into contact with "the strange disease of modern life," and returned to the ravages of time and mortality.

137. Mr. Morgan's Thirteen Galleries of Art: in 1907, John Pierpont Morgan (1837–1913), American financier, built the Pierpont Morgan Library next to his own home in New York City to house his immense collection of manuscripts, books, and art. The library was opened to the public in 1924.

142. Passion Oratorio: a narrative musical performance sung during Holy Week, based upon the sufferings of Jesus.

148. St. John: St. John in this line, as in line 169, might be identified with equal pertinence as either St. John the Baptist or St. John the Divine of Revelations.

154. the pagoda tree: any of several trees of erect habit (characteristic mode of growth) and conical form.

160–164. butterflied the bowels . . . falsies on her buttocks: in his prophetic essay *Democratic Vistas* (1871) Walt Whitman argued that the material and political progress, as he saw it, of the United States was a necessary precondition for spiritual progress, but that without spiritual progress material progress would become morally corrosive. His tone is alternately utopian with regard to the future and denunciatory with regard to contemporaneous American society.

steatopygous: steatopygia is a pronounced development of the buttocks, common among some Hottentot peoples.

Jezebel: the painted harlot of 2 Kings, especially 9:22, and Revelations 2:20.

170. brush turkey: a large, turkeylike bird of the family *megapodidae* that inhabits the wooded regions of eastern Australia. Megapodes are distinguished chiefly for their habit of heaping up piles of vegetable debris in which their eggs are laid and hatched.

175. zone axis of a crystal: a straight line through the center of a crystal, to which all faces of a given plane are parallel.

176. Aristotelian metaphorist: "metaphor consists in giving the thing a name that belongs to something else; the transference being either from genus to species, or from species to genus, or from species to species, or on grounds of analogy . . . the greatest thing by far is to be a master of metaphor . . . it is also a sign of genius, since a good metaphor implies an intuitive perception of the similarity in dissimilars." Aristotle, *Poetics* 1457b–1458b.

179. geometer's horn angle: a figure formed by two plane curves, one within the curve of the other, which touch each other at a single point on the same side of the tangent line. The angle thus formed is without extent (i.e., infinitely sharp) because at the vortex the two lines of the angle are parallel to each other and to the tangent. For Starks the horn angle probably means simply an absolutely precise but elegant figure.

181. waxed stiller than tissues in paraffin: in histology, specimens of animal tissue are saturated with paraffin and hardened before being stained, sliced, and mounted on microslides.

185. *q* in Old Anglo-Saxon: the letter *q* is anamolous in Anglo-Saxon.

186. Danakil Desert: a particularly forbidding large desert region in northeastern Ethiopia.

188. beccafico: Italian, fig-eater; any of various songbirds esteemed in Italy as a delicacy, especially in the autumn, after they have fed on ripened fruit.

196. *a fortiori*: Latin, all the more certainly.

200. jacobin: 1. a political extremist, a radical; 2. a fancy pigeon whose neck feathers are reversed so as to resemble a friar's hood.

208–210. Ike, the painter . . . Nikita, the Art critic: Dwight D. Eisenhower (1890–1969), thirty-fourth president of the United States, had a hobbyist's enjoyment of painting landscapes and other conventional subjects. Nikita Khruschev (1894–1971), prime minister of the Soviet Union 1958–64, maintained, although less ferociously than Stalin, a repressive climate for the arts. He was particularly annoyed by abstract painting, commenting more than once that it was childish, stupid, and pointless.

212. brass-check: in brothels of the late nineteenth and early twentieth century, a customer purchased from the keeper of the house a brass check that, upon presentation to one of the prostitutes, entitled the customer to whatever services had been negotiated. In his pamphlet of that name of 1920, Upton Sinclair used the brass check as a symbol of the moral shortcomings of the Associated Press news service and, generally, the corporate powers of American journalism. Probably because of Sinclair's usage, *brass check* came to mean a bribe paid to a journalist.

218. *Death's Jest-Book*: the play (1850) by Thomas Lovell Beddoes (1803–1849), is based upon Elizabethan tragedy and displays Beddoes's obsession with the macabre, the supernatural, and bodily decay.

219. the Minerva with the Police Gazette Belt: the *National Police Gazette* began publication in 1845 as a weekly newspaper devoted ostensibly to the prevention of crime, but over time became increasingly sensationalistic. After 1870 it was printed on pale pink paper, with a cover that featured large woodcuts, usually of scantily clad women, sometimes wearing a police belt. It was still being published in magazine form in the mid-1960s.

226. Greenland shark: a large arctic shark (*Somniosus microcephalus*) with a small head, small teeth, and weak jaws.

241–244. angrier than Cellini . . . Pantasilea: Benvenuto Cellini (1500–1571), Italian sculptor and one of history's great rogues, is probably as well known for his picaresque *Autobiography* (1558–62) as for his gorgeous bronzes. In book 1, chapters 30–32 of his autobiography, he tells how he and his friend Luigi Pulci both fell in love with the whore Pantasilea. When Cellini witnessed Pulci making love to her, he flew into a rage and tried to kill them both.

247. Francis I of France: Francis I (1494–1547; king 1515–47) was a tactless, disputatious sovereign who conducted a long series of wars against the Holy Roman Empire. He was notable for his love of letters and the arts, and his reign was marked by the introduction into France of the Renaissance.

250. Richelieu: Armand Jean du Plessis de Richelieu (1585–1642), French duke, cardinal, and statesman, lost a brother to dueling and became a determined enemy of the practice.

252–256. *Malakoff . . . "J'y suis, j'y reste"*: the hill and fortress Malakoff, overlooking Sevastopol, was a key position taken by the French (September 8, 1855) during the Crimean War. When the French marshall Marie Edme Patrice de MacMahon (1808–1893) was advised to abandon the position, he responded as quoted by Starks ("Here I am; I'm staying.")

266. cap and bells: part of the costume of court fool or professional jester.

268. ex–Freedom Rider: the janitor was one of the civil rights activists, both black and white, who rode buses through the South during the early 1960s to test and promote desegregation. He may have had to give up his job at Alabama Christian to do so.

278. Empson's classic seven: one of the definitive New Critical studies of irony was contained in William Empson's (1906–1984) book of 1930, *Seven Types of Ambiguity*.

285. Nestor: in Homer's *Iliad*, the oldest and wisest of the Greek generals who fought at Troy, a constant source of sage advice.

289. Taine's smell of the laboratory: Hippolyte Taine (1828–1893), French critic and historian, was a determinist who believed that human nature was the product of heredity and environment. His theories were scientific in the sense that he mistrusted intuition and emphasized formula and system.

296. lactoscopist: a neologism, meaning a scrutinizer of milk.

325. Lionelbarrymorean: Lionel Barrymore (1878–1954) of the famous Barrymore family of American actors, was known for his august presence and emphatic style.

326. Homerized: that is, improvised upon traditional themes, styles, and phrases. Nkomo's "*Sit down, servant*" is a variant of a traditional song.

332–333. scaling motion of clay pigeons from a trap of the *fin de siècle*: that is, rising swiftly and powerfully, as a disklike clay skeet target, launched from an old-fashioned hand pull.

339–342. *Anglo-Saxon Chronicle* . . . Negro: the Anglo-Saxon Chronicle was a monastic record of events in England from the ninth through the mid-twelfth centuries. It has little to say about theories of race.

355. Afroamerican's features of *A Man called White*: the Curator has the appearance of a white person. *A Man Called White* (1948) was the autobiography of Walter F. White (1893–1955), chief executive of the NAACP 1929–1955. Because with his blonde hair and blue eyes he could pass for white, he began his career with the NAACP as a field investigator who infiltrated southern white communities to investigate lynchings or other mob violence.

358. mirror carp: a domesticated variety of carp (which is a soft finned fish), distinguished by having only a few large shining scales on its body.

359–362. Between the ass . . . the skimmers: cf. the lines (85–88) from Matthew Arnold's "Stanzas from the Grand Chartreuse" (1855):

> Wandering between two worlds, one dead,
> The other powerless to be born,

> With nowhere yet to rest my head,
> Like these, on earth, I wait forlorn.

364. *mens agitat molem*: Latin, mind moves matter (or, idiomatically, mind over matter), see Virgil, *Aeneid* 6.727.

365. dried cones of hops: the ripened and dried cones of hops are used in brewing to impart bitterness to malt liquors.

368. *Mens sibi conscia recti*: a mind conscious of the right; see Virgil, *Aeneid* 1.604.

371. a hollow man: cf. note for line 92.

374. green pastures . . . valleys of dry bones: Psalms 32:1–2, Ezekiel 37:1–10. For Starks and his generation "green pastures" would also have a more immediate reference to the folklike play of that name (1930) by Marc Connelly, which, with black actors, scored a great success on Broadway.

377. tailor bird's nest: the tailor bird of Asia, India, and Africa, a member of the warbler (*Sylviidae*) family, pierces leaves and stitches them together to support and hide its nests.

386. the siphons of a Dosinia: dosinia is a genus of bivalve mollusks having a flattened rounded shell, large foot, and united siphons, which conduct water and waste from one side of the body to the other. Cf. line 319.

391–395. cabala . . . "*Quo Vadis*": the referents for this tortuous simile have remained stubbornly elusive. I can speculate that it has something to do with the unlikely alliance of the rival Mexican painters Diego Rivera (1886–1957) and David Siqueiros (1896–1974), who cooperated in producing the murals in the Palace of Cortez in Cuernavaca, but I am not confident of the speculation.

398. Riefler's clock: a high-precision clock with a mercurial pendulum that the mercury adjusts in length in response to the effect of temperature variations.

403. Elektra complex: in psychoanalytic theory, the female complement to the Oedipus complex, by which young girls resent their mothers and develop erotic attachments to their fathers. Such illicit feelings, Freud maintained, make women especially liable to neurotic diseases.

408. Daumier: See note, "Zeta," 46.

413. each a bowl from the Potter's wheel: see Edward FitzGerald's *Rubáiyát of Omar Khayyám*, quatrains 82–90.

414–417. a potter's field . . . silver: Matthew 27:6–10.

419. son of Hagar: see notes, "Kappa," 38; "Epsilon," 23.

428. Niflheim: in Scandinavian mythology Niflheim (mist–home) is the underworld region of endless cold and night, ruled by the goddess Hel.

429. Dutch Schultz: Arthur Flegenheimer, aka Dutch Schultz (1902–1935), was a notorious New York City bootlegger and gangster of the late twenties and early thirties. He was murdered by his colleagues after he insisted too strongly upon the assassination of Special Prosecutor Thomas E. Dewey.

430. Rat Alley: cf. T. S. Eliot, "The Waste Land," ll. 115–16: "I think we are in rats' alley / Where the dead men lost their bones."

440. tala: the yellowish gray hard wood of a timber tree (*Celtis tala*) of Argentina.

447. Kid Ory's trombone in *Sweet Little Papa*: Edward "Kid" Ory (1886–1973), the master trombonist of the New Orleans style, played with Louis Armstrong's Hot Five and other important groups.

448. Caruso: Enrico Caruso (1873–1921), Italian operatic tenor.

452. *La Fin de Babylon*: a semipornographic historical novel, vaguely mystical in tone, *La Fin de Babylone* was written anonymously (ca. 1910) by Guillaume Apollinaire (1880–1918) as part of his duties in editing a series of erotica for the Parisian publisher Briffault.

454. the jut of the *Agamemnon's* prow: five British ships have been named *Agamemnon*, including one that helped lay the first Atlantic cable in 1858 and figured in the British victory at Sebastopol in the Crimean War. Both it and the 1876 *Agamemnon* have prows that form ninety degree angles with the deck.

461–462. a white poet . . . of my fate": William Ernest Henley (1849–1903) lost a foot to tubercular arthritis and wrote a sequence of poems, *Hospital Sketches* (1875), while recuperating. Starks quotes from the most famous of them, "Invictus."

479. the African who had dramatized integration: "You can play a tune of sorts on the white keys, and you can play a tune of sorts on the black keys, but for harmony you must use both the white and the black." This quotation was sufficiently well known to be used as a motto on the title page of *The Treasury of Negro Spirituals*, ed. H. A. Chambers: London [1953], and attributed only to "Aggrey." Tolson's notes make it clear that the image is from Dr. James E. Kwegyir Aggrey, a black South African scholar and educator of Tolson's acquaintance, "the most eloquent speaker I ever heard," to whom he also refers in a column for the Washington *Tribune*. Aggrey seems to have been the source as well for the image of the shape of Africa as a ques-

tion mark and, perhaps, for the story of the eagle who thought he was a chicken that Nkomo tells in "Eta."

481. *tempo di marcia:* Italian, pace of the march.

501. Fats': Thomas "Fats" Waller (1904–1943), jazz singer, pianist, and composer. His forceful "stride" left hand was one of the peculiar strengths of his style.

505. the image of Bast in a royal stable: in Egyptian mythology Bast was a lion- or cat-headed goddess associated with nature and fertility. Since cats were sacred animals in Egypt, her image in a stable would cut through a lot of nonsense and clarify authority in an instant, which is Starks's point.

510. Tin Pan Alley's blues classic: *Rhapsody in Blue* (1924), a work for piano and orchestra by the popular (Tin Pan Alley) composer George Gershwin, was the first important concert work to attempt to bridge the gap between jazz band and symphony orchestra.

511. a buteo: a genus of hawks that soar and wheel high in the air.

513. butcherbird: any of several species of shrikes (*Lanius*), named for their habit of impaling their prey.

520. Alesia: a hilltop town and fortress of Celtic Gaul. Ceasar's defeat of Vercingetorix there in 52 B.C.E. ended Gallic resistance to Rome.

525. Cerebean: in Greek mythology Cerebus was the monstrous, many-headed dog who guarded the entrance to the Underworld.

527. Boston Tar Baby: Sam Langford (1886–1956), middleweight and light heavyweight boxer, who fought more than 500 professional bouts between 1902 and 1924. Because of the racial politics of boxing of the time he was never awarded a title bout, although he did fight Jack Johnson in 1906. He knocked down Johnson, who outweighed him by forty pounds, but lost a controversial decision in fifteen rounds.

530. Jack Johnson's: Johnson (1878–1946) was the great heavyweight boxing champion of 1908–15 whose success and defiant style had journalists openly seeking a "white hope." Like Sam Langford's, his life and career became the stuff of legend.

531. Banquo's ghost: see Shakespeare, *Macbeth* 3.4, 4.1, 5.1.

541. Hippias: a harsh tyrant who ruled Athens 527–510 B.C.E. before being overthrown by the Spartans and forced into exile.

546. Brahui: a nomadic people of Baluchistan, characterized by their short stature and olive complexion.

552–554. Macbeth's . . . mother's womb: *Macbeth* 5.8.7–22.

555. Abraham's bosom: Luke 16:22–23.

557. *The Protocols of the Wise Men of Zion*: the much-circulated forgery *The Protocols of the Learned Elders of Zion* reported the alleged proceedings of a conference of Jews in 1897, at which were discussed plans to overthrow Christianity and rule the world. The document may have been written by the secret police of Czarist Russia. It was widely disseminated by anti-Semites in the 1920s and 1930s.

Phi

THE ARGUMENT

The Curator is left stunned by his reading of *Harlem Vignettes*, even though it is no masterpiece, he thinks, and will earn little posthumous acknowledgment. Rather, it and the memory of its author will "vapor away" like other Harlem vanities. But it hits the Curator hard enough that he thinks he needs a drink. It makes him uneasy in conscience about his accommodations to society and its rituals, at the same time that he feels liberated from them. He dismisses the superficial ceremonies for Mister Starks conducted by the Angelus Funeral Home not with anger or blame but olympian laughter.

His reaction to Starks's manuscript also influences the direction his own poem now takes. He guiltily and perhaps too passively accepts the tacit judgment (which Starks may not have intended and we are not obliged to share) that Nkomo's principled refusal to acknowledge the necessity of compromise about matters racial, social, and artistic made Nkomo the better man. From this point forward *Harlem Gallery* becomes increasingly preoccupied with the definition of race as a key, perhaps *the* key factor, in the ongoing discussion of the imperatives of art.

The Curator begins with a curt dismissal of certain pervasive myths that reduce racial experience to primitivist romance. He insists that the racial past of black people has its own holiness and must be treated with humanity and dignity. His sweeping argument is reexpressed in more immediate and specific terms in the ensuing debate between Shadrach Martial Kilroy, whose fixed idea about race is as reductive as the myth of the Noble Savage, and Dr. Nkomo, who soberly reiterates his familiar point about the complexity of racial identity. Nkomo suggests further that the rhetorical reduction of "plural strains" to a single abstraction is liable to lead an activist to a dead end. To Kilroy's rejoinder that race *is* single and only the context in which social institutions define it variable, Nkomo then asserts, pretty much unanswerably, that responsible individuals will not and should not allow social pressures to determine their behavior. With that, Kilroy, after checking the room for white people, drops his bluster and apparently prepares to engage Nkomo in some straight talk.

As they talk on, a not-so-sober Hideho Heights picks a friendly argument with the Curator, clearly for the purpose of fueling his own creativity, which is, at least in public, geared to the stimulations of the give-and-take. The Curator understands that he is being used, but is cooperative—is, in fact, a conspirator in the creative act. Their companionable ritual of call-and-response results in Hideho's powerful parable of the shark who swallows the sea turtle, a violent, gut-wrenching variation on the story of Jonah, which, as we will learn, Hideho has developed otherwise in his still private poem in the modern vein. Although the imaginative process by which Hideho gave shape to the story began as a response to the "bunkum" of Kilroy and Nkomo and the unacceptable racial symbolism of Dolph Peeler, the story itself is not explicitly about race until the Jamaican bartender pointedly interprets it and explains the personal and historical causes of the intensity of his interpretation.

This moment of creative openness in the carefree atmosphere of the tavern—the poem not only delivered, but conceived and brought to labor in public—inspires Hideho to even more unusual revelations about himself and his creative gift. Perhaps it is the savage caricature of childbirth that could be suggested by the image of the turtle tearing itself out of the shark's innards that leads by association to his childhood memory of witnessing a squalid birth. His subsequent extended comparison between the labors and responsibilities of the parent and those of the poet culminates his most convincing performance in *Harlem Gallery*, a demonstration of the racial logic of art and the apotheosis of what the public poet can and should be.

NOTES

4–7. a second Harlem . . . to Spouse: Edward FitzGerald's *Rubáiyát of Omar Khayyám*, quatrain 55:

> You know, my Friends, with what a brave Carouse
> I made a Second Marriage in my house;
>   Divorced old barren Reason from my Bed,
> And took the Daughter of the Vine to Spouse.

17. charact: not so much character as some mark or sign signifying a special nature.

52–54. Gogol . . . Dickens . . . Rabelais: Nikolai Vasilievich Gogol (1809–1852), Charles Dickens (1812–1870), and François Rabelais (ca. 1494–1553) are apparently grouped here as social critics who did not allow their preoccupation with human failure to embitter them, but were of sufficiently large vision that they saw social issues as part of a grand comedy.

67. Absalom, my son: 2 Samuel 18:33.

77. prongs of Horton's fork: the fork is apparently metaphorical of the Curator's familiar problem of choice, so that the figure could suggest several Hortons. Probably the Curator has in mind James Africanus Horton (1835–1883), a Sierra Leonean scientist and West African nationalist, whose work was rediscovered in 1963. Horton conducted his career as a medical and civil administrator in the service of the British crown at a time when it still seemed possible for African nations to progress gradually under European rule to full political and cultural autonomy. The prongs of his fork might be defined as, on the one hand, his persistent compromises with the attitudes of the white rulers and, on the other, his equally persistent attempts to enlighten and reform colonial policies. See his *West African Countries and Peoples, British and Native, with the Requirements necessary for Establishing that Self-Government recommended by the Committee of the House of Commons 1865; and a Vindication of the African Race* (1868).

78. the horns of Rimbaud's Ogaden: In 1881 Arthur Rimbaud (1854–1891), the French poet, led an expedition into the southeastern Ethiopian province of Ogaden, in the Horn of Africa, which had previously been unvisited by Europeans. Since Rimbaud's career as a trader in northern Africa involved him in some shady activities—including, perhaps, slave-trading—he might leave Tolson, or any admirer of his extraordinary poetry, on the horns of a dilemma about how to judge him.

81. Barmecide feast: an illusory feast, from an *Arabian Nights* tale of a joke played on a starving beggar.

88–89. a specter . . . *Aethiopicus*: cf. Karl Marx and Friedrich Engels, *Manifesto of the Communist Party* (1848): "A spectre is haunting Europe—the spectre of Communism."

90. Banquo's ghost: see note, "Upsilon," 531.

99. Albert Rider: Albert Pinkham Ryder (1847–1917), American painter who developed out of his religious feeling and haphazard training a purely personal style, based conceptually on an anachronistic romanticism but anticipating stylistically many of the methods of modern art.

109. black dog: in addition to the obvious racial reference, Nkomo is using *black dog* in its sense of depression or despondency.

118. a Siamese noun: the Thai language makes use of five distinct tones to distinguish between words that are otherwise identical.

128. *sookin sin*: Russian, son of a bitch.

128–129. like Jacob . . . destiny: Genesis 28:11–19.

169. whirling Ferris wheel: cf. "Delta," 66–72.

172. Centennial of the Emancipation Proclamation: Abraham Lincoln issued the Emancipation Proclamation to be effective January 1, 1863.

185. Remember to remember: Henry Miller's (1891–1980) volume of essays in criticism of American life, *Remember to Remember*, was published in 1947. The theme of the title essay might be summarized by the Curator's comment about tribal anthems. The volume also contained an essay about the redemptive virtues of the African American painter Beauford Delaney.

277. at Dunkirk: the bartender was serving in the British navy during the remarkable evacuation by sea from France (May 29–June 3, 1940) of the British Expeditionary Force, which had been defeated and was surrounded by German armored divisions.

278–280. Churchill . . . Claude McKay: Claude McKay (1890–1948), Jamaican-born American poet and novelist, wrote the sonnet, the first line of which the bartender cites, in response to the Harlem race riots of 1919. In 1940 Churchill read the poem to the British people as a rallying cry during the embattled days of early World War II, and his speech was read into the American *Congressional Record* by Senator Henry Cabot Lodge. In a review of an edition of Claude McKay's poems, Tolson was critical of Churchill for leaving the author of the poem unidentified.

289. a city of refuge: cities of refuge were places appointed by Moses where those who had killed unintentionally could be protected from vengeance while their cases were being heard. See especially Numbers 35:6–34.

Rudolph Fisher (1897–1934) wrote an ironic short story about Harlem entitled "City of Refuge," which was included in Alain Locke's anthology *The New Negro* (1925).

293. Land of the Gray Flannel Suit: *The Man in the Gray Flannel Suit* (1955), the novel by Sloane Wilson (1920–), provided a generic name for the suburban, white-collar, family man of the Eisenhower era.

310. Professor Marotelli's cat: I can't tell you about Professor Marotelli's smart cat. I wish I could.

315. *élan vital*: French, living force.

328. the *howl-howl-with-the-combo* quacks: an apparent reference to the modish bohemian entertainments of the late 1950s and early 1960s whereby often rough-hewn poetry was read to the accompaniment of jazz. Allen Ginsberg's (1926–1997) declamatory poem *Howl* (1956) was a great success of this genre.

329. Eddie Jests and Shortfellows: Edgar Albert Guest (1881–1959), the newspaper poet, and Henry Wadsworth Longfellow (1807–1882) are coupled in shame here apparently as prolific, indiscriminate popular poets without fidelity to their discipline.

Chi

THE ARGUMENT

In this canto the Curator sees through the Hideho Heights of "the racial ballad in the public domain" in ways that Mister Starks failed to do in *Harlem Vignettes*. Hideho is genuinely and admirably a people's poet, or, in the words of the militant Jamaican bartender, a "Poet Defender." His public humiliation of an ecclesiastical Uncle Tom offends the police, but is an act of populist heroism in defense of conscience and integrity. However, the people's Hideho Heights is only half the man and half the artist. He inhabits and vacates that half of himself according to the tyranny of the social institutions of race in the United States, which force upon him the dialectic of "to be or not to be a Negro," even when the alternatives are reductive. His other half is a child of the internationalism and high artistry of his historical moment and its culture. He is a joyful celebrant of the mastery and renewal of poetry, a former expatriate, and a modernist, who has been made ambitious for enduring fame by his recognition of personal mortality.

The Curator is as much concerned with the timing of historical and artistic coincidence as he is with the brute reality of time as duration, and he is startled to learn that Hideho has shared the dreams and experience of his self-consciously aesthetically insurgent generation. He discovers these things when he brings the poet home drunk from a Zulu Club outing and stumbles upon his secret poem in high modernist idiom, *E. & O. E.*, which happens also to be the title of a cognate poem that Melvin Tolson published in *Poetry* in 1951 and which was awarded the magazine's Bess Hokim Prize for that year. The brief exerpts from the poem that are attributed to Hideho in "Chi" are (except for the shift of one article from "the" to "a") verbally identical to Tolson's "E. & O. E.," while the line structure has been adapted to fit the odic prosody of *Harlem Gallery*. Both poems conclude with the same antiheroic stanza.

Tolson's "E. & O. E." is a dense, allusive, psychologically turbulent poem about the power and responsibility of the poet—the poet as prophet—in his particular parenthesis of eternity. It is Eliotic in idiom and in its fear of spiritual inadequacy before the great prophetic tasks. Like all of Tolson's work, it is complicated but not determined by issues of race. In it, Tolson is an ironist, insistently careful to distance himself sharply as poet from the lyric voice which utters his poem, so that it is difficult to calibrate the degrees of irony in the poem's various parodies, self-parodies, hyperboles, and committed modernisms.

The Curator attributes no such ironies to Hideho, who seems here to have entered the confessional. Because of the collapse of distance and the decontextualization of excerpts, he emerges as an inglorious Jonah whose mission has been diverted, both more humbled and more despairing than Tolson's protagonist. At the end of Tolson's "E. & O. E." we are left with a poet who resembles the T. S. Eliot of, say, *Ash Wednesday*, while the Hideho Heights of his *E. & O. E.* is distinctly Prufrockian.

NOTES

3. Hideho's joy was Hasidic: Hasidism is a Jewish movement founded in Poland in the eighteenth century by Baal Shem-Tov, characterized by its emphasis on mysticism, prayer, religious fervor, and communion with God through joyous worship, at times expressed in music and dance.

6–7. aged Istanbul . . . young Beyoglu: Istanbul, ancient Byzantium, was founded by the Greeks in the eighth century B.C.E. Beyoğlu, which lies across the Golden Horn from the ancient core of the city, is the modern section of Istanbul, housing the Turkish government district and many theaters.

17. banzai: Japanese, ten thousand years; used as a salute or cheer. The suicidal Japanese banzai charge was particularly feared by American troops in the Pacific Theater during World War II. It is not clear whether Hideho is being autobiographical or merely metaphorical here. If he has indeed both drunk with Apollinaire (line 171) and fought in the Pacific, he is indeed a remarkable character.

24. not Hamlet's . . . not Simon Legree's: Hamlet's fears of judgment in that undiscovered country that lies beyond the grave differ fundamentally from

the melodramatic projections of guilt by the superstituous Simon Legree, the villain of Harriet Beecher Stowe's *Uncle Tom's Cabin* (1852), but both are mediated and generalized by art.

38–39. From the grandeur . . . home: see Edgar Allan Poe's "To Helen" (1848):

> Thy Naiad airs have brought me home
>   To the glory that was Greece,
> And the grandeur that was Rome.

47. *E. & O. E.*: Tolson's poem, with his notes to it, was published in *Poetry* 78 (September 1951): 330–44, 369–72. In the notes he derives the title from the printer's abbreviation for "errors and omissions excepted."

48. Pasternakian secrecy: Boris Pasternak (1890–1960) Russian novelist, poet, and Nobel laureate, was for years prevented by the Soviet government from publishing his poems or his great novel, *Doctor Zhivago*. He could reach a sympathetic audience only clandestinely, through the illegal *samizdat*, or self-publishing.

54. Black Venus: see note to lines 167–68.

56. Clotho: see note, "Sigma," 115–17.

60. Peach-tree Street: Peachtree is the main street of Atlanta, linking the downtown to the affluent northern suburbs.

65. Omar's *Is* and *Is-not*: FitzGerald's *Rubáiyát*, quatrain 56:

> For "Is" and "Is-Not" though with Rule and Line
> And "Up-and-Down" by logic I define,
>   Of all that one should care to fathom, I
> Was never deep in anything but—Wine.

73. the bark of the toothache tree: the acrid bark of the prickly ash (*Zanthoxylum americanum*) was used by American Indians and early settlers to soothe aching teeth.

75. ondoyant: French, rippled.

79–85. Why place . . . holy grail?: these lines are verbally identical to lines 137–44 of Tolson's "E. & O. E." except that the "a" of line 84 has been substituted for "the." In the original these words are attributed to "the pursy times' Tartufean shill."

82. go to Ninevah: the Lord's command to Jonah, which he resisted. See Jonah 1:2 and *passim*.

98. like sandstone into gneiss: gneiss is a laminated or foliated metamorphic rock formed from either igneous rock or, as with sandstone, from sediment.

116. the Alhambra: the extensive palace/fortress overlooking Grenada, constructed by the Moorish kings of Spain in the thirteenth and fourteenth centuries. The alabaster fountain described by Hideho is in the Court of the Lions.

120. the specter of Amphion in Thebes: in Greek mythology, Amphion was the son of Zeus and Antiope, and one of the builders of Thebes, a musician who played so beautifully on the lyre while the walls were being constructed that the stones slid into place by themselves. He married Niobe and became the father of seven sons and seven daughters. When the children were killed by Artemis and Apollo because of Niobe's boasting, Amphion killed himself.

135–136. Rose La Rose, Mister Minsky's tigress in heat: Tolson told a correspondent (Library of Congress papers) that Rose La Rose was a fictitious character, but she would have thought that was putting it altogether too negatively. She was among the best known strippers of the thirties, who rivaled even Gypsy Rose Lee in popularity and was employed for much of her career, as many of the better exotic dancers were, at Minsky's Burlesque, the famous theater on Second Avenue in the lower East Side of New York City (later on 42d St.), managed by Billy Minsky and several of his brothers.

157–175. I am no ape . . . doesn't care' ": "E. & O. E." lines 194–212.

157–158. I am no ape of Benares: Tolson's note in *Poetry* on these lines reads: "In the interlude before the act of extinction, he [the "man in the poem"] has the remembrance of things past. V. Schopenhauer, *On Women*, the account of the Monkey Temple." In that misogynistic diatribe, the German pessimistic philosopher Arthur Schopenhauer (1788–1860) compares respectfully treated women to "the holy apes in Benares, who in the consciousness of their sanctity and inviolable position, think they can do exactly as they please." Benares, in India, is a city sacred to both Hindus and Buddhists.

159–160. Monthyon prize: "V. Gautier, *Preface to Mademoiselle de Maupin*, the Monthyon prize.[Tolson's note]." Two annual Prix Montyon, one in literature, one in medicine, are awarded by the Institute de France. The prize is named after the philanthropist Baron Jean Baptiste-Antoine Montyon (1733–1820). Théophile Gautier (1811–1872) used the famous preface (1835) to which Tolson refers to argue that art must be free from political responsibility. It is often cited as a key document in the development of the idea of art for art's sake.

167–168. Sorgue's studio with the Black Venus: "V. Salmon, *La Négresse de Sacré-Coeur*. This was the period of the expatriates in Paris, when the Continent felt the impact of Benin art and Harlem jazz [Tolson's note]." The Black Venus, an African dancer in a Montmartre cafe, is the title character of Salmon's novel of 1920, to which Tolson refers. Parts of the novel are set in the studio of another character, the artist Sorgue.

170. drunk piccolo: this drink is unknown; however, in several European countries the Italian word *piccolo* (small) is used as a slang term for a split of champagne.

171–172. Salmon, Apollinaire, MacOrlan, and Picasso: André Salmon (1881–1969), French novelist and poet; Guillaime Apollinaire (1880–1918), French poet and critic; Pierre MacOrlan (1883–1970), French novelist; and Pablo Picasso (1881–1973) were all associated with the cubist revolution in the arts and the great days of Paris bohemianism.

175. Hippoclides doesn't care: "Herodotus tells the story of Hippoclides. Cf. Newman, *Apologia pro Vita Sua*, Part III, 'History of My Religious Opinions' [Tolson's note]."

The Athenian Hippocleides, the favored suitor for the hand of the daughter of the tyrant Cleisthenes, danced lewdly at the banquet at which Cleisthenes' choice was to be announced. When told he had danced away his marriage, he replied "Hippocleides doesn't care." In chapter 3 ("History of My Religious Opinions from 1839 to 1841") of his *Apologia* (1864–65), John Henry Newman (1801–1890) discusses the crisis of his conversion to Roman Catholicism in terms of a balance between individual conscience and respect for ecclesiastical authority.

177. Peak of Teneriffe: Mt. Teide (12,198 ft.), a snow-capped volcano, dominates Teneriffe, the largest of the Canary Islands.

184–200. Beneath . . . Job's cry!": lines 363–70, the concluding lines of "E. & O. E."

199. Barabas's curse: Barabas is the title character, who dies shouting terrific blasphemies, in Christopher Marlowe (1564–1593), *The Jew of Malta* (1592).

Psi

THE ARGUMENT

As the Curator prepares for departure in his final two cantos, he turns away from his narratives and theorizing and speaks directly to his biracial audience about some of the jumping-off-places, not conclusions, which the poem has discovered. In "Psi" he addresses himself in turn to the dialectically opposed *Homo Aethiopicus* and *Homo Caucacicus*; in "Omega' he addresses them together.

The juxtaposition of the separate apostrophes of "Psi" to Black Boy and White Boy allows the Curator to explain each to the other and reinforces his insistence that blackness and whiteness are fictions, which will not withstand the tests of experience. With the authority of a survivor, as well as a handful of puns, he first instructs his idealized Black Boy about the peculiarly American dilemma of being a black artist, whose heritage has been hidden in illusion so that he is left unsure about what tools and stances are available to him. The black American artist, the Curator suggests, has not yet achieved full growth, but remains an exotic primitive, a giant only locally, whose power, mystery, and limitation are evoked by the image of the darkling owl moth. This stunted growth is not a condition of Black Boy's own making, and he must not let himself become acclimatized to it, but it will not be easily overcome. The Great White World and its defenders, the Bilbos, FFVs, and DARs, who rely for security on some reified idea of whiteness, reinforced by religion, fear racial apocalypse above all else and will resist violently anything they perceive to be incursions upon their proprieties of history, biology, or culture.

Dr. Nkomo, with his characteristic verve and sanity, deflates the mythic premises of white supremacy, in particular antievolutionary racist metaphysics, by pointing out (to Black Boy, in the guise of the Zulu Club cynics) that the process of natural selection can be said to have favored the African, and the African could thus be said to represent, in a sense, nature's superior race. Certainly black people will seem superior when their features are contrasted to the apelike vestiges in the physiognomy of the Nordic type, the enumeration of which the Curator has earlier attributed to agnostic Clarence Darrow. Nkomo, however, is in a somber mood and he refuses to rest in his table-turning, or find hilarity in it, or let his audience take comfort in any form of exceptionalism. Racial and social categories are matters of circumstance, he says; people who rely on them will be stripped of their illusions—and their privileged flesh—in the radical democracy of death.

What, then, is the budding black artist to do? The Curator concludes this part of his dual address with a characteristically indirect but elaborate metaphor of wine, the integrity of which demands rootedness in place, continuity of lineage, natural, not chemical, process, and assiduous cultivation. The results are tasty, he says; they invite discrimination; they incarnate maturity.

When the Curator turns to White Boy he unleashes a series of denunciations of racial categories and the crimes of racism. Despite the sly joking and comedy in "Psi," the canto arrives, finally, at the angriest, most anxious statement about race that the Curator allows himself in *Harlem Gallery*. Using himself and his generic Black Boy as putative opposites, he repeats the familiar Socratic "What is it?," this time asking what ineffable common essence defines them both as "Negro." They are not much alike, he suggests, finally making explicit the racial ambiguity that has become increasingly apparent during the poem, that he is white-skinned, blue-eyed, yellowhaired, a Negro only by choice and according to surroundings. His "invisibility" defies the statutory and genetic laws by which the white world seeks to establish sense and order, but it does not change the law of circumstance, which is, as he tells White Boy, that in the United States blacks and whites are pretty well dependent upon each other, as the wick is on the oil if the lamp is to work.

The process of association by which the Curator mockingly attempts to understand the definition of the Negro leads, through the idea of working together, to the stereotype of the black cook, which leads in turn to a comic description of cookery, not so much by, as of, the Negro. The Curator's bravura catalog of improbable foodstuffs, apparently incompatible flavors, and diverse appetites is juxtaposed to the metaphor of the wine in the apostrophe to Black Boy. It also shifts the Curator's broodings, through analogy, into the horrors of historical memory. Just as a variety of improbable ingredients are blended by the mysterious syncresis of cooking into something recognizable as chop suey or mulligan stew, so disparities of blood and color, racial amalgams beyond name, are blended through the invocation of race into something called "the Negro."

The old slave life that spawned such riddles of identity was unholy. The Curator's brief, bitter vision of it fuses the themes of moral darkness, violence, blood, death, and vulnerability that have been slowly emerging during the canto and leads him to identify their modern counterpart. He argues not so much that America might be engaged in some moral equivalent of Nazi genocide, as that the name Buchenwald, whether metaphor or warning, gives shape and the force of presence to the pervasive dread that haunts American black people, as the Curator, with all his defenses, must acknowledge that it continues to haunt him. It lurks just beyond the control of will or reason, to trouble sleep with fearful dreams wherein the precarious balance of racial roles is lost, and everything collapses into a vacant whiteness.

NOTES

2. Table of Fifty Sounds: the precise number is in dispute, but standard varieties of English contain approximately fifty phonemes, or discrete sounds.

9. Lot: because he did not look back, he survived the Lord's angry destruction of Sodom. Genesis: 19:1–29.

12. Sodom of Gylt: "gylt" is the archaic past participle of both "guilty" and "gilded."

18. Zuexian grape: the Greek painter Zeuxis (ca. 400 B.C.E.) is said by Pliny to have painted grapes so realistically that birds were deceived by them.

22. American Dilemma: the title of a classic study (1944) by the Swedish economist (Karl) Gunnar Myrdal (1898–1987), in which the American dilemma is defined as race.

23. trying plane: a carpenter's tool used for precise finishing work.

32. Brazilian owl moth: *Erebus agrippina*, the largest known moth, with a wingspan of ten inches.

40. *ignoti nulla cupido*: Latin, what is unknown is not desired: Ovid, *Ars Amatoria* 3.397.

43. Buteo: see note, "Upsilon," 511.

49. the herb of grace, the rue: rue is a strong-scented European herb (*Ruta graveolens*) with yellow flowers and bitter-tasting leaves, associated symbolically with penitence. It is also called *herb of grace*.

50. Job's comforter: Job's comforters could be said, in the contemporary idiom, to blame the victim. See Job 16:1–11.

53. Broken Orange Pekoe: i.e., tea of the best quality.

54. *What* is he: Dr. Nkomo has Job (7:17, 21; 15:14–16) on his mind too.

66. *Dies Irae*: see note, "Eta," 307.

68. Boas and Dephino, Blumenbach and Koelreuter: Franz Boas (1858–1942), German-born American anthropologist and ethnologist, who did seminal work in anthropometry and Native American linguistics; Johann Friedrich Blumenbach (1752–1840), German zoologist and anthropologist, often called the father of modern anthropology, who first classified human species as Caucasian, Mongolian, Ethiopian, etc.; Josef Gottlieb Koelreuter (1733–1806), German botanist who did pioneering work in hybridization and cross-fertilization of plants. These scientists would differ in their sympathies (Boaz was liberal on questions of race; Blumenbach a white supremacist) but they are gathered here for their work in the definition and classification of species. Their position on guard around such a rare specimen as Bilbo is probably nothing more than a joke. Dephino has resisted identification. Michael Bérubé (*Marginal Forces/Cultural Centers*, 1992) suggests persuasively that he is one of Tolson's puns.

71. Bilbo: Theodore Gilmore Bilbo (1877–1947), governor of Mississippi (1916–20, 1928–32) and United States Senator (1935–47), was a southern Democrat whose name became a byword for white supremacist bigotry and demagoguery. He died of mouth cancer.

77. rams' horns from Jericho: which brought down the walls. See Joshua 6:4–20.

78. facies: the word, which means *face*, doesn't seem to work in Tolson's context. He may have meant *fasces* in its sense of the authority symbolized by the physical fasces of Rome or as it is related etymologically to the word *fascicle*.

84. barley bird: a member of the woodpecker family, known more familiarly as "wrynecks," a name derived from the peculiar jerking or twisting head movements used in courtship or defense.

85. sounding brass: 1 Corinthians 13:1: "Though I speak with the tongues of men and of angels, and have not charity, I am become as sounding brass, or a tinkling cymbal."

90. F. F. V.: First Families of Virginia, the designation loosely applied to the squirearchy on the British model that dominated much of the political and cultural life of Virginia from colonial times until well into this century. The term has become a common symbol of quasi-aristocratic exclusiveness and pretentiousness.

92. the rising tide of color: *The Rising Tide of Color against White World-Supremacy* (1920) by (Theodore) Lothrop Stoddard (1883–1950) was only one of this American author's contributions to the racist menace-literature of the 1920s and 1930s.

94. D. A. R.: Daughters of the American Revolution, a conservative women's organization, limited in membership to descendants of soldiers or patriots of the American revolutionary period. Its reactionary racial policies attracted considerable attention in 1939 when, despite the urgings of Eleanor Roosevelt and her subsequent resignation, the organization refused to allow the African American singer Marian Anderson to perform in its Constitution Hall.

94. Heraclitean flux: see note, "Eta," 253.

96. Crispus Attucks: see note, "Lambda," 20.

100-103. old Darrow . . . God Almighty's: the reference is to the famous Scopes trial of 1925, in which the radical attorney Clarence Darrow (1857–1938) defended the high school teacher John Scopes against prosecution (led by William Jennings Bryan) on charges of violating state laws against teaching the theory of evolution. As part of his defense Darrow argued that Charles Darwin's models of the development of species were compatible with some interpretations of the bible. That argument did not prevail in fundamentalist Tennessee.

104. Catarrhine ape: of the superfamily of the order *Primates*, a group that includes Old World apes and monkeys as well as human beings.

105. the C from a Canada goose: the Curator appears to be playing with the substitution for the Greek *k* in the etymology of *Catarrhine*, which is derived from the Greek *katarrhina*. *Canada* is derived from *kanata*, a Huron-Iroquois word for *village*. Because these native languages were not written, the orthography of the word is known only as it is recorded in the journals of the explorer Jacques Cartier. Surely all this is not without meaning.

114. Aramis: one of the swashbuckling three musketeers in Alexandre Dumas's (1802–1870) romance of that title (1844) and its sequels.

128. as Herodotus marvels: in his *Histories* the Greek historian Herodotus (5th c. B.C.E.) describes many marvelous Egyptian, Libyan, and Ethiopian tribes, several times noting matter-of-factly that the sun has made them black, but otherwise has little to say about natural selection. Probably Nkomo has in mind Herodotus' assertion in his third book that Ethiopians are the tallest, best-looking, and longest lived of men.

138. Logos: Greek, *word*, often used metaphysically. See note, "Lambda," 22.

143. if Adamness has made him half blind: Dr. Nkomo may be commenting on the Curator's Pelagianism (l. 359).

144. Marah: the bitter spring that Moses, with the Lord's help, made sweet. Exodus 15:23–25.

145. Elim: the lush oasis where the Israelites rested during their journey in the wilderness. Exodus 15:27.

148. Sardou: Victorien Sardou (1831–1908), French dramatist of light comedies and historical pieces, whose great popularity was short-lived.

150. feverfew: a perennial European herb (*Chrysanthemem parthenium*), once used to ease fever.

153. Hardyesque artistry: cf. "Rho," 75. This time only Thomas Hardy is implied.

158. Tower of Silence: a circular stone wall of 20 to 30 feet in height, 200 to 270 feet in circumference, on which Parsees expose their dead to be consumed by birds.

168. Parsees': Indian Zoroasterians, the descendents of Persian refugees.

174–175. Asscher's . . . Cullinan Diamond: at a weight of about 3,255 carats, the largest diamond ever found, discovered in the Transvaal in 1905 and named after its discoverer, Sir Thomas Cullinan. It was subsequently cut into nine large stones, including the Star of Africa, and about 100 smaller ones. The proverbially tense work of cutting was done by I. J. Asscher and Company of Amsterdam.

178. with Omar: see note, "Chi," 65.

184. Bordeaux: the wine-producing region in southwest France that has traditionally been regarded as the source of the most distinguished wines.

197. *a capriccio*: Italian, in re music: at the performer's pleasure.

208–209. the Republic does not guarantee . . . Château Bottled: that is, the Republic of the United States does not, unlike the Republic of France, which insists upon and supervises strict consistency of information in labeling wine. *Château Bottled* means that the wine is the product of a particular vineyard and estate, and its label is imprinted with the name of the vineyard and its owner. Such designations are reserved for the finest wines. *Clos Saint Thierry* (line 216) is an example (*clos* meaning a particular kind of vineyard, here the famous Saint Thierry vineyard, north of Reims).

222. the flatted fifth and octave jump: among the characteristics of the new "bop" or "bebop" jazz introduced by Charlie Parker, Dizzy Gillespie, and other veteran jazzmen in the 1940s were chromatic harmony and a new, complex system of rhythms. Bop jazz also featured long, individualistic—a skeptic might say, exhibitionistic—breaks, or solo performances.

240. Socrates' *"Tò tí?"*: see note, "Alpha, 41."

243. moutaba tick: probably the moubata tick (*Ornithodoros savignii*), which can cause fatal illnesses in human beings. It can survive long periods without a blood meal and has been found in the cracks in walls in human dwellings.

259. xanthein: either a neologism, based on the root *xanth-*, meaning *yellow*, or a misspelling of xanthene or xanthin, both of which have to do with yellow pigmentation.

279–283. races . . . in antipodal places: the Curator refers to the theory, much discussed in the late 1950s and early 1960s, that human races were not derived from a common ancestor but had separate geneses and had evolved separately. It was most influentially argued in the work of the American anthropologist Carleton Coon (1904–1981), especially his *The Origin of Races* (1962).

290–291. like Kant . . . grammar straight: Immanuel Kant (1724–1804), German idealistic philosopher. The slur on his grammar may be nothing more than an observation about the German language.

294. pitch wheel: a toothed wheel that engages another toothed wheel in a machine.

300. disease of kings: probably gout, a chronic inflammation of the joints that is exacerbated by rich diet.

314. an ola-podrida: *olla podrida* (the Spanish means, literally, *rotten pot*) is a spicy soup or stew made of one or more meats and a variety of vegetables, usually including chick peas.

338–339. a Gordian knot without . . . Alexander's sword: in Greek mythology, King Gordius fastened the yoke and pole of his wagon, the symbol of his kingship, with a bark knot; he who untied it, an oracle declared, would rule all of Asia. When Alexander came to Gordium as a conqueror he simply cut through the knot, which had frustrated all previous attempts to untie it, with a sword.

341. *vitro de trina*: Italian, *lace glass*, Venetian glassware in which white threads are worked into transparent glass with a lacelike effect.

342. the old-oaken-bucket's: the title of the sentimental poem of 1826 by Samuel Woodworth (1785–1842), which became famous after being set to music by Frederick Smith.

345. not a dog moved his tongue: in Exodus 11:7, Moses reports the promise of the Lord that not a dog shall move his tongue against the children of Israel as all the firstborn of the Egyptian masters die.

346. not a lamb lost a drop of blood: Exodus 12:3–14 describes the first feast of Passover. The Lord instructs the Israelites to mark their houses with the blood of the passover lambs, so that the Israelites may be spared the slaughter of the firstborn.

348. Xenos of Xanthos: the Greek roots would mean something like *yellow foreigner*. *Blonde stranger* probably would come closer to Tolson's intention.

353. *Buchenwald*: during the Second World War, one of the most infamous of the Nazi concentration camps, located near Weimar in central Germany.

357. that Lonesome Road: this folksong of (in Carl Sandburg's phrase) "a desperate heart" exists in many versions. The Curator has in mind the most familiar of them, with its refrain, "Look down, look down that lonesome road before you travel on." But compare the version Sandburg records in *American Songbag* (1927).

359. a Pelagian: a follower of the British (or Irish) monk Pelagius (ca. 360–ca. 420) who argued against the doctrines of Original Sin and innate depravity. His views were condemned as heretical by church councils in 416 and 418.

362. the Yazoo tiger's: the small Yazoo City is located on the Yazoo River in Yazoo County in west central Mississippi.

373–379. Scylla and Charybdis: see note, "Eta," 293.

378. *Vanitas vanitatum!*: Latin, *vanity of vanities*; see Ecclesiastes 1:2–3.

Omega

THE ARGUMENT

After the low point at the conclusion of "Psi," the Curator seeks in "Omega" to recover the invigorating hopeful vision he had several times glimpsed during the course of his long narrative. His departing address is set in the Gallery, among the paintings of the exhibition he and Dr. Nkomo had opened in "Iota," and is a final celebration of the redemptive powers of art. It is also an apologia for the special role of curators in making art real and accessible, even, or perhaps especially, in a society so fundamentally attuned as the United States to the logic of money. Lurking mischievously in the shadows of it all, never quite articulated, is an apologia for long, hermetic, modernist poems.

By reversing the tactic of "Psi" and addressing himself simultaneously to both black and white communities, the Curator emphasizes his conviction, which remained understated in "Psi," that, willy-nilly, American black people and American white people share a common lot, even while their capacities for renewal—so the final stanzas suggest—are disproportionate. He claims the authority to speak about such things not from his education or professional status but from experience and cunning. Those who have gained perspective, he says, have the responsibility to bring vision and nourishment to the other "children" who are still in need of instruction.

Curators must not be distracted by size or prominence. It is their duty to intercede so that when the painter arrives at the inevitable crossroads he need not feel constrained to choose the path of the merchant, with its vulgar displays, but instead meet there, in the knowledge and presence of death, a curator as friend to friend. Curators understand the principles of timing by which art achieves its best effect and may thus help to release both its healing powers and its great capacity to nourish. In a tacit acknowledgment of the lesson of Mister Starks's *Harlem Vignettes*, the Curator crosses one of his previously uncrossed t's by reversing the position he had taken in his predawn debate with Nkomo about the relative virtues of the allegorical whole milk and its components.

Neither cater to an elite, he says now, nor condescend to the masses. Rather trust the imagination to guide artists and curators through an unpredictable, dangerous world, whose perpetual newness entails the pain of succession as well as the tonic of fresh beginnings. Art imitates the violence as well as the sweetness of the primal creation's design, so that the artist requires something of the primal freedom of the designer and is not to be restricted in subject or method. That godlike passion also infects the scholars and critics who rally to the support or explication of art. Although these subalterns do not always function in entirely fruitful or wholesome ways, they can help art stand against the forces of officialdom, which insists on a system of values and a version of truth all its own.

Nkomo, as pointed and eloquent as ever, is now summoned for his final appearance. He responds with a fresh version of a familiar lesson, that the uses of art are to create new ways of knowing, new enlightenments, and thus new roads through life's only apparently familiar terra incognita. Prompted by Nkomo's wistful acknowledgment that he is not himself an artist, the Curator affirms his own reconciliation with his limited role as an ally and facilitator and proceeds to his final iteration of his personal credo.

He has drawn his characters, he says, in their ambiguous dusk of dawn in a spirit of racial celebration, but with half an eye out for the Great White World. Although he is frustrated almost to exhaustion by being forced to make do with too little—send bucks, he says bluntly—and ground down by the unremitting philistinism of the regents, he sees through and can endure their alternate enmity and enticements. The dialectics of history, race, and art will continue their endless, formative interactions; that knowledge is both burdensome and encouraging. The Curator chooses to work in the service of the future, which can be radiant only in the light of the present, just as the present can be intelligible only in the light of the past.

The final two stanzas express the Curator's personal faith, often embattled, in the character of his people and the humanizing powers of art. In a newspaper interview, Tolson expressed satisfaction that at the last he had planted the flowers of renewal and hope—the white heather and the white almond—not in the white, but the black community. And so, on to the next fold of the future.

NOTES

3. Tyche: see note, "Theta," 74.

16. Nestor: see note, "Upsilon," 285.

22. Pelagians: see note, "Psi," 359.

32. a lesser dog: astronomically, the lesser dog is the constellation *Canis minor*, but the Curator is speaking metaphorically about a much less visible light in the far distant sky.

33. Palomar's eye: the world's largest reflecting telescope on Mount Palomar in southern California.

34. Schaeberle: John Martin Schaeberle (1853–1924), German-born American astronomer, a particularly avid and prominent observational astronomer.

37. Lhote: André Lhote (1885–1962), French painter, teacher, and critic, identified with Fauvism and, later, cubism, who founded the Academie Montparnasse.

42. *nawiht*: Anglo-Saxon, nothing.

44. thirty pieces of silver: see note, "Upsilon," 417.

47. Admirable Doctor: because of his unusually great learning and curiosity, the English philosopher, scientist, and Franciscan friar Roger Bacon (ca. 1214–ca. 1294) was known as *Doctor Mirabilis* or *Admirabilis*. Cf. "Omicron," 41–50.

49. Jack Dempsey: William Harrison "Jack" Dempsey, the Manassa Mauler (1895–1983), American heavyweight boxer, champion of the world 1919–26.

51. Godavari of Art: the Godavari River, sacred to Hindus, with several stations for pilgrims on its banks, arises in west India and flows southeasterly to the Bay of Bengal. It is fed by numerous tributaries and opens into a huge delta about fifty miles from the coast.

53. the Decan trap: the Decan (or Deccan) Trap is a geologic formation of basaltic lava covering vast plateau areas in India.

64. "lesser breeds": see the imperialistic prayer-poem, "Recessional" (1897) by Rudyard Kipling (1865–1936):

> If, drunk with sight of power, we loose
>   Wild tongues that have not Thee in awe—
> Such boasting as the Gentiles use
>   Or lesser breeds without the Law—

75–77. Cézanne . . . Daumier: see notes, "Kappa," 103; "Zeta," 46.

79. Hogarth: William Hogarth (1697–1764) English moralist and satiric painter, famous for his anecdotal paintings satirizing personal vice and social abuses.

81. Ushas: in Hindu mythology, the perpetually young goddess of the dawn.

83. Gobelin arras: the Manufacture nationale des Gobelins was founded as a dyeworks in the mid-fifteenth century, a tapestry works added in 1601. Since that time Gobelin tapestries have been famous for excellence of materials, dyes, and workmanship. An arras is a pictorial tapestry of fourteenth- to fifteenth-century Flemish origin.

84–85. Degas . . . rue Victor Masse: Edgar Degas (1834–1917), the reclusive French impressionist painter, was in 1912 almost totally blind and saddened by the recent death of Henri Roaurt when evicted from his lodgings in rue Victor Masse.

89. the dread hand: See note, "Theta," 17.

91. Tokay: the image appears here to involve the grape or grape flower, although *tokay* properly refers only to the wine, which is made from several grapes.

97. buffalo bird: any of several small birds of the starling family that perch upon buffalo and cattle in search of parasites, often warning the host of danger.

102. Tyrean: also Tyrian: of the ancient seaport of Phoenicia, famous for its colorful dyes.

103. the huzzy thrown from a window to the dogs: Jezebel; see 2 Kings 9:30–37.

104–105. red pallets . . . Aragon's shield: the shield of the kings of the Spanish kingdom (11–15 cent.) of Aragon was divided into equal vertical thin bars (pales or pallets) of alternating colors.

107. metaphor-maker of Naishapur: Omar Khayyám. The oblong leaf probably refers to illuminated manuscript pages but could refer to the quatrain itself, particularly since it was Omar who developed this form and its lovely triple rhyme.

109. *cyma reversa*: a type of molding, the profile of which is formed by a continuous line in a double curve. The concave portion of the curve is nearest the wall.

110–111. the mosaics . . . San Vitale at Ravenna: San Vitale, a Byzantine church at Ravennna, Italy, was constructed between 530 and 548. Its many mosaic decorations are especially prized as monuments of Byzantine art.

113. Purbeckian marble: marble from the Purbeck Beds of England was a favorite of medieval architects, used in Westminister Abbey and other English churches. This unmetamorphosed marble is often marked with interesting color contrasts or fossil remains.

120. *chef-d'oeuvre*: French, masterpiece.

121. By Room: the term would appear to mean an underground enclosure, part of a network of caverns, that sits apart from the main cavern after the model of a side or private room in a house. Robert Huot suggests that Tolson may rather have had in mind the enormous (fourteen-acre) Big Room in the southern section of the Carlsbad Caverns in New Mexico.

131. Masoretic texts: the Masorah is a vast body of annotations about such textual issues of the Hebrew bible as diction, style, sources, and especially pronunciation, written in the margins and at the end of texts by Jewish scholars by the mid-tenth century.

133. fid: a square bar used to support a topmast or topgallant mast by stabilizing its heel.

140. robes of the Medici: the Medici family directed the fortunes of Florence from the fifteenth to eighteenth centuries. The patronage by many members of the house of the arts, literature, and learning made Florence one of the great repositories of European culture.

143. Cheops: Greek form of Khufu (26th c. B.C.E.), king of Memphis in Egypt, second ruler of the fourth dynasty, who is most famous for building the Great Pyramid at Giza.

148–149. from Giverney . . . Jardin d'Eau: Claude Monet (1840–1926), French impressionist painter, lived on his estate at Giverney from 1883 until his death. The water garden there became one of his dominant subjects, and later paintings of it show the bridge built over it. Monet painted it, as he did other subjects, in series, to show effects of changing light or the passing of time.

155. Cliffs of Etzetat: Etretat (correct spelling) was a French beach and summer resort that Monet and other artists frequented in the late nineteenth century. Monet painted its waters, beach, and cliffs many times, including the series of twenty-four paintings of cliffs, done in 1898.

155. Coins of Rivière: this puzzling and elusive title may be written in two languages. If indeed its first and third words are French, it probably has to do with serial paintings of aspects of the river, the Seine, as it fascinated Monet and other impressionist painters. If the title is to be read in English—well, there were engravers, perhaps of coins, named Rivière. But it is hard to see what their craft has to do with Nkomo's dream.

163. gilbert: the basic centimeter-gram-second unit of magnetomotive force, equal to .7958 ampere turns, named for Sir William Gilbert (1540–1603), English physicist.

168. God's acre: the cemetery.

178. all-God's-children-got shoes: a line from the final verse of the spiritual "All God's Children Got Wings." See note, "Mu," 133; and *The Book of American Negro Spirituals*, ed. James Weldon Johnson (1925).

179. the moving finger: FitzGerald's *Rubáiyát*, quatrain 71:

> The Moving Finger writes, and, having writ,
> Moves on, nor all your Piety nor Wit
>   Shall lure it back to cancel half a Line,
> Nor all your Tears wash out a Word of it.

199. in spite of sounding brass: see note, "Psi," 85.

200. the words of Archbishop Trench: Richard Chenevix Trench (1807–1886), English clergyman and philologist, who is quoted here from *English, Past and Present* (1855).

204. Haroun-al-Rashid: the taste and hospitality of Haroun-al-Rashid (763–809), the most famous Caliph of Baghdad (786–809), made his court a center of wit, learning, and art for the Moslem world.

209. characin: a white substance with a moldy odor, found in some fatty algae.

212. 666: the number of the beast, in Revelations 13:18.

216. hetaera: a sophisticated courtesan or woman of the demimonde.

219. Selika's invisible choir: in the opera *L'Africaine* (1864) by Giacomo Meyerbeer (1791–1864) Selika, an African queen, in love with Vasco de Gama even though he has made her his slave, kills herself as Vasco sails away. An invisible chorus comments that in death all are equal.

224. deep-sea Harriotta: *Harriotta raleighana* inhabits the deep northern regions of the Atlantic. It has a daggerlike snout (the rostrum) which is hooked at the end.

226. *kind gallows* at Crieff: Crieff, in central Scotland, was until 1770 the site of a famous cattle fair. There may be an unwitting pun behind the name of the kind gallows, since they were commonly used for the execution of Highland cattle (kine) thieves.

227. *Illuminations*: the prose poems of Arthur Rimbaud (1854–1891) were published in 1886 by Paul Verlaine as *Illuminations*. Rimbaud was running guns to combatants in a civil war in Ethiopa at the time, and it is not known if he ever saw a copy of the book.

228. Djami: Rimbaud's Abyssinian servant and constant companion during his ten years in Ethiopia, the only person to whom Rimbaud showed any affection. When Rimbaud left in 1891, Djami begged to accompany him, even at the cost of abandoning his own family.

230. faithful Harrari: a citizen of Harar in eastern Ethiopia, where Rimbaud made his headquarters off and on during the 1880s. The Curator seems to think that the Abyssinian Djami was Harrari.

236. Ararat: Genesis 8:4.

242. Syncorax' brew: the evil witch Sycorax (correct spelling) was the mother of Caliban and imprisoner of Ariel in Shakespeare's *The Tempest* (ca. 1611).

244–245. white heather . . . white almond: in many cultures, the almond, the first flower of the year, is strongly identified with springtime, fertility, and renewal. The tiny flowers of the heather are prized because they blossom in otherwise barren or rugged environments.

246. hyacinth: see note, "Beta," 64.

247. asphodel: in Greek mythology asphodels grow in hell and are associated with Persephone and the quasi life of the dead. As William Carlos Williams might have reminded Tolson (in "Of Asphodel, That Greeny Flower," 1962), they also grow in urban New Jersey.

249–251. Cleobulus . . . Pittacus: the Seven Wise Men of Greece, all of whom flourished ca. 600–ca. 550 B.C.E. These pre-Socratic kings, lawgivers, poets, and philosophers were admired for their practical rather than speculative wisdom.

254. Mantegna: Andrea Mantegna (1431–1506), Italian painter and engraver, many of whose paintings have a sculptural emphasis, as if their figures were less painted on canvas than carved out of stone.

The Published Works of
MELVIN B. TOLSON

Books

Caviar and Cabbage: Selected Columns by Melvin B. Tolson from the "Washington Tribune," 1937–1944. Ed. Robert M. Farnsworth. Columbia: Univ. of Missouri Press, 1982.

A Gallery of Harlem Portraits. Ed. Robert M. Farnsworth. Columbia: Univ. of Missouri Press, 1979.

Harlem Gallery: Book I, The Curator. New York: Twayne, 1965.

Libretto for the Republic of Liberia. New York: Twayne, 1953.

Rendezvous with America. New York: Dodd, Mead, 1944.

Poems and Articles

"Abraham Lincoln of Rock Spring Farm." In *Soon, One Morning: New Writings by American Negroes,* ed. Herbert Hill, pp. 57–77. New York: Knopf, 1963.

"African China." *Voices* 140 (winter 1950): 35–38.

"Alpha," "Beta," "Gamma," "Delta," "Epsilon," "Zeta," "Eta." *Prairie Schooner* 35 (fall 1961): 243–64.

"All Aboard!" *New Letters* 39 (summer 1973): 3–37.

"The Auction." In *Negro Voices,* ed. Beatrice M. Murphy, pp. 152–53. New York: Henry Harrison, 1938.

"The Black Rapist." *The Oracle,* Oct. 1938, 14, 15, 18.

"The Braggart." *Common Ground* 4 (summer 1944): 74.

"The Breadline." In *Sonnets: An Anthology of Contemporary Verse*, ed. Ralph Cheyney, p. 97. New York: Henry Harrison, 1939.

"The Cabin's Victim." *The Lincolnian* (Yearbook, Lincoln High School, Kansas City MO), 1917, pp. 52–55.

"Caviar and Cabbage." *Washington Tribune*, 9 Oct. 1937–24 June 1944. On microfilm, Moorland-Spingarn Research Center, Howard University.

"Claude McKay's Art." *Poetry* 83 (Feb. 1954): 287–90.

"The Contributor's Column." *Atlantic Monthly* 168 (Sept. 1941): v.

"Dark Symphony." *Atlantic Monthly* 168 (Sept. 1941): 314–17.

"Dr. Harvey Whyte." *Modern Monthly* 10 (Aug. 1937): 10.

"E. & O.E." *Poetry* 78 (Sept. 1951): 330–42, 369–72.

"Five Essays." *New Letters* 48 (summer 1981): 103–19.

"Five Poems." *New Letters* 42 (summer 1976): 164–69.

"The Foreground of Negro Poetry." *Kansas Quarterly* 7 (summer 1976): 30–35.

"Goodbye Christ." *Pittsburgh Courier*, 26 Jan. 1933, 10–11; 2 Feb. 1933, 10–11.

"Hamuel Gutterman." *Modern Monthly* 10 (Apr. 1937): 7.

"Harlem." *The Arts Quarterly* 1 (Apr.–June 1937): 27.

"Jacob Nollen." *Modern Monthly* 10 (May 1937): 10.

"Kikes, Bohunks, Crackers, Dagos, Niggers." *The Modern Quarterly* 11 (autumn 1939): 18–19.

"From *Libretto for the Republic of Liberia*." *Poetry* 76 (July 1950): 208–15.

"From *The Lion and the Jackal*." *Okike* 1 (May 1967): 8–16.

"A Long Head to a Round Head." *Beloit Poetry Journal* 11 (summer 1952): 19–21.

"A Man against the Idols of the Tribe." *Modern Quarterly* 11 (fall 1940): 29–32.

"The Man from Halicarnassus." *Poetry* 81 (Oct. 1952): 75–77.

"Miles to Go with Black Ulysses." *New York Herald Tribune Book Week*, 20 Feb. 1966, 2, 12.

"Modern Poetry under the Microscope." *Midwest Journal* 7 (spring 1955): 113–15.

"The Negro Scholar." *Midwest Journal* 1 (winter 1948): 80–82.

"The Note." In *Eros, an Anthology of Modern Love Poems*, ed. Lucia Trent, p. 69. New York: Henry Harrison, 1939.

"Notes on the Trombone of the West." *Voices* 140 (winter 1950): 50–52.

"The Odyssey of a Manuscript." *New Letters* 48 (fall 1981): 5–17.

"The Past, Present and Future." *The Lincolnian* (Yearbook, Lincoln High School, Kansas City MO), 1918, p. 31.

"A Poet's Odyssey." In *Anger and Beyond*, ed. Herbert Hill, pp. 181–95. New York: Harper & Row, 1966.

"Quotes or Unquotes on Poetry." *Kansas Quarterly* 7 (summer 1973): 36–38.

"Rendezvous with America." *Common Ground* 2 (summer 1942): 3–9.

"Retrospection." *The Lincolnian* (Yearbook, Lincoln High School, Kansas City MO), 1917, pp. 28–29.

"Roland Hayes." In *Negro Voices*, ed. Beatrice M. Murphy, pp. 151–52. New York: Henry Harrison, 1938.

"Richard Wright: *Native Son*." *Modern Quarterly* 11 (winter 1939): 19–24.

"She Can't Take It." *Flash* (Washington DC), 31 Aug. 1939, 6.

"Six Poems." *New Letters* 43 (spring 1977): 11–18.

"Recipes of the Success of Black Men." *The Oracle* (n.d.).

"A Song for Myself." *Phylon* 4 (1945): 351–52.

"The Tragedy of the Yarr Karr." *The* (Wiley College) *Wild Cat* (1926), pp. 193–98.

"Uncle Walt." *Modern Quarterly* 10 (Mar. 1938): 10.

"Unpublished Poems of Melvin B. Tolson." *Y'Bird* 1, no. 2 (1978): 82–97.

"Vergil Ragsdale." *Modern Quarterly* 10 (winter 1939): 48.

"Wanderers in the Sierra." *The Lincolnian* (Yearbook, Lincoln High School, Kansas City MO), 1918, pp. 20–26.

"Wanted: A New Negro Leadership." *The Oracle*, Sept. 1937, 10–11.

"Will the Real Moses Stand Up." *New York Herald Tribune Book Week*, 30 May 1965, 5, 8.

"The Wine of Ecstasy." In *Negro Voices*, ed. Beatrice M. Murphy, p. 153. New York: Henry Harrison, 1938.

"*Woodcuts for Americana*: 'Old Man Michael,' 'The Gallows,' 'The Man Inside,' 'When Great Dogs Fight.'" *Common Ground* 3 (spring 1943): 38–43.